GOD NEEDS NO PASSPORT

Also by Peggy Levitt

The Transnational Villagers

The Changing Face of Home:
The Transnational Lives of the Second Generation
(with Mary Waters)

GOD NEEDS
NO PASSPORT

IMMIGRANTS AND THE CHANGING

AMERICAN RELIGIOUS LANDSCAPE

Peggy Levitt

THE NEW PRESS

NEW YORK
LONDON

Requests for permission to reproduce selections from this book should be mailed to:
Permissions Department, The New Press, 38 Greene Street, New York, NY 10013.

Published in the United States by The New Press, New York, 2007
Distributed by W. W. Norton & Company, Inc., New York

LIBRARY OF CONGRESS CATALOGING-IN-PUBLICATION DATA
Levitt, Peggy, 1957–
God needs no passport: immigrants and the changing American religious landscape / Peggy Levitt.
p. cm.
Includes bibliographical references and index.
ISBN 978-1-59558-169-3 (hc.)
1. United States—Religion—1960–   2. Immigrants—Religious life—United States.
3. Emigration and immigration—Religious aspects.   I. Title.
BL2525.L484 2007
200.86'9120973—dc22   2006030951

The New Press was established in 1990 as a not-for-profit alternative to the large, commercial publishing houses currently dominating the book publishing industry. The New Press operates in the public interest rather than for private gain, and is committed to publishing, in innovative ways, works of educational, cultural, and community value that are often deemed insufficiently profitable.

www.thenewpress.com

Composition by dix!
This book was set in Walbaum MT

Printed in the United States of America

1   3   5   7   9   10   8   6   4   2

CONTENTS

TO ROBERT—"IF NOT FOR YOU..."

ACKNOWLEDGMENTS

This book would not have been written without the generous support of many individuals. First and foremost, I thank N. Rajaram, Waldo Cesar, Breda Gray, and Mehtab Karim, who worked with me in India, Brazil, Ireland, and Pakistan, respectively. They taught me much of what I know about their countries and expanded my world in ways I never expected. I also thank the many immigrants who opened their homes and hearts, including Pankaj and Parul Bhaghat, the Anitia family, Imran Khan, Imran Qidwai, Imran Sayeed and his family, Hasan and Naheed Usmani, Vera and João Freitas, and Father Ted.

Many students worked on this project during its long arc; several have gone on to become successful teachers and researchers in their own right, including Jill Jeffries, Sunaina Maira, Irene Bloomraed, Rafael de la Dehesa, Poonam Ghandi-Moirangtham, Shivani Kolhatkar, Neha Shah, Karen Chai, Teena Purohit, Ayn Cavicchi, Adriana Jacykewycz, Avanti Patel, and Jay Dater. A special thanks to Erin Collins, who did the lion's share of the work on the Irish piece of this project, and to Wasim Rahman, who worked closely with me on the Pakistani case.

Ruth Ann and John Harris, Ashu Varshney, Adil Najam, Heloisa Galvao, and Myron Weiner helped get me started. Sally Merry, Manuel Vásquez, Michele Dillon, Michele Lamont, Nancy Foner, Paul Lichterman, Wendy Cadge, Sara Curran, Diana Wong, Nina Glick Schiller, Sanjeev Khagram, Sarah Alvord, Suzanne Koven, Karen King, Jessica Hejtmanek, Josh DeWind, Srilatha Batliwala, Peter Dobkin Hall, Marshall Ganz, and Rainer Bauböck are among the many people who read drafts of these pages and helped clarify the ideas in them. Miriam and

David Weil, Stephanie Roeder, Hans Poppel, Jill Block, Wade Ruben-
stein, Kathleen Sills, Anne Mathew, CC King, and other Conantum and
Concord friends cheered me on around the dinner and picnic tables. I
also benefited a great deal from my conversations with colleagues at
Wellesley College, the Hauser Center for Nonprofit Organizations and
the Weatherhead Center for International Affairs at Harvard University, the Ford Foundation's Working Group on Progressive Values and
Religion, and the Social Science Research Council's Project on Religion
and Globalization. I received generous funding from the Ford Foundation, the Yale University Center for Religion and American Life, the
Hauser Center, the Weatherhead Center, the Wellesley College Faculty
Research Fund, and the Rockefeller Foundation. Lots of ideas got
thought through on wonderful hikes with Philip Genty, Joe Swingle,
and Shawn La France. To my dear friends Jody Tannenbaum, Judy
Waksberg, and Debbie Wengrovitz I owe enormous thanks.

Three people were special guardian angels of this project. Connie
Buchanan of the Ford Foundation has been a patient supporter from
the beginning. I am deeply grateful for all I've learned from her. Marc
Favreau edited this book with skill and kindness, and pushed me, I
hope, closer to my goal of speaking to a broader audience. Nadya Ja-
worsky has been a brilliant, tireless research partner. This book is
much, much better for her contribution, and I know she will go on to
write wonderful books of her own.

My parents, Fred and Claire Levitt, and my mother-in-law, Mary
Lou Levers, are always there for me. My children, Dylan and Wesley,
are the lights of my life. I hope they will forgive the many hours spent
away from them to write these pages and think it worth it if they somehow help to make the world a better place. And most of all, I thank my
husband, Robert, whose generosity and spirit make it all possible and
worthwhile. This book is for you.

GOD NEEDS NO PASSPORT

Prologue

President George W. Bush claims to be doing God's work when he fights what he calls "the axis of evil."[1] On the other side of the world, Arabs and South Asians are embracing Islamic leaders who they see as succeeding where their national leaders have failed. Religion is alive and well, despite predictions it would wane in the twenty-first century. And while many people applaud these trends, others tremble at them.

Immigration is also at the heart of many heated conversations. Immigrants make up one-quarter of the American public along with their American-born children. They are not only transforming cities like Houston and Atlanta, they are remaking suburban and rural America as well. One side argues that they steal jobs, overuse services, and hold values that are antithetical to the American way. Immigrant supporters counter that they do jobs the native born don't want to do, stimulate the economy, and enrich our cultural heritage.

In several fundamental ways, these debates are based on assumptions that are out of sync with our national reality. They do not reflect dramatic shifts in the social landscape that are transforming our nation. They also fail to fully grasp the strong connection between changes in immigration and changes in religious life. When we talk about how religion influences American culture and politics, we still really mean Protestantism. When we think about what religion is, where we look for it, and how it works, we tend to think in traditional terms. Jews and Catholics are represented, though they hardly dominate the design. Islam, Hinduism, and Buddhism are barely visible. Today's immigrants, however, are remaking the religious landscape by introducing new faith traditions, and Asianizing and Latinoizing old ones. By doing so, they are transforming what it means to be American.

The stories in these pages reveal a striking paradox. For one thing, many immigrants don't trade in their home country membership card for an American one but belong to several communities at once. They become part of the United States and stay part of their ancestral homes at the same time. They challenge the taken-for-granted dichotomy between either/or, United States or homeland, and assimilation versus multiculturalism by showing it is possible to be several things simultaneously, and in fact required in a global world. For another, just as the local Gap clothing store is part of an extensive global corporate network, so more and more local mosques, temples, and Pentecostal churches are also global operations. The values immigrants express and the faith communities they belong to are shaped by factors inside and outside our borders. American religious life is no longer just American.

These changes scare many among us. The passage of the USA PATRIOT Act and the increasing cases of religious profiling reported in the news reflect a deep suspicion toward the darker-skinned, non-Christian newcomer. Global tensions are manifesting themselves on local street corners. We have entered a period of collective soul-searching about how to protect national security and continue to be a country of immigrants at the same time.[2]

But the conversations I had to get a better handle on these dynamics with Muslims from Pakistan, Hindus from Gujarat State in India, Catholics from Ireland, and Protestants from Brazil who live in the Boston area should be reassuring. Many people did hold commitments and values that may seem foreign to many Americans. Yet when I asked people how they want to act on their faith and put it into practice, their answers echoed many of the opinions expressed by the native born. There was a small group who believed they held a monopoly on the truth and it was their job to convince the rest of us. They represented the religion of the margins, not the middle. The vast majority care much more about affordable housing, education, and health care. They want to live where they can walk down the street without being afraid and where government officials can be trusted. Even people who said they wanted religion to play a central role in public life didn't want to impose it on the rest of us. Treating Islam, Hinduism, or evangelical Christianity as if they are one-size-fits-all categories is to make the same mistake as saying all Christians are equal. Newcomers come in all religious shapes and sizes. In general, they broaden and steady the religious boat rather than rock it.

I met many people in the United States and the countries where I traveled while writing these pages who had strong feelings about religion. Alice represents one view I often encountered. She is a friend, in her fifties, who teaches anthropology in Boston.[3] We often get together to talk about our work and families. One February afternoon, when I was just beginning this project, as we walked home in the snow from lunch, I told her I planned to write a book about religion. "Why would you study that?" she asked. "Don't you realize that only causes problems? Those of us who care about making the world a better place don't seem to get much help from that quarter."

The more I spoke with people, the more I realized that Alice's views were fairly common. Alice thinks of herself as a good liberal. She has dedicated her life to promoting social change. She reads widely, has traveled extensively, and is well informed about the world. And her trips and reading have convinced her that religion is up to no good.

Alice is like many intellectuals and liberals who believe faith only wreaks havoc. To them, religion at its most benign gives people permission to think they alone know the truth and, at its most potent, grants them permission to kill people who disagree. Antireligionists, like Alice, wish that religion would just go away or at least stay in its own corner.

Antireligionists like Alice don't just live in America. They also live in Pakistan, India, Brazil, and Ireland. In Brazil, the people I met worried about the rising number of evangelical Christian legislators. In Karachi, they bemoaned the fact that more and more women wore head scarves. They felt that religious institutions wielded far too much power and that religious leaders' voices were far too loud. They wanted a secular public sphere where they could continue to live their secular lives.

I met Luis, who epitomized a second stance toward religion, at a meeting on migration and development organized by the Rockefeller Foundation in Mexico. Like Alice, Luis, a foundation staff member in his thirties, travels widely and reads a lot. He has also dedicated his life to making the world a better place. But although religion is all around him, and deeply meaningful to the people he works with and who live next door, he refuses to acknowledge its influence. He passes by the places of worship in his neighborhood every day without noticing them. Luis is blind to the people driving to Mass on Sunday when he goes out for his morning run. It would never occur to him that religion might help him get his job done.

Because they are not religious, secular humanists like Luis have a hard time taking religion seriously. They equate being modern with being secular, despite the overwhelming evidence that religion is alive and well all over the world. They are afraid to bring religion into the picture because, like antireligionists, they assume that believers will try to impose their views on everyone else.

Florence's views exemplify a third attitude toward religion that I encountered repeatedly. She is a fifty-seven-year-old mother of two who just welcomed her fifth grandchild into the world. She lives in a small, neatly painted, colonial-style house in a middle-class neighborhood in Lowell, Massachusetts. Her living room is filled with knickknacks and photos of her large family. There is a shamrock on the door, in honor of Saint Patrick's Day, and freshly baked Irish soda bread and tea waiting on the dining room table when I visit.

Florence grew up in Lowell. Her mother worked as a kindergarten teacher, and her father was an accountant at a textile mill that has long since closed. As a child, Florence went to church every Sunday and has continued to go throughout her married life. If anyone wants to find her, they can count on her being at the 11 o'clock Mass. Over the years, she taught Confraternity of Christian Doctrine classes, sang in the choir, and served on the parish council.

When I asked Florence to talk about how Lowell has changed over the years, she began with a big sigh. When she was little, she said, there was a thriving downtown. Men worked in the mills, and on Saturday afternoons, the streets were packed with families out for a good time. In those days, it was mostly Irish, Italians, and French Canadians. They each had their own churches, but they all got along because they "all shared their love of Christ." But in the 1950s, Lowell's luck ran out. Most of the mills closed and unemployment soared. Pretty soon, the downtown "was like a ghost town." And that was when the immigrants began moving in.

Today, Florence said, you can't even recognize Lowell for all the Cambodians, Puerto Ricans, and Indians that live here. Many new stores have opened downtown, but she never patronizes them. How can you feel welcome in a store where all the signs are in a different language? At Saint Marie's, the old French Canadian parish, they say Mass in Spanish, and the old Episcopalian church on the north side is now some kind of Hindu temple. "I'm glad that Lowell is bouncing back," she said, "but I liked it better in the old days. To be honest, I'm not really comfortable with all these new people and their different faiths. Between you and me, they don't believe in Christ."

Unlike Luis, Florence knows that religion is all around her. It is a positive force in her own life and she believes it plays a positive role in society at large. She just wants it to be her kind of religion. Religious pluralism is OK, except when it steps outside the boundaries of Christianity, Florence's alarm goes off. She wants to re-Christianize America rather than de-Christianize it. Spreading "the word," for her, means spreading the vocabulary she is accustomed to.

There were also many people like Florence in the countries that I visited. These "exclusivists," who are Muslim and Hindu as well as Christian, believe they are tuned in to God's word and that everyone else just needs to change their channel. Since they think they know the right way to live, it is their job to change others rather than arrive at some respectful compromise. What is right and true is not up for discussion.

Wasim, who lives on the other side of the world, articulated a fourth stance toward religion. I met him at the Sheraton Hotel in Karachi. The hotel's lobby looks like most upscale chains around the world. The sight of the "S" on the side of the building's prominent, concrete-slab wall was comfortingly familiar. As a woman, an American, and a Jew in the post–September 11 world, I was nervous about my trip. Even many of my Pakistani friends warned me to keep to myself and not go out alone. I was happier than usual to find the same coffee shop, lobby chairs, and health club I had encountered over and over in my travels.

Granted, it was not an exact replica. The faux Middle Eastern arches, hanging down from the walls of the sunken lobby, softened what would have been the square, stark angles of a Western hotel. Because alcohol is prohibited in Pakistan, there were no bars serving free hors d'oeuvres during happy hour. The sauna and Jacuzzi had separate hours for women and men. But although I didn't see many other women sitting alone when I went down to breakfast each morning, the hotel was filled with Pakistani businessmen by day and Pakistani upper-middle-class families by night. Here was at least one place, I told myself, where the East coexists with the West.

The next morning, I was less optimistic. One of the first people I met during my visit was Wasim, the thirty-four-year-old founder of one of Pakistan's first venture capital firms. Wasim studied at Pakistan's premier business school, worked abroad in Hong Kong for two years, and then returned with his family to make a go of it. He spoke enthusiastically about Pakistan's growing economy and the Pervez Musharraf government's positive role in turning his country around. But when it came to international affairs, he was bleak.

> I think we are at a point where Samuel Huntington's *Clash of Civilizations* may really become true.[4] I, for one thing, am wishing that it won't. But for a number of reasons, I think that will happen and that there will be a lot of bloodshed. I hope it won't happen in my lifetime but I fear that that time is probably not too far away. Twenty years ago, it appeared that the world was completely secular. Now it appears that religious fundamentalists are everywhere, whether they be Christians, Jews, or Muslims. . . . That is all the more reason to worry about how Islam is represented today. I don't want bin Laden to represent me. I want myself to represent myself. But thanks to radicals here and in the West, he is portrayed as the only representative of Islam—that is a very scary for me. There is a similar thing happening on your end. All the good things about American society are being eroded one after the other. I see a pretty scary end to all this. There is not much hope at the moment. There is nothing I can latch on to. I wanted to share these things with you because it is important that the American people hear this. Our only hope is that by talking with one another, things can become clearer and maybe things will change.

Wasim recognizes the salience of religion. He has strong religious beliefs of his own. Yet unlike Florence, he appreciates diversity and does not expect everyone to believe in the same things he does. Instead, he knows that religion's role is changing, and he is struggling to figure out what it should be and what he should do about it. Wasim doesn't want religious extremists to control the radio dial. He wants an open, respectful conversation between people of different faiths who agree on common goals and work toward them together. Religion, he says, shows us the right way to live and inspires us to be tolerant. It's not a license for self-righteousness.

This book is written to the Alices, Luises, Florences, and Wasims of the world. Antireligionists and secular humanists can no longer afford to act as if religion will just go away. Nor should exclusivists like Florence go unchallenged. Religion is here to stay, driven by forces inside and outside our borders. Right now, conservative religious voices control the airwaves. We can't just turn off the radio because we don't like the program. We have to make sure that more secular, humanist, moderate, and progressive religious stations, reflecting a wider range of views, are on the air.

Wasim raises the critical question. He knows that religion has a dismal track record, but he also sees its potential. He worries about its growing strength, although he also believes in its potential to be a moral compass in a world set dramatically off course by materialism, individualism, and fundamentalism. He doesn't like that Osama bin Laden and George Bush represent faith's public face, but he's not sure what a new cast of characters would look like or what their message would be. He knows, though, that it is much more complicated than the daily headlines lead us to believe. It's not just about what is happening inside America. It doesn't just boil down to bin Laden versus the pope, or the West versus the rest. To be sure, there are some "mini Osamas" out there, just as there are saints. Most people, however, fall somewhere in between. True religious pluralism means making more than just superficial room for their voices. Given current world events, and that religious extremism is so often behind them, we can't afford not to listen.[5]

1

Redefining the Boundaries of Belonging

Spring quietly announced its arrival on an early New York morning in March. New buds softened the stark winter branches. Business owners swept the sidewalks, and arranged their fruits and vegetables, as I walked down street after nearly empty street. Fathers sleepwalked through their Saturday morning routine of taking the baby out to the local coffee shop so their wives could sleep in. Early spring in New York—comfortingly predictable.

But New York, like the Sheraton Hotel in Karachi, is always about surprises as well as the familiar. There is the main attraction, taking place in Times Square, at Rockefeller Center, or Ground Zero, and then there are the myriad small performances going on off-Broadway at alternative theaters that reveal much more about the heart of urban life.

I was on my way to a memorial service for Reverend Pandurangshastri Athavale, the leader of the Swadhyaya movement in India, who died in November 2003. The members of the *Swadhyaya Parivar* or "Swadhyaya family" in Lowell who I befriended while writing this book had invited me to attend the ceremony. As I made my way over to the Jacob Javits Convention Center, I noticed the many little preparations under way that I would have missed had I not had "tickets." Cars crammed full with large extended families hurried to find spaces in the neighborhood parking lots. Dozens of yellow school buses transported Swadhyayees from all over the region to the convention center doors. And groups of followers, wearing name tags written in Gujarati pinned to the lapels of their winter coats, were being shepherded over from Penn Station. While New York woke up, and grew busy with shoppers, tourists, and antiwar protesters, the curtain was rising on an important yet barely noticed sideshow.

And it was a wonderful, enlightening performance. When I arrived at the convention center, a long line of visitors slowly wending their way into the building greeted me. Two queues fed into two long stairways leading into a large exhibition hall, a banner strung over its entrance announcing "Memorial Service for the Rev. Pandurangshastri Athavale," or, as his followers call him, Dadaji. Swadhyayees, who are famous for managing multiday events attended by millions in India, have masterfully adopted their crowd control skills to the United States.

One turn away from the entrance to the meeting room, we arrived at a carpet. Men dressed in white shirts and dark trousers, to identify them as part of the organizing team, distributed plastic bags for visitors to store their shoes. These were then hung, three to four deep, on coatracks lined with strings to make improvised "shoe checks." One always removes one's shoes before entering a Hindu holy place, and in India, public temples have shoe racks as a matter of course. But in New York, Swadhyayees had to be creative, and to do so in a way that at the end of the day, thousands of visitors went home with their own footwear.

Once barefoot, followers entered and moved through the auditorium along two carpeted pathways. Between them were twenty or so photographs of Dadaji as well as his niece and successor, Didiji. Designs made out of flowers and flower petals adorned the floor in front of each portrait. Some were just decorative while others formed Gujarati phrases. Chanting filled the room, although I was not sure where it came from.

Each line moved slowly toward a set of stairs ascending to a stage hidden from view by a curtain. Eight men sat on the other side of the curtain, all wearing white. They were the chanters, singing line after line of *slokas* or prayer verses they read from mimeographed sheets in loose-leaf binders. At the center of the stage, a bronze urn containing Dadaji's ashes rested on a pedestal. Beyond that, Didiji greeted the receiving line. All through the month of March, she presided over similar events in Chicago, Toronto, Los Angeles, and other North American cities where there are large Swadhyaya communities. By the end of this day, more than ten thousand Indians from the East Coast would pay their respects to their leader. A representative from the mayor's office, who attended a special commemorative ceremony in the afternoon, declared March 20 Dadaji's day on New York City's calendar.

Similar gatherings, also below the radar of most Americans, happen around the country on a regular basis. The Brazilian Protestant community in New England holds a day of prayer and celebration at the TD Banknorth Garden (formerly the Boston Garden) in Boston each year where preachers from Brazil are invited guests. Leaders of the International Swaminarayan Satsang Organization (ISSO), a Hindu community that many of the Gujaratis in this book belong to, greet overflowing crowds of followers at football stadiums around the country each summer.

America is likely to remain a Christian country. And migrants who settle definitively in the United States will always outnumber migrants who continue to be active in their homelands. But groups like Swadhyaya, albeit at the margins, are changing the face of American religion and religious life around the globe. They signal important changes on the way.

Scholars like Diana Eck, Martin Marty, Robert Wuthnow, and Alan Wolfe applaud our country's increasing religious diversity. They nevertheless see it as a product of forces operating inside the United States.[1] But like the Swadhyayees, many migrants belong to religious communities that simultaneously promote their integration into the United States, keep them connected to their ancestral homes, and link them to religious movements around the world. American religious diversity, therefore, is sometimes shaped as much by forces at work outside our borders as within them.

Our deeply held assumptions about immigration and religion don't reflect this reality. We assume that what happens in America is made in America. We expect newcomers to assimilate, becoming part of "our" community by severing their ties to their homelands. And we tell ourselves we are religiously diverse even when our expectations about what religion is and where to find it are based on Christian models. Protestantism is what Martin Marty calls "the wallpaper in the mental furnishing department in which America lives, always in the room but barely noticed."[2] While American culture claims secularity and tolerance, it in fact demands religiosity, and that of a certain kind, which leaves increasing numbers among us out.

We need a wider lens that sees American religious pluralism as an integral piece of the global religious puzzle.[3] Just as corporate CEOs would be out on the streets in a heartbeat if they did not understand that their companies are part of the global economy, so we miss the boat by insisting that religion and culture stop at the nation's borders. Just as we recognize the U.S. economy is made up of worldwide production and distribution networks, so we must see the local mosque or Pentecostal church as part of multilayered webs of connection where religious "goods" are produced and exchanged around the globe.

Immigrants' everyday experiences drive home the need for this broader view. Many continue to vote, invest, raise children, and pray in their homelands while they put down roots in the United States. They come from places where it is difficult to separate religion from culture and where the state plays an active role in regulating religious life. They are used to combining elements from different faith traditions in their worship and belonging to several groups simultaneously. Because mixing and matching is the rule, not the exception, religion is a permission slip for belonging to several communities at once.

True religious pluralism requires making room for these varieties of religious experience and understanding what they mean for religion's role in public life. It means taking a hard look at some of our taken-for-granted assumptions, and acknowledging honestly who they welcome and who they render invisible.[4] And I am talking about pluralism, not just about tolerance. Tolerant people acknowledge difference. They are willing to live side by side with people who are not like them, but are unwilling to be changed by them. Pluralists believe that no single religion has absolute authority over a single religious truth. They are willing to engage with and be changed by others, creating something new along the way.

God Needs No Passport

Many religious institutions were founded on universal claims and have always been worldwide in scope. In this current period of globalization, however, religion's universality and globalism often take precedence over its national forms. Religion, like capitalism or politics, is no longer firmly rooted in a particular country or legal system.[5]

This happens, in part, because religion is the ultimate boundary crosser. God needs no passport because faith traditions give their followers symbols, rituals, and stories they use to create alternative sacred landscapes, marked by holy sites, shrines, and places of worships.[6] For some people, these spaces are less important than the actual political geography. Others belong to faith-based global movements that coexist easily with their national and ethnic identities. Still others place more significance on the religious landscape than its secular counterpart. Minarets, crosses, and sanctuaries, rather than national monuments or historic structures, are the salient landmarks in these imaginary terrains. What happens in Bombay, London, Johannesburg, Sydney, or Trinidad, for example, matters much more to some Swadhyaya members because these are the boundaries of a sort of "Swadhyaya country." Religion also transcends the boundaries of time because it allows followers to feel part of a chain of memory, connected to a past, a present, and a future.[7] That is why Cubans in Miami, say, bring their newborns to be baptized at a shrine they built to their national patron saint. There, they induct their children into an imagined Cuban nation with a past in their ancestral land, a present in Miami, and a future they hope to reclaim again in Cuba.[8]

Among the more than 80 percent of U.S. residents who call themselves Christians, the majority are Protestant (about 52 percent), followed by Catholics (about 24 percent).[9] Those who claim "no religious preference" comprise about 10 percent of the population.[10] Although the numbers of Muslims and Buddhists have doubled in the past decade, and the numbers of Hindus have tripled, non-Christians still represent a fairly small portion of America.[11] Jews and Muslims represent only 2 and 1.5 percent of the population, respectively, and "Eastern" religions, such as Buddhism and Hinduism, weigh in at less than 1 percent each.[12]

But while their numbers are small, their cultural influence is great. Especially after September 11, the social impact of these non-Christian newcomers is much larger than their numbers would suggest. And America's increasing religious diversity is evident on more and more street corners. The sign at the local Protestant Church now includes a line in Korean or Chinese to attract newcomers to the ethnic congregations that worship there. In between the Subway and Dunkin Donuts at the strip mall is a new Swadhyaya meeting hall. Religious groups that were once tightly connected to one immigrant community have become "disengaged," abandoning their particularistic commitments in favor of a more universal and inclusive approach. When the White House hosts Divali and Eid celebrations each year, it is sending a clear signal to the American public that our religious rainbow is changing.[13]

Putting Religion in the United States and around the Globe on the Same Map

New immigrants introduce new faiths as well as Latinoize and Asianize well-established denominations. By belonging to religious communities, they make a place for themselves in the United States and maintain connections to people around the world. A 1996 pilot survey of "new immigrants" conducted by Guillermina Jasso and her colleagues found that Catholicism (42 percent), Christian-Protestant (19 percent), and "No Religion" (15 percent) were their top religious preferences.[14] By some estimates, newcomers from Mexico and other Latin American countries account for nearly 40 percent of the country's Roman Catholics.[15] Between 1990 and 2001, the proportion of newly arriving Asian Christians fell from 63 to 43 percent while those professing Asian religions increased from 15 to 28 percent.[16] Jasso and her colleagues also found that four times more respondents professed faiths other than Judeo-Christianity than the native born—nearly 17 versus 4 percent. Surveys conducted in 2004–5 found a continued rise in non-Christian religious preferences.[17]

Incorporating newcomers is an age-old story for Catholics, who had lots of practice turning Irish and Italian immigrants into American Catholics, and use many of the same techniques to incorporate Brazilians and Vietnamese. But mainline and evangelical Protestant faiths are not as experienced at integrating newcomers, although they face great incentives to do so, given the sharp declines in their native-born membership.[18] Many new immigrants are the product of missionary work done in Latin America and Asia during the 1900s.[19] The descendants of those who converted bring their own version of Christianity back to the United States, asking to practice their faith alongside their denominational brothers and sisters. How they ultimately do so is a major engine of religious change.[20]

Other immigrants belong to global religious movements uniting members, who happen to be living in the United States, with fellow believers around the globe. Charismatic Catholics, for example, belong to small communities of prayer and fellowship that connect them to other followers worldwide. The Tablighi Jama'at, one of the largest transnational Islamic movements, is now believed to be comparable in size and scope to Christian Pentecostalism.[21]

Migrants and nonmigrants who follow particular saints, deities, or religious teachers also form imagined global communities of connection. One of the fastest-growing religious shrines in Mexico, for instance, is Santa Ana de Guadalupe in Jalisco State, where Saint Toribio, who guides migrants safely across the border, is believed to have been born. Santa Ana grew from a former backwater into a major tourist destination for people who feel an affinity to the saint and a sense of kinship toward each other.[22]

Finally, religious leaders and teachers meet, virtually and actually, to form religious public squares where they debate what constitutes appropriate practice in the twenty-first century. Long before they emerged in the West, Muslim scholars and public figures created these kinds of arenas in what are now Indonesia, Pakistan, and Egypt. In their contemporary form, scholars and professionals develop networks, attend conferences, participate in chat rooms, and establish institutions to figure out how universally shared faith and values can be translated into local contexts.[23]

But it is not just the cast of characters, or who they are connected to around the world, that is redefining the boundaries of religious belonging in the United States. The ideas migrants bring with them about the meaning of faith and what it looks like also drive these changes. The separation of church and state is so firmly embedded in the American psyche that people in the United States tend to treat religion and culture as more distinct than they actually are. But many newcomers come from places where religion and culture go hand in hand. They cannot sort out Irishness from Catholicism, Indianness from being Hindu, or what it means to be Pakistani from what it means to be a Muslim. Faith guides how they live their everyday lives, whom they associate with, and the kinds of communities they belong to, even among people who say they are not religious. Their ideas about tolerance and diversity are shaped by experiences where states actively regulate religious life, and where expectations about relations between "us" and "them" are quite different from those in the United States.

As a result, many immigrants bring a much broader understanding of what religion is and where to find it to the table. When people adorn their refrigerator doors with "saint magnets," hang cross-stitched samplers with religious teachings on their walls, light candles in honor of the *Virgen,* or decorate their rearview mirrors and dashboards with photos of their gurujis, they imbue the quotidian with the sacred. The religious and the spiritual also spill over into the workplace, the school yard, the health clinic, and the law office. When a Latino family celebrates its daughter's fifteenth birthday or a Hindu son invites his elderly father to live with him in the United States, they are performing religious as well as "cultural" acts. For some newcomers, American values are in part religious values. And these values are made not just in the United States but around the world.

Migrants also bring different understandings of what membership in a religious community means. Some people belong to an official congregation with a leader who espouses a version of faith his or her followers share. But many others do not form part of one religious community with whom they pray on a regular basis—they have no ongoing relationship with a leader who tells them what to think and feel. There is no one right way to practice that everyone subscribes to. Many are comfortable worshipping at any church, temple, or mosque. Faith is an individual affair not a collective experience. You can practice it at home or in the park just as well as in an official sanctuary. So when Muslims silently say their prayers while stopped at a traffic light because there is no place nearby to pray, they are transforming the practice of Islam in America and talking back to Christian expectations about faith. They also tell people back home about their experiences where religious practice is also changing.

And just as the walls of religious buildings are permeable, so are the boundaries between faiths.[24] Many people come from countries where religious practice has always combined elements from different traditions. Brazilian Catholicism, for example, has long included indigenous, African, and Christian practices, giving followers permission to be many things at one time. Similarly, many of the Gujaratis in this story had no problem belonging to several communities at once because all the pieces fit under the broad Hindu umbrella. For these individuals, boundary crossing or combining elements from different faiths is an accepted part of their everyday religious experience. The American context, with its wide array of religious choices, strongly encourages this kind of mixing and matching.

What's more, religion has never obeyed political or ethnic boundaries. The Crusaders resurrected Christianity in a range of dominions, kingdoms, and principalities claimed by Muslims. Incan, Mayan, and Aztec traditions across Latin America were forcibly absorbed by Hispanic Catholicism. The British spread Anglicanism to the four corners of their empire. Even the birth of the modern nation-state system has not required God to use a passport. There are one billion Catholics around the globe—just less than the population of China. India's population of 966 million is only slightly bigger than the number of Sunni Muslims worldwide, at 900 million.[25] The Catholic Church has the most sophisticated, far-reaching system of global governance, linking its members around the world through its National Conferences and social movement chapters. But many denominations, such as the Baptist World Alliance and the ISSO described here, are creating administrative structures that are increasingly global in reach.[26]

These changes in religious demography are transforming the balance of power within global religious institutions. At the last ten-year meeting of the Anglican Communion, Third World bishops challenged the traditional authority of English and American prelates, and their positions on homosexuality, abortion, and the ordination of women. The center of political gravity in Roman Catholicism, dominated until only recently by Italian leaders, is slowly shifting as more and more cardinals from Africa, Asia, and South America are appointed to positions of power.[27]

Making More Room Is What the United States Is About

The American story has always been a religious one with a diverse cast of characters.[28] People in the United States attend church more frequently than any other nation at a comparable level of development—nearly five out of every ten Americans go to religious services each week. According to Will Herberg, whose book *Protestant, Catholic, Jew* is still one of the classics on immigrant religious life, immigrants were expected to abandon their nationality and language, but were not expected to abandon their faith. In fact, through religion, immigrants and their children carved out a space for themselves in America.[29] To be American was to be religious. Asserting a religious identity was an acceptable way to be different and be American at the same time.[30]

Moreover, immigration and religion in the United States have always been part of larger global processes. This country was founded by religious people looking for religious freedom. Its story is about successive waves of successful religious accommodation that were each global in their own way. What is happening today is a third wave of "moving over" to make room for non-Christian voices—a reasonable next chapter in our ongoing saga.

The first encounter between people of different faiths involved different kinds of Protestantisms. The Christianity they brought with them was neither completely homegrown nor simply transplanted but inherently transnational because they continued to carry it back and forth across the Atlantic.[31] The Puritan heritage so strongly associated with New England, and considered seminal to the awakening and development of a distinctly "American" religious identity, underwent continual interactions with Catholicism in France and Spain. It was fertilized by and itself nourished religious thought, belief, and practice all over the world. We must see religious development in America, urges historian David D. Hall, with a "double vision," as being dependent on but independent of its European counterparts—cosmopolitan and provincial in the same breath.[32]

Seventeenth-century New Amsterdam, where eighteen different languages were spoken, is often cited as an early example of modern American pluralism. Although most of its residents came in search of the economic opportunities the new land offered, not for religious freedom, the Dutch West India Trading Company made the Dutch Reformed Church officially responsible for the colony. After a few short years, religious diversity expanded to include Jesuits, Anabaptists, Mennonites, Presbyterians, Puritans, and Lutherans. In fact, in spite of Governor Stuyvesant's reservations, the company's directors insisted on a policy of tolerance, and prevented him from banishing Quakers and Jews.[33] And while the religions of early America imported ideas, they also exported notions of their own. What has been analyzed separately as the American Great Awakening, the English Evangelical Revival, and the Scottish Cabuslang Wark was perceived by many of its participants as part of a single God-inspired phenomenon.[34]

The transnational face of the Catholic Church in America, beginning with the massive influx of southern Europeans in the nineteenth century, represents the second wave of religious accommodation, during which Catholics and Jews have been included to various degrees into the Protestant mix. Again, transnational flows moved in both directions. On the one hand, an array of ethnically particular traditions were exported and maintained inside and outside of immigrant enclaves in the United States. In 1892, for example, Antonín Dvořák had no trouble following the prayers at Saint Wenceslaus's parish in Spillville, Iowa, which he visited on his vacation, just as today, people visiting from Brazil feel perfectly comfortable worshipping at Saint Tarcisius in Framingham, Massachusetts.[35] At the same time, the structure of the Catholic Church in America changed from one that tolerated a range of ethnic traditions into what some called a "national" church. Although sometimes reluctantly, the Vatican accepted American Catholic positions on authority, procedures, and church order reflecting the unique democratic, individualistic, and liberal culture of the United States.[36]

Nor were Protestant churches immune to transnational religious influences during this period. Denominations constantly changed in response to newly arriving members. The Lutheran Church experienced continual schisms and bouts of Americanizing and de-Americanizing. In early eighteenth-century New York, its official language changed from German to English, only to change back again to German following a pre–Civil War influx of immigrants.[37]

Many European churches remained strongly connected to their expatriate members because they still felt responsible for them, and because they wanted their political and financial support. Others, fearing migrants would convert in the United States, contributed money, clergy, and resources to create ethnic churches.[38] The Hungarian government, for example, directly subsidized loyal churches, priests, schools, and newspapers, regardless of their members' ethnicity, to dampen opposition among those living abroad.[39] During the first two decades of the 1900s, Chinese Protestants successfully persuaded Chinese Americans to support a republican government in China. Using evangelical teachings, they criticized China as a backward, pagan land that would become modern and democratic only if it became Christian. "The immediate aim of our effort is the salvation of souls by preaching of the gospel," one leader remarked in 1917. "The ultimate aim is the redemption of China through the earnestness of our converted young men when they return to the homeland."[40] Other churches feared migrants and returnees, anxious that converts would proselytize or stir things up by challenging their authority. In fact, returnees normally did not treat priests as deferentially as they had before they left. Thousands used the political organizing skills they learned abroad to create village organizations, labor unions, and even political parties, which challenged church power.[41]

What we are witnessing today, then, is the logical next step along a broadening continuum of religious diversity that has always been driven by forces inside and outside our borders. Asking Protestantism to make room is not to discount its fundamental role in laying the foundation for religious tolerance in this country. The nonprofit sector has been influenced strongly by Protestant associational archetypes. Common governance and organizational forms are based on the Protestant polity. As Peter Dobkin Hall writes, "Far from being a 'second-order phenomenon,' religion (in particular, liberal Protestant values) was integral in the development of American corporate technology. The rationales and methods of bureaucratic and corporate organization actually emerged from the domain of religion and spread from there to the economic, political and social institutions."[42] These templates have deep roots and profoundly shape American public life. They are not likely to go away, nor necessarily should they.

Instead, challenging Protestant privilege is to bring to light these routinized aspects of American life to see whom they help and whom they hurt. It is to call attention to the subjective experience of being among the "unprivileged" or what it feels like to be on the wrong side of the default category. Just as women internalize a certain minority status when the operative pronoun is "he," so Muslims, Hindus, and Buddhists, and for that matter Jews and Catholics, feel like outsiders when Protestant cultural references and practices are the automatic norm. It is also to challenge us to live up to the high bar set by Protestantism's legacy. If the American story is about effectively making room for successive waves of religious newcomers, it is a heritage worth perpetuating.

Thinking Outside the National Box

Grasping that people earn their livings, participate in election campaigns, or raise children across borders is challenging because many of us take for granted that the world has been and always will be organized into sovereign nation-states.

But such a view is short on history. Capitalism, imperial and colonial regimes, antislavery and workers' rights campaigns, illegal pirating networks, and of course religions have always crossed borders. The modern nation-state system did not even exist until after the Treaty of Westphalia in 1648. In the early 1900s, there were barely 130 sovereign states; the remaining 65 percent of the world's political entities were colonies and protectorates. Three-quarters (150) of the more than 200 countries recognized today came into existence in the past century.[43]

Assuming that social life automatically takes place within a national container blinds us to the way the world actually works. Assuming that political outcomes are decided nationally doesn't give enough credit to political and social movements involving activists from around the world. Taking literally the label "Made in the U.S.A." ignores the fact that some piece of that garment was probably made in Latin America or Asia. Eberhard Sandschneider, the research director at the German Council on Foreign Relations in Berlin, got it right when he told the 2005 Davos delegates, "What we are increasingly seeing is a multidimensional system in which states and state-based multilateral organizations work with businesses and civil society through a dense web of international and interdisciplinary networks."[44] Bush administration officials, who told the members of the 9-11 Independent Commission that what happened was completely beyond their imagination because they could not envision a terrorist operation organized across borders, nor did they have the capacity to respond to one, got it dangerously wrong.

To pick up on these dynamics, one has to trade in a national lens for a transnational one. It is not to deny the continuing importance of nation-states nor the fact that states continue to regulate many aspects of life. Nor is it to argue that everything is produced by factors operating outside national borders. Indeed, in many cases, cross-border forces play only a small supporting role in the story. It is to say that to understand today's world, one has to ask how individuals and groups actually organize themselves, without assuming, a priori, that they fit neatly within a national box.

Let me explain briefly why I talk about the transnational rather than the global.[45] World-systems research, as well as much recent work in globalization studies, has a lot to say about transnational forms and processes. But much of this "globalist" scholarship treats all kinds of cross-border relationships and phenomena as if they were the same. Structures and processes that differ in strength and character are depicted as comparable.[46] The existence of bounded social units is taken for granted without asking why certain kinds of groups form at certain times. The integration of the system is highlighted, while its diversity and contradictions get short shrift.

Furthermore, institutions and processes are portrayed as if they were unconnected to any territory, when in fact they are rooted in particular places but also transcend their borders. States are ignored or dismissed, although they are alive and well, even if they don't do what they have always done. People and structures operating at different scales and scopes are lost in a picture painted with too broad a brushstroke. They are lumped together into categories, like "worker" or "migrant," that don't take into account the racial, national, or class differences that shape what people think and do.[47]

Research on "the local" also contributes to a transnational perspective. It drives home the importance of paying attention to the sociohistorical context, and the danger of making universalistic generalizations that wash out critical shades of color and tone. It underscores the fact that local agency, knowledge, and cultural practices still matter. But much of this work comes up short by failing to link everyday lived experience with the larger social processes that influence it. A great deal is learned about a particular site and time, but not enough about how the local is historically connected to other places, levels, and scales of social experience.

A transnational gaze begins with a world that is borderless and boundaryless, and then explores what kinds of boundaries exist, and why they arise in specific times and places. It tries hard not to overemphasize the global or the local but to hold these social layers, along with everything in between, in productive conversation with each other. The world is too broad, deep, and complex to be captured by a lens that focuses on a single level of experience. A transnational perspective tries to look at all layers of social life simultaneously and understand how they mutually inform each other. It recognizes that some social processes happen inside nations while many others, though rooted in nations, also cross their borders.

Using a Transnational Lens to Understand Migration

Understanding migration as a transnational process, and that people will simultaneously belong to this country and their homelands for the long haul, reveals several important things.[48] For one, sometimes migration is as much about the people who stay behind as it is about people who move. In some cases, the ties between migrants and nonmigrants are so strong and widespread that migration also radically transforms the lives of individuals who stay home. They don't have to move to participate across borders. People, money, and what I have called social remittances—the ideas, practices, social capital, and identities that migrants send back into their communities of origin—permeate their daily lives, changing how they act as well as challenging their ideas about gender, right and wrong, and what states should and should not do.[49] In response, the religious, social, and political groups they belong to also begin to operate across borders.

Nonmigrants hear enough stories, look at enough photographs, and watch enough videos of birthday parties and weddings filmed in the United States to begin imagining their own lives elsewhere. They covet clothes and accessories that are now a standard part of the dress code. They want to play by the rules they imagine are at work in the United States—which they learn about each time they talk on the phone, receive e-mail, or someone comes to visit. In such cases, migrants and nonmigrants, though separated by physical distance, occupy the same social space. What happens to those in the United States cannot be disconnected from what happens to people who stay home because their fates are inextricably linked. When a small group is regularly involved in its sending country, and others participate periodically, their combined efforts add up. Taken together and over time, they are a social force that can transform the economy, values, and everyday lives of entire regions.

One factor propelling these changes is the enormous amount of

money that migrants send home. According to the World Bank, workers' remittances have doubled in the past decade (to $232 billion in 2005
alone, of which $167 billion went to developing countries). Official fig-
ures, though, probably represent only half the funds people actually
send. The global remittance market may be as large as $300–$400
billion annually.[50] Countries like Albania, Bosnia and Herzegovina,
Croatia, El Salvador, Haiti, Samoa, Yemen, and Jordan are among the
thirty-six where remittances exceed private and official capital inflows,
and are the primary source of foreign currency.[51] They depend so heavily on remittances that their economies might collapse if they declined.
To make sure they do not, numerous governments now offer emigrants
some form of long-distance, long-term membership. States as diverse
as France, Ireland, Greece, the Dominican Republic, Brazil, Italy, Por-
tugal, and China give emigrants and their descendants full rights when
they return to their homelands, even if they are passport holders of another country. Colombia even grants political rights to emigrants who
are abroad by allowing expatriates to elect representatives to the
Colombian legislature.[52]

Looking at migrants and nonmigrants transnationally also drives
home that their lives are influenced by people and organizations in
many other places. Salvadoran villagers and their migrant family
members in Los Angeles are not simply connected by their personal relationships. They are also connected by political and social organizational ties that link these two settings. Further connections arise from
ties between the Salvadoran and U.S. governments and the Salvadoran
and U.S. Catholic Church.[53] Similarly, understanding the religious lives
of Brazilians in Massachusetts requires looking beyond the connections
between specific congregations in Boston and Brazil and placing them
in the context of the thick, multilayered web of denominational connections linking the two countries.

Finally, seeing migrants and nonmigrants as occupying the same social space also drives home dramatic changes in the meaning of incorporation. The immigrant experience is not a linear, irreversible journey
from one membership to another. Rather, migrants pivot back and forth
between sending, receiving, and other orientations at different stages of
their lives. The more their lives are grounded in legal, health care, and
pension systems on both sides of the border, the more likely it is that
their transnational lives will endure.[54] Increasing numbers of newcom-

ers will not fully assimilate or remain entirely focused on their homelands but will continue to craft some combination of the two.[55]

A Blessing or a Threat?

Many Americans feel that keeping one foot in the United States and one
foot in the country that you come from will only lead to trouble. They
believe it is impossible to pursue American and homeland dreams at the
same time. As Wasim was well aware, Samuel Huntington's 2004 book
Who Are We? warned us that we are headed toward an internal "clash
of civilizations" because (primarily) Mexican immigrants do not assimilate Anglo-Protestant values, and because they remain behind linguistic and political walls.[56]

To survive and thrive as a nation, many believe, America needs newcomers to "become Americans," subscribe to a core set of values, and
abandon their ancestral homes. Especially after September 11, they
argue, aren't those who are loyal to two countries suspect? Transnational
institutions like the United Nations threaten U.S. sovereignty, these critics claim, rather than enhance global understanding. "Would we want
decisions about the war in Iraq to be made in Paris or Geneva?" the
speakers at the 2004 Republican National Convention repeatedly asked
listeners. Choices affecting America should be decided in America.

That religion encourages multiple loyalties really makes people's
blood boil.[57] So many acts of terrorism and violence are perpetrated in
the name of God.[58] Not just al-Qaeda but Hindu, Christian, and Jewish
groups espouse versions of faith that leave little room for argument.
The Alices and Luises of the world claim that religion makes us com-
placent about social injustice. Besides, they ask, how can you support a
Catholic Church that opposes condoms, or a pastor or imam who
preaches that women are inferior to men?

Again, my most promising conversation partner is Wasim. He asks, if
religion often sharply divides us, why can't it also be the bricks with
which we bridge these divides? Clearly, we should be afraid when religious extremists want to make the world over in their own image and
are willing to commit suicide to do so. We should worry when secular
public space, narrowed in the name of God, compromises basic rights.
But the vast majority of people in the world, whether in the East, West,
North, or South, are not religious extremists. They live transnational

lives not to perpetrate atrocities but to achieve something better for themselves and their families. In India, Pakistan, Brazil, Ireland, or the United States, most of the people I talked with were concerned about raising their children, helping their communities, and being able to live safely and securely in places where the schools and police departments work. Their stories could not be reduced to simple punch lines with clear heroes and villains. Their dreams are ones we can all agree on. And as these pages will reveal, while there were those who felt they owned the religious truth, the majority were willing to discuss what that truth is and how we should use it to make the world better. This book is about helping them raise their voices, and about how the conversation changes as a result.

2

Transnational Lives

More than one million people arrived in the United States during the first and last decades of the twentieth century—two "bookends" that bracket the immigrant experience. The people who came in the 1990s hailed from different parts of the world than those who came at the turn of the century. In the early 1900s, the top five countries sending immigrants to the United States were Italy, Russia, Hungary, Austria, and the United Kingdom; one hundred years later, they were Mexico, the Philippines, China, India, and the Dominican Republic.[1]

These trends have dramatically altered U.S. demography. Immigrants and their native-born children make up more than one-quarter of the nation's population.[2] In 1900, most of the foreign born came from Europe—nearly 9 out of 10 million.[3] In 2000, nearly 54 percent of the 33.5 million foreign born were from Latin America.[4] Today one out of every eight residents of the United States is Latino. By 2100, these numbers could increase to one out of every three.[5] In 1900, just over 120,000 foreign-born residents were from Asia.[6] In 2002, there were 13.1 million Asian-born people in the country, representing a more than eightfold increase in less than forty years.[7]

New immigrants are moving to places where newcomers have not traditionally settled. While in 1910, New York, Chicago, Philadelphia, and Boston were the destinations of choice, today's most popular destinations are the Sun Belt and the West.[8] Although most migrants still move to large urban centers, increasing numbers are moving to smaller cities, suburbs, and rural areas. In New England, the foreign born were responsible for nearly half the total population growth in the 1990s. North-central Massachusetts and southern New Hampshire are now

dotted with South Asian and Latino grocery and video stores catering to this influx. Other migrants move farther off the beaten path. Between 1990 and 2000, the number of foreign born in the South and Midwest grew by 88 and 65 percent, respectively. Much of this growth took place in small towns that have little experience with immigration. Whether they pack poultry in the Carolinas or raise cattle in rural Nebraska, migrants are diversifying areas that previously knew little heterogeneity.[9]

While the conventional wisdom tells us that migrants' ties to their homelands weaken as they become part of this country, this has never been true. Migrants have always stayed connected to their homelands while they became Americans, and not just through their membership in faith communities. Between 1880 and 1920, an estimated one-quarter to one-third of all immigrants repatriated.[10] Many people also circulated between their home and host countries, working seasonal jobs during the warmer months and returning to Europe during winter layoffs. Like their contemporaries, they saved money to buy land, build homes, or support family members back home. Hometown clubs funded improvement projects, provided famine relief, and aided communities ravaged by war. In fact, remittances to Italy were so high between 1900 and 1920 that the secretary of the Society for the Protection of Italian Immigrants claimed that Italians in New York contributed more to the tax rolls than some of the poor provinces in Sicily and Calabria.[11]

Today's migrants are just continuing a long-standing though unacknowledged tradition. And telephones, e-mail, and airplanes make it easier and cheaper for them to do so. The numbers of people who participate regularly in homeland affairs are fairly small. Sociologist Alejandro Portes and his colleagues found that only about 5 to 10 percent of the Dominican, Salvadoran, and Colombian migrants they studied were active in homeland economics or politics on a regular basis.[12] But many more occasionally took part in a range of home country–oriented activities, particularly during elections, economic downturns, natural disasters, or important life-cycle events. Doing so is part and parcel of living in a global world.

Most national debates about immigration overlook this key fact. They assume that if we just get a handle on what is going on inside the United States, our problems will be solved. But you only have to walk down the streets of Flushing, New York; South Central Los Angeles; Lowell, Massachusetts; or Nashua, New Hampshire, to recognize this is only half the story. The many ethnic grocery stores, travel agents, churches, political party headquarters, and money-sending agencies that line their sidewalks are the proof in the pudding. To understand the immigration experience, we have to look at what is happening in the United States and the places that migrants come from because, increasingly, they are two sides of the same coin.

Valadarenses

> I named my cows Kennedy and Clinton because America has been so good to my family.
>
> —Luisa, seventy-year-old woman
> in Engenheiro Caldas, Brazil

You can see the Pico do Ibituruna, the small mountain overlooking Governador Valadares, from anywhere in the city. Strong and depend-

able, it is one of the few stable elements in a place that has changed dramatically in the past thirty years.

About 255,000 people live in Valadares, located in the Brazilian state of Minas Gerais.[13] The city is relatively new. Lutheran migrants from Germany established it in the 1930s. As a result, unlike most Latin American cities, which are overwhelmingly Catholic, it is not built around a main cathedral or central plaza. Protestantism was present at Valadares's founding, and is alive and well today.

As recently as 1980, 88 percent of the Brazilian population claimed to be Catholic, although few regularly attended Mass. By 2000, 15 percent identified as Protestants, including an estimated 85 percent who were Pentecostal/Evangelical.[14] A broad spectrum of Protestant groups is represented in Valadares today. In fact, in one neighborhood of about four thousand residents, we counted more than thirty churches. The churches ranged from tumbledown storefronts to large, new buildings that could seat over a thousand. Even congregations that were clearly struggling to survive had plaques outside their doors announcing their ties to sister congregations in Massachusetts.

A long history connects Valadares to the United States. North American mining company executives first went there during World War II. The Rockefeller Foundation funded large public health projects to protect the mining employees from endemic diseases. After the war, "the Morrison," as locals refer to it, came to the city to build a railroad. The company's employees socialized with the Valadares elite, introducing them to the washing machines and dishwashers they brought with them, and establishing organizations like the Rotary Club. They also awarded scholarships to promising young Valadarenses, who became the first to migrate to the United States. One story goes that migration to Boston began in earnest when mining executives went back home and took young women with them to work as domestic servants. Others say it began when a soccer team went to Boston to play a match and never came back.

Once in place, migrant networks notoriously spread. When the economy, which revolves largely around ranching, declined sharply in the 1970s, Valadarenses took advantage of these connections and moved en masse to the United States. Migration increased considerably in the 1980s, following a failed economic stabilization program that hit hard at the middle and working classes. According to estimates from the Brazilian Ministry of Foreign Affairs (Itamaraty), in the late 1990s, 1.9 million Brazilians lived abroad, mostly in the United States, Paraguay, Japan, and Europe. The majority left Brazil in the 1980s and 1990s, settling primarily in Massachusetts, Florida, and New York.[15] Although Itamaraty estimates of the numbers of emigrants hover near 800,000, according to the 2000 U.S. Census, there were only 181,076 people of Brazilian ancestry nationwide, with just 30,583 residing in Massachusetts.[16] There is no doubt, however, that the Brazilian population has grown tremendously in the past decade, with the numbers quadrupling in the Boston metropolitan area alone.[17] An estimated one-quarter of the Brazilian immigrant population lives in New England.

During my visit in 1997, many people told me that at least half the families they knew had relatives in the Boston area who had settled in suburbs west of the city like Framingham, Clinton, Hudson, and Marlboro. Although back then it was rare for people to own their own homes in the United States, many still had property in Brazil. They said that

when something happened in Engenheiro Caldas, a small town outside
of Valadares, they found out about it faster in Framingham than they
did in Ipatinga, a town twenty miles away. Migration fever was endemic
among the youth. Finding someone who spoke fluent English was easy.
And not surprisingly, in each town I went to, everyone knew the houses
where migrants had come back to live or where someone was home for
a visit.

One husband and wife, with their three young children, had moved
back from Danbury, Connecticut, over two years ago. Gracia worked as
a housecleaner, and her husband worked as a maintenance person at a
public housing complex. They liked life in the United States, but felt
that their children would get a better education in Brazil. When their
first child entered kindergarten, they returned, using money they saved
to buy a ranch. They also hoped to use their savings to fix up Gracia's
family's grocery store.

Another returnee, Heloisa, in her thirties, was not so optimistic.
After seven years in the United States, she returned to Brazil and filled
her house with the accoutrements of the American middle class—
Legos, popcorn, and a new DVD player. After two years back, she feared
her family would not make it financially or emotionally. "I don't fit into
this society anymore," she claimed. "I don't respect Brazilian ways.
Everything is so formal. Everyone is always gossiping. You can't even go
to the shopping center without getting all dressed up." Sara, in her early
twenties, back for a visit from Pompano Beach, Florida, where there is
also a large Valadarense community, agreed. A housecleaner, she was
happy to come back for a visit and be pampered by her family, but she
swore she would never return to live. Life here is too slow. She's glad she
has learned to live on her own. Milton, on the other hand, a twenty-
eight-year-old musician from Hudson, Massachusetts, feared he might
have to come back because it was getting so hard to make a living in the
United States. The photos he proudly shared with anyone willing to
look showed him playing guitar at one of the many Brazilian barbeque
or rodizio restaurants that had become so popular around Boston. His
gigs were becoming fewer and farther between because so many restaurants were closing.

Valadares has the feel of a southern European city. Its founders had
the good sense to plant sycamore trees, which are now so big they blan-
ket the street almost completely from the midday sun. There is the old

"American barrio," with its ranch-style bungalows built by the engineers and managers who worked for the Morrison Company. There is the downtown area with businesses like the Boston Café and Framingham Lunch—inspired by their owners' experiences in Massachusetts. There are many new neighborhoods of three- and four-story apartment houses, built by migrants returning from abroad who invested in real estate as their key to a secure future. And there are the older neighborhoods, alternately populated by modest, well-kept houses sitting next to the new or renovated homes, almost palatial by comparison, that were built with remittances from the United States.

During one visit, Gilse, a forty-year-old return migrant, took out a well-worn copy of a now-defunct English-language immigrant community newspaper in Massachusetts, to show me an article in which he was profiled.[18] In the United States, it reports, he made over $160,000 and returned to Valadares to build six apartment houses, which he now rents. He said that he came back because he was afraid his son was being "corrupted" by American influences. He had to work so much that they hardly spent any time together. Yet while he thanks God every day for his good fortune, like Heloisa, his reentry into Brazilian life has not been smooth. His son has different interests than his "sports fanatic" classmates and has had trouble fitting in. Gilse also feels the constant attentions of his neighbors, explaining, "There [in the United States] you are a fish in a river but here you are a fish in an aquarium." Because so many other returnees also built apartment buildings, real estate has not produced the windfalls he had hoped for. When we met, his savings were disappearing fast and he was contemplating a return to Boston.

In this region of Brazil, emigration was on everyone's mind, but so far it had not become central to national debates. Emigrants make up just over 1 percent of the Brazilian population.[19] People leave from specific regions.[20] Brazil still thinks of itself as a country of immigrants rather than one that exports its citizens. Accepting otherwise would mean acknowledging that Brazil's *grandeza*, or greatness—a central pillar of former dictator Getúlio Vargas's program—was not as big or grand as everyone thought.

Although emigration is not front-page news, the government has put into place policies that encourage strong emigrant ties. Former president Fernando Henrique Cardoso made the Consular Affairs Office into a General Directorate in 1995.[21] In 1996, consular offices began organizing councils of citizens to address the community's problems in cities with large Brazilian populations. They also created "mobile consulates" designed to bring consular services "to the people" by periodically holding office hours at convenient locations. That same year, in a largely symbolic move given the haphazard methods employed, the administration conducted a census of Brazilians living abroad, also underscoring their continued membership in the Brazilian nation.

These efforts have regional parallels in areas of significant outmigration. The Valadares economy has grown so dependent on *Valadolares* (or Valadollars—what people call remittances) that when the Brazilian government devalued its currency in 1999, Valadares was the one place in Brazil said to benefit. The mayor of Valadares visited several East Coast cities in the late 1990s. Just as he visits his constituents in Valadares, he said, so he should visit Valadarenses in the United States. The publisher of a Valadares daily newspaper, *O Diario Rio Doce,* added a two-page section with news and advertising from community members in Massachusetts. Articles about weddings, births, and social events held by Valadarenses at home and in the United States were regular features. The Banco do Brasil, in partnership with the mayor's office, set up a special investment fund offering higher than average interest rates to contributors. Its profits were earmarked for regional development projects. The Federacao das Industrias do Estado de Minas Gerais (the Federation of Industries in Minas Gerais) offered technical assistance to return migrants who are planning to set up businesses in Brazil. It also organized a trade fair at the Massachusetts Institute of Technology to encourage graduates to return.

One of the principal destinations at the other end of this migration stream is Framingham. Once a quintessential New England town with its common bordered by white-steepled churches, it has seen better days. Framingham was settled in 1647, in part by refugees from the Salem witch trials. Once filled with large plantations, it soon became an important stopping point on the main road between New York and Boston. Industrialization quickly followed, and Framingham became home to companies such as Denison and General Motors. Company managers lived on the north side of town while Irish and Italian immigrant workers built modest homes on the south side. By the 1950s, Framingham's once-thriving commercial center was largely deserted.

Shopper's World, the country's first mall, opened in 1951, and its mom-and-pop clothing and shoe stores could not compete with the new department stores and chain stores. General Motors and Denison moved on as well. When longtime residents of surrounding communities remember the Framingham of the 1960s and 1970s, they recall a crime-ridden ghost town.

Not so in the eyes of the Brazilian entrepreneurs who began moving to the area in the 1980s. Instead, like other immigrants before them, they saw opportunity for the taking. Soon downtown Framingham was resuscitated by the grocery stores, insurance brokers, and check-cashing and travel agencies they opened in the vacant storefronts. Others found jobs cleaning houses or cars or working in hotels and restaurants.

Not everyone is pleased about the "Brazilianization" of Framingham. While some take pride in the low vacancy rates and the repopulated sidewalks, others feel as Florence does about Lowell. They balk at the signs in Portuguese, claiming they feel unwelcome. Framingham's town leaders want a revitalized downtown, but one that looks like "Framingham in the old days." They hold Brazilians and other residents of color responsible for the town's continuing struggle with crime and drugs.[22]

Valadarenses keep close tabs on what is happening in Brazil. Nearly everyone (90 percent) said they read the Brazilian newspaper regularly, or watched Brazilian television and movies (60 and 75 percent, respectively). Eighty-five percent said they phoned home on a regular basis. But their ties to their homeland have also changed over time. At first, like so many immigrants, no matter how long they had lived in the United States, they insisted they would go back to Brazil. And in fact many did return to build apartments, buy ranches, or open small businesses. Like Gilse, however, they often found it tough going. It was hard to find renters because the real estate market became saturated. It wasn't any easier to make a living at ranching than it had been before they left. After earning U.S. salaries, it was hard to go back to earning reales. And many realized they had grown accustomed to life in America. They liked the fact that rules were rules, and that who you knew didn't help you get around them. They liked the way the government functioned. While Brazil seemed to be falling deeper and deeper under the weight of crime and insecurity, they had felt safe in Framingham. Each successive government promised to lift the average Brazilian out of poverty but it never delivered. Before they knew it, their savings were depleted and they were back to square one.

As a result, in the early 2000s, community leaders saw a shift toward more permanent settlement. They noticed that more and more people wanted to regularize their tax status or buy real estate in Massachusetts rather than in Brazil. Naturalization rates seemed to be increasing. Several organizations came on the scene to address the challenges of the immigrant experience. The Brazilian Business Network promoted small business development. The Brazilian American Association promoted political involvement. Community members joined forces with state representatives to improve relations between Brazilians and long-time Framingham residents.

Barbara Valadares, a forty-five-year-old native-born educator married to a Brazilian, said she noticed people becoming more interested in something other than just "work, work, work." "People now line up at 6:00 a.m. for the 8:00 a.m. opening of registration for English as a second language classes. A few years ago, they couldn't even get enough people to fill a class. I think now they have ten classes, and still have a waiting list of over four hundred people. That's only here in Framingham."

Some people, like Daniel Sales, found being divided between Brazil and Massachusetts too difficult; it hurt one's chances of success. The forty-year-old business owner, who is also studying to be a pastor, said he made up his mind to remain in the United States about a year ago.

An American pastor went to the institute where I study and said, "Do you know why the majority of Brazilians here suffer? Because they come here but continue carrying Brazil on their backs. The day you leave Brazil there and understand that you are here, you will live a little better."

I said to myself, "My God! I can't believe that I needed to hear that. I've been in America for eighteen years, and it is just now that I am discovering how to live in America." For me, the best way I discovered to live in the United States is understanding that I have no more business with Brazil.

Others are making a commitment to the United States and maintaining ties to Brazil at the same time. They still go back on a regular basis to see family, and to purchase an annual supply of their favorite foods and medicine because they are so much cheaper than in the United States. They are holding on to the homes that they own in Valadares even as they purchase property in Framingham.

"I see a big change among a lot of us," said Roberta, a thirty-five-year-old mother of three.

> People are definitely recognizing that they are here to stay. Now for some that means turning away from Brazil and never looking back. But for me, and a lot of my friends, really, that means becoming part of America and being part of Brazil at the same time. In this day and age, why should you have to choose? I can be a very patriotic, loyal member of this community and still care about Brazil and help Brazil at the same time. Look at me, I own a business here, I'm an active leader of the Brazilian community, but I also have business interests and give to charity in Brazil. I mean if Coca-Cola can do it, why shouldn't I?

Living Across Borders: The Gujarati Experience

The suburb of expensive homes with neatly trimmed lawns and sport-utility vehicles seems like any other well-to-do American community. But the mailboxes reveal a twist: almost all are labeled "Patel" or "Bhagat." Over the past twenty years, these Indian immigrants have moved from the villages and small towns of Gujarat State on the west coast of India, initially to rental apartment complexes in northeastern Massachusetts and then to their own homes in subdivisions outside of Boston. Watching these suburban dwellers work, attend school, and build religious congregations here, casual observers might conclude that yet another wave of immigrants has succeeded at the American dream. A closer look, however, reveals they are achieving Gujarati dreams as well. They send money back to India to open businesses and improve family farms. They support the Bharatiya Janata Party and the Indian American Political Forum. The temples and religious schools they build are changing the Gujarati and U.S. religious landscapes. And their influence is not lost on Indian politicians, who energetically encourage their involvement in Indian political and economic life.

Dipa Patel and her husband, Pratik, exemplify people who keep their feet in the United States and their homeland at the same time. And by all accounts, they are enjoying a good deal of success. Nearly six years ago, Pratik left Bodeli, a town of approximately ten thousand, to marry Dipa. He had a bachelor's degree in computer science from an Indian university, and he and his cousin were partners in a computer school franchise. When he first moved to America, Pratik found a job on the assembly line of a large telecommunications firm. Rewarded for his hard work, he moved quickly back on to the engineering track and has ascended the corporate ladder steadily ever since. The company, which during its heyday packed over eight thousand cars into its parking lot each morning, now employs fewer than a thousand people. Pratik is still among them.

Nothing deters Pratik and Dipa from their pursuit of the American dream. As soon as he completed the mandatory five-year residency requirement, Pratik filed for citizenship. He and Dipa now have two young daughters, who are much more conversant in American children's songs and folktales than they are in Indian stories. Pratik takes classes toward his master's at a satellite campus of Boston University in the evenings. Dipa works as a quality insurance supervisor at a computer manufacturing company. Her parents, who live with them and speak little English, are also important players in the extended family's strategic plan. Pratik's mother-in-law found a job at a Pizza Hut, and his father-in-law works at a local quarry. Each month, they go to BJs Warehouse to purchase one more piece of American middle-class life. A large-screen television fills one entire wall of their living room. They drive a spotless Honda Accord. With their new camcorder, they tape endless hours of footage of their children at the park, the temple, and birthday parties so Pratik's parents, who still live in Bodeli, can get to know their grandchildren from afar. And last fall, they finally achieved the pièce de résistance: their own home in a new subdivision in southern New Hampshire.

But Pratik and Dipa are steadfast in pursuing Gujarati dreams too. Physical separation has only strengthened the bonds of the extended family. They send most of the money Pratik's parents use to support themselves back in India. His father closed the watch repair stall he ran in the Bodeli market for over twenty years because the remittances he receives from his son far exceed what he earned before. Pratik is still a

partner in the computer school. He sends money back to buy new equipment any time he has something to spare. And before buying their home in America, the family's first project was to build a second story on to the house in Bodeli, including a separate bedroom suite and Western-style bathroom, which sit empty except when they visit.

One way that Pratik and Dipa's lives transcend national borders is through religion. They belong to the ISSO, a Hindu denomination based in Ahmedabad in Gujarat State that has interconnected chapters all over the world. They spend most of their weekends at the Lowell temple, an old church where the altar is now home to several Hindu deities rather than a cross. On Saturday evenings, there are *sabhas* or prayer sessions followed by a large communal vegetarian meal. There are frequent weddings and holiday celebrations. Pratik and Dipa's children attend religious school classes and youth group meetings each Sunday. Most of their friends are fellow Swaminarayan members who stand in for the extended family they sorely miss in the United States. The community is a limitless fount of social support when a new baby is born, a family moves into a new home, or there is an illness or death. By being Swaminarayan, Pratik and Dipa make a place for themselves in the United States.

At the same time, belonging to the ISSO is very much about maintaining a home in India. Pratik constantly consults with religious leaders, not only about temple business, but about difficult decisions he faces in his personal life. When he was deciding whether he should invest in a small grocery store, he called India. When the community was unsure about whether to participate in a citywide relief drive for Asian tsunami victims, Pratik also called to discuss the pros and cons. In fact, the directors of the temple consult their leaders back home about most important decisions. They also host a steady stream of visiting dignitaries from India and other ISSO communities around the world. By being Swaminarayan, Pratik and Dipa also carve out an enduring place for themselves in their ancestral home.

During one of my trips to India, I visited Vasna, the village where Dipa was raised. Even though it is only seven kilometers from her home in Bodeli, it takes almost two hours to get there. The driver of the 1970s car we rented could go only about ten miles an hour. It was over one hundred degrees outside. The trip would be long and uncomfortable. Still, Dipa's mother- and father-in-law, her sister-in-law and small niece, and her cousin and baby daughter all piled in to accompany my colleague Rajaram and me. The children were dressed in the clothes that Dipa sent from America. That a friend of Dipa's came all this way would signal to the families we visited how well Dipa and Pratik are doing. That Dipa's in-laws put so much time and effort into our visit is one way they could thank their children for their generous support.

After a delicious six-course meal, we set off in the early afternoon. Deciding which houses to stop at, where to take food rather than just water or tea, who would sit on the swing chair—considered the best seat in the house—and how long to stay are all major political calculations. Each decision says something about where the visitor and host stand in relation to each other in the social hierarchy.

Visitors to Vasna are greeted by a large whitewashed, two-story structure, decorated with real and imaginary carved wooden figures. The village's second-largest building is a long, one-story house, with a screened porch extending along its entire length. What looks like a single house are actually five separate, adjacent apartments that open onto this common space. Five brothers live side by side, together and separate. Each family's section is deep and narrow. Mahendra Patel, the eldest brother and thus our official host, offers to take us on a tour. The first room off the porch area is for cooking and eating. Lentils and rice are stored in big metal canisters placed on shelves high up in the eaves. When mealtime comes, the men sit on the floor in a row behind large, round aluminum trays covered with small bowls for dal and vegetables. The women move back and forth down the line, ladling food into each container, eating only after the men finish. The next two rooms are sleeping areas, separated by three-quarter partitions rather than full walls, to allow as much light and air into the part of the house farthest away from the windows and doors. During the daytime, these rooms are nearly empty. The sleeping mats and metal bed frames on which they are rolled out each night are stored away each morning. The back door of the house opens onto a sunlit garden, planted with vegetables, where each family has its own washing area and outhouse.

After our tour, the four brothers still living in the village assemble on the porch to receive us. Mahendra is clearly in charge. He wants me to know that he and his family, and their neighbors in the villages around them, own rich farmland known throughout the region for its fertile soil. They used to grow cotton but now grow cash crops like bananas, tomatoes, and tobacco. Irrigation and modern farming methods have helped them earn more. Yes, Mahendra acknowledges, labor costs are rising, and young people do not want to farm, but they don't have to go to America to make a good living. Nor does he need his relatives in America to support him. Mahendra estimates that only 10 percent of the families in Vasna live off the remittances they receive. Others get money every so often. He personally, he is not ashamed to admit, looks down on those who have left. If you stay here and work hard, you can do very well. Those who have gone, in his opinion, made a deal with the devil. They have forgotten what is important in life and care only about making money.

Mahendra is a Bhagat, an endogamous subcaste from the Baroda District in Gujarat State whose relatives share the same last names as those printed on the mailboxes in suburban Boston. The Uda Bhagats follow Kabir, a sixteenth-century saint admired by Hindus and Muslims alike. Kabir was a *julaha* or weaver, born in Utter Pradesh, who was left by a river, where he was found and raised by Muslim parents. When he grew older, he became a pilgrim, traveling around India to preach against the caste system and social hierarchy. He did not claim to be a god but an intermediary between Ram, an incarnation of God, and his devotees, the Kabirs. On one of his journeys, he met a prince who had rejected worldly concerns and run away so he didn't have to be married. The prince asked to be initiated as a follower, becoming Jivanji Maharaj. Jivanji Maharaj and his descendants, the Bhagats, reject many Brahmanic rituals or Kharma Khand. They do not require a bride's family to pay a dowry or that a priest officiate at their wedding ceremonies. They reject the caste system, and refuse to wear the thread signifying a person is twice born or has been reincarnated.[23]

Today, followers of Kabir live in the Mehsana, Saurashtra, and Surat Districts of Gujarat as well as in Baroda. Jivanji Maharaj's descendant Swami Jagdishchandra Yadunath leads the Baroda community from his throne or *ghadi* in Punyiad, about fifteen miles from Baroda. In 2002, the Bhagat Samaj in Baroda included nearly ten thousand members; about two thousand lived outside India.[24] Dr. Bhagat, the swami's first cousin who lives in Edison, New Jersey, heads the Uda Bhagat organization in the United States.

The Leuva Patels, another subcaste, come from the Charotar area of central Gujarat. They are both endogamous and hypergamous. People who come from one group of six villages, called the Cha Gam, are supposed to marry one another. Boys from these high-status villages, because they are located where the land is very fertile, can also marry girls from the Bavis Gam or twenty-two villages, or the Satyavis Gam or twenty-seven villages, provided the young woman's father can pay the higher dowry required to make this "better" match. Cha Gam girls are not allowed to marry down. Truth be told, however, migration has totally shaken up the status hierarchy because anyone with a green card, regardless of their "home place," automatically rises to the top.

Caste and religious identities often overlap. Many of the Bhagats now belong to Swadhyaya, the group that held the memorial service for Dadaji at the convention center in New York. The Leuva Patels are also well represented among Swaminarayan followers. In addition to the ISSO, which Pratik and Dipa belong to, many others belong to a second Swaminarayan denomination, Bochasanawasi Shree Akshar Purushottam Swaminarayan Santha, which is headquartered in and around Ahmedabad but also has chapters throughout the United States.

After several cups of tea and a snack of mango pulp, we move on to the next village. By 11:00 p.m., when we return to Bodeli for the night, we have been introduced to so many people and drunk so much tea that I cannot bear the thought of another cup. Our visits uncovered a portrait of village life changed dramatically by emigration. In Nana Amadara, where there were about forty Bhagat families, nearly 10 percent of the households had moved en masse to the United States. In another third of the households, at least one member had migrated. Not one belonged to the seventy or so Scheduled Caste families living in the village. In Chhatrali, more than 40 percent of the families had emigrant members living in Massachusetts, New Jersey, and Pennsylvania. Again, there were no emigrants from the "other backward classes" households.

Relatives bring back Mickey Mouse children's dishware and Hello Kitty toys as gifts, although most times, they sit gathering dust on the shelf, considered too special for everyday play. Unopened American shampoo, toothpaste, and perfume line the shelves of many bathrooms. Gujaratis also support hometown improvements. In Nana Amadara, they built a school and a dispensary. Most people, though, prefer to give money directly to needy relatives because they are suspicious of group fund-raising efforts. How much money is raised largely depends on the persuasiveness and reputation of the *Sarpanch* or local village head. In the early 1990s, the residents of Kundanpur collected $500 from each emigrant household and built a small temple that has since become something of a pilgrimage site.

Many of my hosts were anxious to tell about a sister or a daughter who lives in Massachusetts. They took out well-worn pieces of paper, tenderly folded and refolded, with an address written in pencil, to see if I knew where it was. Like in Valadares, there was always someone visiting who was quickly summoned to meet me and compare notes. In fact, before we left Vasna, we met Sonia, a young woman, dressed in jeans and a T-shirt, who grew up in New Jersey yet came back to her grandfather's home to get engaged. She had only seen her fiancé in a photo, but the next day she would dress in her best sari and jewelry to meet him in the flesh, with all the Bhagats from miles around attending the celebration. In the moment we had alone, she confided to me in English that she was afraid she would not pass muster. Although her mother schooled her in Indian culture, she realized the next day was her big debut and that everyone would be watching to see if she got it right.

Not everyone emigrates from a village. Many families had already moved to small towns like Bodeli and Anand, or even to Baroda, so their children could attend secondary school, before going to the United States. Unlike their village counterparts, they come with high school and college diplomas, and even some graduate education. According to Kirin Patel, a sixty-year-old engineer in Massachusetts, "Most Gujaratis are very scientific. In the old days, you were either an engineer or a lawyer. The third son who, by that time, didn't listen to the parents, went into business."

Manish Patel left from Dabhoi, a small town of about 55,000 residents located around thirty kilometers from Baroda.[25] Manish still owns a house in Dabhoi and land in a nearby village that his brother takes care of. Since he "was the bright one," his parents invested in his education and sent him to Massachusetts to get a graduate degree. Manish and his brother, though, still maintain something of a transnational joint family household whose members share income and plan together for the future.

Manish, says his sister-in-law, Shefali, who lives in Dabhoi, is very attentive to his family. He paid for the new addition and bathroom they built on the house last year. When he comes to visit, he always notices what is missing. Last time, he realized it was hard for them to reach the phone from their new second floor, so he later sent a cell phone. He also brought them a VCR. Shefali and her husband, Ganesh, on the other hand, take care of and support their parents, which is really Manish's responsibility since he is the eldest son. When Manish and his family come to visit, Shefali gives them saris and clothing that, last time, she calculates cost over 10,000 rupees or $230. She and Ganesh hope to move to the United States in the next five years. Shefali's son, Ramchandra, wants to be an engineer like his uncle, and his ambitions are part of the collective family plan. Although she knows no English and has never worked outside her home, Shefali is sure she will be able to get a job in the United States. "Elder brother," she declares, "will take care of it. We will be able to stay with them when we get there so we will not need anything. My husband has told his brother that he does not want to work for anyone and Manish told him, don't worry, I will buy you a store that you can manage on your own."

The current wave of Gujarati emigrants, then, includes people from a range of class and religious backgrounds. The pioneers were college educated who left the towns and cities of Gujarat to pursue higher education and professional careers. Many landed in Lowell, where the newly established outpost of the University of Massachusetts was all too happy to educate these prospective engineers. As Florence described, Lowell offered lots of low-rent apartments and storefronts abandoned by workers who lost their jobs when the mills shut down. Once these newcomers established themselves, they sponsored their relatives, thereby broadening the emigrant profile to include people from rural areas with less education and skills.

Gujaratis are no strangers to emigration. Many went to East Africa in the early 1900s to work as indentured laborers and traders. Subsequent generations moved into managerial jobs.[26] The community flourished in Africa, occupying the middle ground between the poor, native Africans and the white colonials. But like other "middleman minorities," they stuck to themselves, living, socializing, and marrying one another.[27] The local population grew to resent their success and expelled many South Asians during their struggles for independence. Gujaratis who for generations had visited India only occasionally now scrambled to find a home there. Others chose to make new lives in the United States or England.

India, in that era, was firmly oriented toward the Soviet axis. The West was suspect. Few products entered the country from outside its borders. Foreign currency exchange limits were tightly enforced. But a sea change began in the 1990s. Even prior to her assassination, Prime Minister Indira Gandhi began to distance herself from her policies of economic self-sufficiency and strict trade regulation. Prime Minister Rajiv Gandhi, followed by Narasimha Rao, opened the country to global trade. Since then, India has enjoyed tremendous growth, particularly in the service, manufacturing, and agricultural sectors. Western clothing, food, appliances, and cultural goods have flooded the market and become the required trappings of Indian middle-class life.[28]

The role that nonresident Indians play in economic development is not lost on the Indian government. In 2003, the state approved selective dual citizenship, allowing emigrants in the United States and the United Kingdom to retain their Indian passports even after they became naturalized citizens of the United States or the United Kingdom.[29]

January 9 was designated Non Resident Indian Day. Since January 2003, the government has organized a major nonresidents conference (called Pravasi Bharatiya Divas) to stimulate investment and sociopolitical involvement that thousands attend each year.[30]

Gujarat also wants residents to visit regularly and stay active in its economy. To encourage them, Chief Minister Narendra Modi launched a set of state-level initiatives paralleling those at the national level, which take place during the Gujarati festival of Navratri.[31] Gujaratis around the world received invitations through their hometown associations.[32] A Web site and magazine were launched to keep them up-to-date on new developments. A government official works twenty-four hours a day answering e-mail inquiries from potential investors. Interested emigrants can stay at government-run hostels and get help negotiating the Indian bureaucracy from state employees. The government also produced a Gujarati-language instructional CD for their children.

To encourage charitable contributions and investment, Gujarat State also launched a half-and-half scheme that divides project costs equally between the state and local groups.[33] Gujarati officials want nonresident Gujaratis not just to help their own villages but to fund the construction of law schools, hospitals, and export-processing zones as well. The government reserves medical school slots each year for nonresidents who can pay in dollars. It also signed a Memorandum of Understanding with eleven countries so medical students from around the world can come to Gujarat to study Ayurvedic medicine. The Non Resident Gujarati Foundation, with board members in more than fifteen countries, was set up to oversee these activities.[34]

In Massachusetts, and now in southern New Hampshire, there are increasing signs of the American side of this Gujarati transnational equation extending out from its roots in Lowell to surrounding cities and towns. Most obvious are the growing number of South Asian grocery stores where one can also rent the latest Bollywood hit. Neighbors in garden apartment complexes with names like King Arthur's Court and Tudor Village, or in the suburban neighborhood where Pratik and Dipa bought their home, continue to share food, help raise each other's children, or get together for prayers. Their children speak Gujarati when they play together on the street, and their elderly parents, visiting from India, drink tea together during the day while their sons and daughters are at work.

Living Across Borders, Pakistani-Style

The room looks like any other hotel meeting room in America. It has the requisite equipment for PowerPoint presentations; the pastel-colored tablecloths; and the glasses, pitchers of ice water, and candy dishes on each table. But this conference center is unique. Just as Chinese restaurant owners in New York discovered a thriving market for Kosher Chinese food, so the managers of the hotels in the suburbs surrounding Boston realized money could be made catering to South Asian immigrants. Both the Pakistanis and the Gujaratis in this story host a seemingly endless round of weddings, baby showers, and professional events with specific dietary and cultural requirements. Gone are the chafing dishes of pineapple chicken and braised beef with peppers. Instead, the buffet table overflows with steaming samosas and chicken kabobs. And it is not just the food that has changed. A special room is available for prayers during the meetings. No alcohol is served.

One event I attended in late May 2004 was sponsored by OPEN (Organization of Pakistani Entrepreneurs of North America). Its five founders created the group in 1998.[35] Several years ago, OPEN's directors decided it should expand its horizons. In addition to encouraging business development in the United States, the group would build business ties between the United States and Pakistan. Some members had already done quite well outsourcing parts of their businesses abroad. Malik Rahman, for example, prints most of his marketing materials in Pakistan. Other OPEN members do research and development for new products there. And during the 1990s, when the high-tech boom produced a shortage of qualified engineers in the Northeast, Ahmed Sayeed recruited thirty employees to work for his company. Other members want to be the intermediary between potential U.S. and Pakistani business partners. OPEN has since set up chapters in Silicon Valley and Washington, DC, and, if all goes well, it plans to open a chapter in England in the near future.

One challenge OPEN faces is how to meet the changing needs of its members as the Pakistani community grows. Its founders, who are already well-established businesspeople, attend meetings to socialize and give something back to the community. The younger generation is hungry for tips on venture capital and business strategies. And the teenage children of the group's founders, largely raised in America and still in

high school and college, can barely be enticed to attend, renaming the group's acronym "Old People Eating Nonstop."

There are now close to 2,400 Pakistanis living in Massachusetts and an estimated 6,000 living in the New England area. By and large, the Pakistani community is the most successful immigrant group in this story. Unlike the larger Pakistani community in New York, well known for its strong presence among the ranks of the city's cabdrivers, most Pakistanis in Massachusetts come from well-off families in Lahore, Islamabad, and Karachi.[36] They speak English fluently, and many came to this country with college degrees. A steady stream has passed through the halls of MIT and Harvard. More than half earned a bachelor's degree or higher, and 25 percent have master's or doctoral degrees. After graduating, they started businesses that have by and large flourished. A large number of Pakistani doctors as well as financiers and investors also live in the area.

Unlike Valadarenses, who cluster in Framingham, Allston, and Somerville, the Pakistani community has no residential center. Most families live and work alongside native-born Americans in the suburban neighborhoods that surround the city. Since there is no Pakistani shopping district, they make periodic pilgrimages to grocery stores specializing in halal meats along with South Asian fruits and vegetables. They see one another often, though, at dinner parties and holiday celebrations, weekly prayers and Sunday school, cultural events, and professional association meetings hosted by a range of Pakistani groups.

The Pakistani immigrant community consists of at least two groups. The first are the pillars of the community who established OPEN, mortgaged their homes to build the Islamic Center, and still organize many of its cultural events. The second, in their late twenties, thirties, and forties, attended U.S. universities and befriended many of their native-born classmates. While some in the first group dislike socializing with native-born non-Muslims who drink, smoke, and eat pork, members of the latter tend to be comfortable going to cocktail parties and having a Coke, or even ordering a drink themselves.

Both groups keep in touch with Pakistan but in different ways. The peer group they relate to at home and the Pakistan of their memories are quite different. Members of the older group recall a tolerant Pakistan, where ethnic and religious diversity was valued and women occupied a social place more or less equal to that of men. The "younger" cohort left a Pakistan that, although more globally influenced, was less tolerant of difference.[37] Both groups, however, have family members and former classmates in high places whom they can call on when they want to get something done. Both groups are periodically involved with Pakistan, although some members, considered "hard core," are in touch on an almost daily basis. In fact, the Pakistanis had the highest percentage of respondents who telephoned (87 percent) or e-mailed (80 percent) their homeland on a "regular" basis (at least once a week or more). Over 70 percent read ethnic newspapers, and more than half watch Pakistani movies or programs on television. The way you can tell how hard core people are, one OPEN member confided, is by how much time they spend reading the English-language Pakistani newspaper, *Dawn*, on the Internet.

Karachi, where I conducted the sending-country interviews with this community, is a sprawling, dry port on the Arabian Sea. Its population has grown tremendously in the past twenty years, jumping from almost 5.5 million in 1981 to close to 10 million in 1998.[38] The vestiges of colo-

nialism are visible in the architecture, the church spires that peek out
behind locked gates, and the old exclusive Sindh or Gymkhana Clubs,
where one can still imagine Britons sitting on the veranda drinking
their gin and tonics. Much more prominent are the many minarets that
dot the skyline. Karachi's growth has brought with it the familiar roster
of problems that plague most developing-country cities: water short-
ages, frequent blackouts, and horrendous traffic. Still, most of the family members I visited lived comfortably, if not lavishly. The majority
had cooks and servants who wheeled in snack trays laden with sweets
and savories along with strong tea. Air-conditioning and ceiling fans
eased the discomfort of the Karachi heat.

This image helps capture the contrasts that are Karachi. A young
mother of two, whose conversation is peppered with Koranic verses,
said that to understand her city, one should visit the McDonald's in the
Gulshan-e-Iqbal and Defence sections of the city. Both are well-off
neighborhoods, but in Gulshan-e-Iqbal you see women in head scarves
and robes as well as boys and girls sitting separately, and in Defence you
find boys and girls sitting together, unsupervised, wearing tank tops and
jeans. So goes the alleged clash of civilizations in Karachi between the
modern, religious conservatives and their more Westernized counterparts. Both are well connected to the world outside of Pakistan, but they
engage with it in different ways.

Karachi's elite is a thin, inbred slice of Pakistani society. Normal
small talk at the beginning of a visit touched on the social connections
the host and the visitor had in common, what school one's children attended, and where one worked or studied in Asia or the West. Their social views varied along a continuum. Those on the Left used words like
"liberal," "modern," or "Western" to describe themselves. The majority lives in the Clifton or Defence neighborhoods. The saying goes that
when you cross over the bridge into the rest of Karachi from these areas,
you enter into another world.[39]

On weekends, this group shops at the Park Towers Shopping Mall,
where the bright lights, expensive stores, and pop music playing in the
background could be anywhere in the world. At the Karachi Boat Club,
another former British bastion, there are signs on each table requesting
that visitors check their cell phones with the maître d'. Several people
told me about warehouses where you could buy any kind of alcohol.
While they might identify strongly as Muslims, they wanted to keep

their religious lives private. They did not want religious mullahs telling them how to express their faith. They sent their children to "progressive" private schools, where boys and girls even attended parties together. Going to the States or Canada for higher education was an expected right of passage. They were well informed about who was studying where and what kinds of jobs their children might find once they graduated.

Sarah, a middle-aged woman whose cousin lives outside of Boston, used to live in Dubai, which, she says, is "the best of the East and West." Eight years ago, her husband moved the family back to Pakistan—a decision she deeply regrets. He has had a tough time finding work in his field. Although he finally got a job in real estate, he has been unable to recoup the family's former status. She recently started her own event planning company. Her first big job was a national car show, where car manufacturers and suppliers from all over the world exhibit their products.

Things in Pakistan are difficult, she said. The cost of land and real estate has skyrocketed. Food has also become more expensive. The city had been "dry" for the last three or four months, and the last time she organized a fund-raiser for a local hospital, all the glasses were empty. Both her children studied abroad. Her daughter was back in Pakistan, just having completed her law degree, but would return to the United States at the end of the year to be married. "I don't know how she would feel if she were staying here for good," remarked Sarah, "but since she knows she is leaving, she is having a grand old time."

Those on the other side of the social divide, also equally well off, declared their faith more openly. What they believed in and how it shaped their lives was central to their conversation. They were more likely to live in some kind of joint family arrangement.[40] They were also more likely to send their children to schools where "religious values" were a centerpiece of the curriculum. Their children did not necessarily go abroad to study. They were proud of Pakistani institutions and believed that young people could get a fine education at home. When they talk about the increasing competition between money and faith, they clearly came out on the side of values.

This does not mean they are any less modern than those who label themselves as such. Nadia is a twenty-eight-year-old woman who grew up in Dubai and only returned to Pakistan in high school. In her early twenties, she and her younger sister began to talk about wearing the hijab. Although their mother does not cover her head, Nadia felt this was what she was supposed to do. For a long time, she found herself "standing at the edge of the pool, looking at the water, but not jumping in." Her impetus came when a cousin from England, who is quite religious, stayed with her family for three weeks. Out of respect, she covered her head, thinking she would see what it felt like. Even after he left she continued, gradually adopting more conservative clothing. Six years ago, there were few women veiling themselves, but now Nadia finds she is in good company.

Nadia has dressed this way for her jobs as an information technology specialist at Citibank, Procter and Gamble, and the Pakistani company she now works for. She drives herself each morning and works alongside men. She travels alone on business trips when necessary, both in Pakistan and abroad. All of this, she says, is ordained by Islam. Her faith figures large in her professional life. There is a prayer room for men and women at her office. Meetings are scheduled so they do not interfere with prayer times.

Both types of Karachiites were equally well connected to the outside world and their emigrant relatives scattered around it. Even before cable television came to Pakistan in the late 1990s, dramatically transforming how the Pakistani masses experience the world outside their country, most of these families had satellite dishes. Family ties are reinforced by the fairly widespread practice of marriage between cousins. Even distant relatives tend to see one another during the wedding season, when it is not unusual for over five hundred guests to attend several days of celebrations in large marriage halls put up specifically for this purpose. Most people have traveled outside Pakistan themselves or their relatives come back to visit often. They said they were in constant contact, especially now that phone cards and Skype have become widely available. Others kept in touch by e-mail, thus allowing young people to get acquainted with their cousins growing up far away.

Aside from the emotional pain of separation, most of the people I talked with in Karachi didn't feel that emigration had a big effect on their lives. They already enjoyed the global lifestyle of the world's upper middle class. But, many reflected, life in Karachi was changing, both because "people go out" and because of globalization. Young people like to wear jeans. They want to eat pizza and burgers instead of the traditional foods their mothers put in front of them. They don't respect their parents in the same way that their parents did. "We never raised our voice to our parents," said Mehtab, a fifty-year-old banker. "Our parents decided who we would marry and what our jobs would be. We never thought twice about it because we knew it would be that way from the time we were very young. My son is not like that. He told me that he wanted to study computers and that is what he is doing."

What people perceive as positive change occurs as well. Tariq, a young man in his twenties, came to the United States on contract to work for a high-tech computer company. In fact, there are several Pakistani-born employees in his office who also came to work on long-term contracts. They introduce their work culture to their American colleagues and carry back things they observe to Pakistan. These sector-specific social remittances spill over into related industries. As Tariq explained,

What's happening is—it's slow, and it's subtle, but at least in this new sector, people say to themselves, "I need to do good if I want to be a good computer scientist. I need to work hard, be honest, meet deadlines. I won't get promoted because of who I know but because of how I do my job." I have friends in Karachi who work in electrical engineering and when we get together, we discuss things. So it disseminates ideas and crossbreeds them.

Most people, though, saw these changes as touching the fringe of Pakistani life rather than its core. While emigration to the Middle East, involving the poor and the working classes, has transformed whole villages, the emigration of the elite does not.

The uneven impact of migration is replicated at the national level. The nearly $4 billion in remittances that Pakistan receives each year is certainly appreciated.[41] After September 11, when some Pakistanis living in the United States no longer felt welcome in their adopted home, there was a big, onetime influx of expatriate capital. Remittances surged to record levels, both because more people transferred money home and they did so using official money transfer systems, fearing U.S.

government surveillance.[42] Real estate prices soared as more expatriates bought land and homes in urban Pakistan. A 5,500-square-foot lot in the center of Islamabad, the nation's capital, now sells for as much as $800,000.[43]

Still, compared to other governments, Pakistan has done little to reach out systematically to its diaspora. The Higher Education Commission, claiming the country suffers from a shortage of qualified professors, created a program in 2004 to attract people of Pakistani origin back to Pakistan (although theoretically anyone can apply). Candidates were to be paid the equivalent of $4,000 to $5,000, over eight times the average salary of locals—a disparity not lost on those who have opted to stay home despite many opportunities to work abroad. "We still have this feeling that anything that is homegrown is inferior and everything that comes from abroad is better," an urban economist said. "It takes a long time to recover from colonial consciousness." The Ministry of Labor instituted a new "Remittance Book" program that rewards people who send at least $2,500 or more annually with free and expedited passport issuance, special treatment at the airport, and an increased baggage allowance. The only problem, one businessperson noted, is that "the customs officials don't want to give it to you." [44]

There are also private and state-backed efforts to promote charitable giving. The Edhi Foundation runs programs in Pakistan, the United Kingdom, the United States, and Canada, including shelters for abandoned women and children, maternal and child health centers, a cancer hospital, drug rehabilitation centers, and a nurse training school. Its thrift shop in Queens, New York, gives away household items and clothing to the poor.[45] Since 1999, the Pakistani community in Boston has organized a yearly conference where emigrants get to "put in their two cents" about Pakistani national development. Ad hoc commissions visit Pakistani to advise labor and education ministers. Those in high places get an earful when they meet their former classmates visiting during the wedding season.

A recent study commissioned by the Pakistani Centre for Philanthropy in Islamabad found a community solidly rooted in the United States that gives generously to both American and homeland causes, and increasingly demands to know how its money is being spent.[46] The average household among the estimated five hundred thousand Pakistanis living in the United States contributed about $2,500 in money and goods, and approximately 435 hours of volunteer time, amounting to $250 million in cash and in-kind giving and the equivalent of $750 million in volunteered time—a total of $1 billion annually. About 40 percent ($100 million) went to Pakistani causes in Pakistan, another 40 percent went toward causes unrelated to Pakistan, and the remaining 20 percent went toward Pakistani causes in the United States. More than half of the volunteer hours, the equivalent of 13,500 full-time employees, went toward causes not related to Pakistan, such as soup kitchens, school associations, and community groups. Most of the remainder went to Pakistani-related social, cultural, and philanthropic endeavors. Donors were equally motivated by faith and issues. In fact, faith inspires Pakistanis in much the same way it inspires Americans— it's the *reason* they give, rather than the destination.[47]

Inishoweners

> The most important thing to me is that my family has ties to America that go back four generations. My great-grandfather went out, my grandmother came back. Now I have three brothers in Boston. I have America in my blood.
> —Liam, middle-aged bar owner, Buncrana

The road to Malin Head, on the Inishowen Peninsula in county Donegal, is long and winding. It passes thin, uninterrupted ribbons of sandy beach and rocky harbors shaped like pieces of a jigsaw puzzle. It climbs steeply through hills covered with wildflowers before descending into the small village with whitewashed houses and hedges thick with roses. Inishoweners think of their corner of Ireland as way off the beaten path—you don't have to pass through this part of the country on your way to anywhere. They complain the government neglects their roads and services. Partition only exacerbated this, cutting them off from the closest city—Derry.

As local wisdom has it, nearly every family in Inishowen has relatives in America. Many live in Boston. Some migrated recently, as part of a second wave of "new Irish" who came in the 1980s and 1990s. Others left during the early part of the twentieth century, or are the second- and third-generation descendants of those who did.

Most people in Inishowen either fish, farm, or work in construction.

The textile industry also has deep roots. Before electricity arrived in the 1950s, women took in piecework at home, often organizing sewing parties to make the work go faster. Several factories, which manufactured shirts for the English market, remained open until the 1970s when Britain placed an embargo on Irish goods in an attempt to save its own textile industry. In the early 1990s, Fruit of the Loom opened a plant in Inishowen, which at its height employed more than eighteen hundred workers. The grandmother of the company's president is said to have emigrated from the peninsula in the early 1900s. In the last few years, however, many workers lost their jobs when the company relocated to Morocco after the tax breaks expired that attracted it to Inishowen to begin with.

Malin Head is located at Ireland's northwesternmost point. Thousands of tourists travel each year to visit its lighthouse, perched dramatically on a high, rocky cliff with waves crashing below. Teahouse, pub, and bed-and-breakfast owners make their living from these visitors. But some community members believe that Malin Head's tourist potential has not been fully realized. Their concerns found a receptive audience in Thomas Clarke, a fiftyish businessperson from Boston whose mother emigrated from Malin Head in the early 1920s. Although clearly proud of his Irish American heritage, Thomas never thought much about the Irish part of who he was while growing up. He was unexpectedly smitten during his first trip back to Ireland ten years ago and overwhelmed by the warm reception he received from even distant relatives. He felt he had discovered a piece of himself he hadn't realized was missing. So he listened avidly when his relatives and their neighbors told him about their scheme. Thomas promised to help, even using his contacts among Irish Americans in Boston on their behalf.

Rosemary Wahlberg, a seventy-year-old, second-generation married woman with children, also returned to Inishowen late in life. She traveled with her friend Peggy, who frequently visits her relatives on the peninsula, and was treated like one of the family. But Rosemary wanted to find her own family, and she eventually did.

Peggy has an aunt who is like ninety-eight. And Peggy said to her, "Rosemary would really like to find the house her mother lived in, up in Malin Head." Her aunt said, "How old would she be if she was alive?" and I said, "I think she'd be like almost a hundred." And then she talked about what it was like then, how cold and hungry and poor it was, and I thought I'm listening to a voice telling me what my mother really lived through. So she says, "Peggy, take her to so-and-so's house. She'll know." So that's what we did; we went to the next cousin's house. And they drove me to where my mother came from. I was so unnerved by them knocking on stranger's doors and interrupting them, and having the stranger say, after Peggy would say, "This is my friend Rosemary, she wants to find her mother's, and she lived in Glenngale." And they would say, "Oh. My mother-in-law is right next door. Try her, she'll know." I'm trying to say, no, maybe we shouldn't do this, out comes the mother-in-law, she was wearing boots. And she was very nice; she said the one you need to get ahold of is McLachlin and she tells Peggy how to get there. And we get there, and the young man lived for seven years in Field's Corner [an Irish neighborhood in Boston]. Of course, I'm calling him young; you wouldn't have called him young. . . . Ah, maybe fiftyish. And he said to me, so help me God, he said, "Did you have an Uncle Willy who lived in

Charlestown, and fell out the window and died?" I said that happened in 1933. He said, "Then you're my cousin."

The majority of those who left Inishowen between 1920 and 1950
fled abject poverty. After all, you couldn't eat the scenery, and there was
little work and little money to buy food. Extra children were sometimes
loaned out to farmers, sometimes kin and sometimes not, because their
parents simply could not support them if they stayed home. Everyone
knew that when children came of age, they would be better off going to
America. It would mean fewer mouths to feed and, with any luck, better opportunities. The night before someone left, the community held
what they called an American wake, expressing the expectation that
migrants would never return. Since so few knew how to read or write, it
was difficult for them to let anyone know they arrived safely.

In this Ireland, the church reigned supreme. No one questioned its
authority. "When the priest came over," Charlie, in his seventies, recalled, "we would run to the back of the house because we were too
scared to speak to him. It was OK for our parents to give him tea, but we
wanted nothing to do with it." Irish religiosity consisted not only of
going to Mass but also of pagan folk practices. People visited holy wells,
marched in Corpus Christi parades, and placed medals on trees to express gratitude and appreciation.[48]

While some, like Rosemary's mother, got on the boat and never
looked back, in most families there were usually one or two people who
kept in touch. Even without the benefits of visits, telephones, or airplanes, the people who stayed home had a vision of life in Boston and
the people who emigrated kept up-to-date about Inishowen news. According to Aidan Burns, the unofficial historian in Malin, there are several now-deserted towns like Bally Hillion, also known as Little Boston,
because so many residents left there to go to the United States. There
were men who knew the towns of Roxbury and Dedham who had never
been to Buncrana, only five miles away.[49]

As a boy, Aidan says, everyone could tell you who their people were
and where they lived. "We had a tradition of storytelling. Everyone
knew their own family tree, from the king to the spade, and used to sit
around at night and pass around stories. I could tell you my own family
tree ten generations back. When migration started, the cast of characters just moved across the pond." The tradition of naming grandchil-

dren after their grandparents also made it easier to keep track across the generations. And as the place mats that are ubiquitous in restaurants throughout Ireland indicate, the Doherty and McLachlin clans are native to the Donegal area. That each family has its own nickname also makes remembering who is who easier.

The first wave that went to Boston created a close, tight-knit community. The young men did manual labor while the young women worked as nannies and maids. They met at the Metropolitan or Hibernian dance halls on Saturday evenings. After they married, they moved on to raise their kids in the streets and alleys of Charlestown, South Boston, and Dorchester. Saint Brendan's Church in Dorchester became known as Little Inishowen because so many emigrants from Donegal attended Mass there. Everyone noticed if you skipped a Sunday. Their children attended the same local parochial schools. They stopped off at the same pubs on their way home from work. Since no one had a car, they spent most evenings and weekends chatting on the front steps or playing in the street. Sometimes, there was a subway ride to Franklin Park. In summers, groups of families rented small cottages next to one another in the working-class towns of the Massachusetts shore.

A shared hatred of Britain, the continuous round of wakes they attended, and their deep appreciation for Irish music and dance united this community. Its members were fascinated by the Kennedys and claimed their successes as their own. "JFK is nearly the same as the pope because he's powerful, Catholic, and Irish. It made my hair stand up on the back of my head to see it," declared sixty-two-year-old Michael Doherty about his visit to the Kennedy compound in Hyannis. "Everyone helped each other and looked out for each other," according to Catherine, a fifty-year-old woman whose parents emigrated from Ireland. She remembers having money passed on to her by friends and family members. "The parents would have nothing, but you'd never give it to the parents, you see. They might be too proud to take it, so you could pass it along to the children, you know what I mean?"

Before the 1960s, traveling back to Ireland was rare. Nevertheless, Inishoweners constantly traded news of home on the street, at church, at funerals, or on the beach. Maryann, in her seventies, recalls "the letter going back and forth was regular because at that time, Ireland, as bad as the depression was here, in some ways, it was worse there and people always tried to put a little something aside to send home." This trickle of mail was enough to keep immigrants and those who stayed behind connected to one another until people started visiting regularly. Direct flights between Boston and Dublin began in 1964. Both sides found it easy to pick up where the letters had left off.

> I remember when we went to visit Uncle Pat, and like you mentioned before, Helen, he had all these mementos from his two sisters. Keep in mind, he was only probably like nineteen when they left and he was the youngest. It was so heartbreaking for him; he said he used to wait by the water for them to come back. In his little drawer there, his mementos, he brought out a letter, and it was on blue paper and that was one that I had written, for mama, and I can remember writing the letter. And they always wrote about news, like of people they would have known from home. . . . We went the first time in 1978, when we went to Ireland we went to see, this would have been my father's sister Grace Ann who we communicated with all the time. She went to her kitchen drawer and she brought out an envelope flap, and it said 137 Bunker Hill Street. And that's where we had lived, and she said, "I've had this for so many years and I didn't know if anyone would come." The sad thing was that my mother had died before any of us went to Ireland. (Bredge, seventy-eight-year-old woman, Boston)

The "Yanks" came back curious. In an old shoe box in the attic, in the mailbox, in the picture of the Sacred Heart that hung over the mantelpiece in their parent's living rooms, there had been Ireland waiting for the taking. The second generation found that it knew a lot about Ireland without realizing it. Bob Doherty, a fifty-six-year-old, said the first time he went back to Carndonough, he looked at the people's faces and they looked just like those in Charlestown. "You go to the pubs, and you wouldn't be there five minutes and somebody would be talking to you. 'Where you from, Yank? Oh, and I've got a brother who lives there. I've got a cousin who lives in Arlington or Somerville.' Those people over there know more about their relatives over here then we know about them."

Besides discovering additional members of their families, they also found something of themselves. Mary Murphy, in her eighties, said that when she returned to Ireland, she finally understood why she was a Democrat and a liberal. Although the rest of her family wasn't political, she always felt the need to fight for her neighborhood and community. It wasn't, she believed, just something that came from being Irish in America. She realized that it came from how close people were in Inishowen and how they all tried to help each other out. Ben Craig, in his thirties, also described the way his father changed when he began visiting Ireland after thirty-four years. "My dad was like Dr. Jekyll and Mr. Hyde. In this country, he was very shy, and then he'd get off the plane and he was like a different guy. In this country, if he needed directions, he would never ask for them. But in Ireland, he would go in, find out where we're going, and he'd talk to people. He was just really a different personality in Ireland—came out of his shell."

What those like Mary and Ben's father did with their new insights varied. For most people, they simply reinforced their Irish American roots. Others began making yearly pilgrimages back to Ireland to learn more about their families. But a small number, like Thomas Clarke, became transnational activists. John Doherty, for example, saw business opportunity in Ireland. He realized there were many Inishoweners like himself who had grown to love the place and were longing for an "authentic" Irish experience. Why not build those old-style thatched-roof cottages, complete with the sod in the fireplace, so the Yanks could get what they came for?

Emigration to America declined in the 1950s. Men went instead to harvest potatoes and wheat in England and Scotland. Some were gone for as many as fifty weeks a year. But in the 1970s, as agriculture became mechanized, the need for manual labor declined and once again Inishoweners set their sights on America. These emigrants, especially those departing in the 1990s, left behind a totally different Ireland. The Celtic Tiger was roaring. Ireland joined the European Union (EU) in 1973. Many see Ireland's standard of living, the new housing construction, and the lifestyle as comparable, if not better, than the United States. In fact, in recent years, the government stations officials at airports at Christmastime to distribute pamphlets about job opportunities in Ireland to people coming home for the holidays.[50] The government allows dual citizenship and the expatriate vote.[51]

New emigrants also keep in close touch with Ireland. When sixty-

year-old Colleen's father passed away in the late 1940s, she didn't get
the news until four days later. "Today," says her son-in-law, "you get on
a plane and it is like traveling from Cork to Derry. It's only a five-hour
flight from Boston to Ireland so it feels like it's around the corner." Even
with Ireland's current economic good fortune, the habit of emigrating
dies hard. "To go out" or "to have an adventure" is a deeply rooted rite
of passage. While local jobs enable young people to make good, steady
money for the first time in anyone's memory, most people just can't recover from emigration fever.

Moving to Boston is fairly easy because the first wave did all the hard
work. The Irish presence in Boston's archdiocese is palpable. The Irish
church sends out priests to serve the new Irish and partially supports a
network of pastoral centers to care for them. The ninety-eight-year-old
Donegal Association may be for "fuddy-duddies," as Bernadette, who
returned to Inishowen after living in Boston for thirty-two years, called
them, but the new Irish still go occasionally to its dances. Everyone
knows about the Irish bakery where people looking for work wait each
morning to see if someone is hiring. Every bar along Dorchester Avenue attracts young people from a different county. The Democratic
Party is still part of the Irish trinity, but Fianna Fáil and Fine Gael have
always found supporters among Irish Americans in the United States.[52]
The same organizations that solidified Irish American identity in the
past do double duty today by also reinforcing transnational attachments. The parish, the bar, the sports club, and the hometown association broadcast messages about being Irish and being Irish in America
that each individual selectively tunes in to.

Some new Irish, like Donal and Ian, are young and single, out for a
good time, and not particularly concerned about what the future will
bring. They live in nearly empty bachelor apartments. There's plenty of
construction work to be done by day and drinking to be done by night.
Everyone supports everyone else's Gaelic football team and buys each
other's raffle tickets, no matter what county they come from. These
twenty-somethings actively avoid serious conversations about the future. They are just having fun, they say, and they don't have a plan.
"You've always got home in the back of your head," Donal said. "Basically, I could settle in about three years. I want to see the world. Get to
know a city and move on, like. I've seen New York, had enough of it.
Boston now, like. We've no ties. We can get up and go tomorrow if we

want to. Get up and go somewhere else. Next stop, I'd like to see France for a year."

It's when people get married and start having children that decisions need to be made. According to Father Patrick, one of the priests sent over to care for the community, people with families end up staying. If they go home, they tend to go before their children start school. After all, if their kids learn soccer and football rather than baseball or basketball, they won't fit in.

According to thirty-five-year-old Colm, for example, nearly thirty people he used to go to dances with in Inishowen now live in Boston. Almost everyone had family already living in the United States. At first, the women worked as housekeepers and in child care; the men worked as carpenters. Although they hung out with people from all over Ireland, they much preferred being with their own. Most have married and now own houses in Dorchester and Quincy. They go to Saint Brendan's on Sundays. They are here to stay. Jackie and her family, on the other hand, decided to move back to Inishowen. She worked at Wendy's in Boston, and she and her husband opened a fast food restaurant called Boston Burger when she returned, although she swears she wasn't capitalizing on the Boston-Inishowen connection. Everyone thinks it is better to raise kids in Inishowen, she explained. Your family is nearby; it's safer and healthier. "I wanted my kids to grow up with my same traditions," she said.

Church authority in the Ireland that Donal, Colm, and Jackie said good-bye to has radically diminished.[53] Vatican II dramatically changed things. It turned the priest around to face his parishioners and obliged him to speak in their language. There are altar girls as well as altar boys. Many of Catholicism's strict rules, like not being allowed to read the Protestant Bible or eating meat on Fridays, were repealed. These changes transformed people's worldviews because what was forbidden was what had distinguished them from their neighbors.[54] Though the priest still commands respect, the younger generation is not above challenging him, especially given the scandals plaguing the church in recent years. Those claiming "no religion" have increased steadily in the past half century.[55] Many people expressed frustration over what they see as the church's complacency. "They never fail to ask you for money," said Donald Brenna, a returnee in his late thirties, "but they never take a role fighting for anything if they don't have to."

Living Across Borders

Many people are hard at work inventing ways to belong globally. They divide their energies and loyalties between the countries they move to, the places that they come from, and the many places beyond and in between.[56] They care more about some places than others at different points in their lives. The same person who paid little attention to his or her ancestral home as a teenager becomes an activist across borders in middle age. Religion is key to how people make places for themselves in the world. It plays a starring role in immigrant incorporation. It ranks high as a tool for staying connected to a homeland, either directly, through membership in a homeland-based religious community, or by belonging to social and cultural groups infused with religious values. It also connects people to fellow members of the same religious communities around the world.

What's more, religion doesn't just work locally, at the level of everyday experience at the mosque or temple. That mosque or temple is often connected to national and international networks that link people to fellow believers as well as real and imagined landscapes far away. Religion also speaks to the many levels of people's daily lives. It comes equipped with stories and strategies that span the universal and the particular, bring together the global and the local, and combine homogeneity with diversity. It speaks to the transcendent and the ordinary at the same time. As such, its message resonates with people's everyday experiences, the global world they live in, and the cosmos that created it. What better tools with which to meet the challenges of living in a global world?[57]

If so many people live transnational lives, how do they respond when people ask the question "Who are you?" And more important, what do they do about it? How do people actually participate in a global world? Where do they turn for protection and representation? What do they think they should give back in return? Luis is just waking up to these dynamics. For Alice, there is already too much religion in this story. She wants what she sees as an oppressive, evil force to go away rather than spread its tentacles even more. Florence is convinced that you can't possibly belong in several places at once without falling down somewhere on the job. She worries that some people will care more about Muhammad or Dadaji then they will about the president of the United States. Wasim admits that she's probably right for a small group. But he also believes that people who claim the religion of the middle are doing their best to be responsible members of all the communities they belong to.

Let's see who is right.

3

Between the Nation,
the World, and God

The pages of an atlas—with its thin black lines separating the light pink, blue, and green countries—still define the mental and physical maps most of us use to think about the world. The globe is clearly divided into nation-states, and people are expected to belong to just one. Identity equals territory, and proposals to the contrary often meet with strong resistance. Witness the EU's unsuccessful attempts to make Europeanness more important than being French or German. Closer to home, think of recent proposals to erect more walls between the United States and Mexico so that only documented Americans live in America. For some people, one land, one membership card, and one identity is a secular version of the Holy Trinity.

But Valadarenses, Gujaratis, Pakistanis, and Inishoweners, to name a few, don't live that way. A straightforward national "identity card" does not reflect the reality of many of the people described in the previous chapter. Instead, their stories were about how they combined political citizenship with other kinds of belonging. If people have lots of food in their pantries, what are the main ingredients they cook with every day, and what do they use only occasionally? How do the recipes they prepare change as a result?

About a third of the people I talked with were good old-fashioned national citizens. They felt either American or part of their homelands, or some combination of the two. They were the first to bring apple pie to the Fourth of July picnic or samosas to the Indian Independence Day celebration. Some, who identified as dual nationals, did both. Others, who considered themselves ethnic Americans, invented new dishes, adding masala spices to the ketchup they put on their hamburgers or using chai to make their iced tea.

Cosmopolitanism represented another type of identity, claimed by another third of the people I spoke to. These immigrants felt at home everywhere in the world, or they felt rooted and rootless at the same time. They were either real-life jet-setters, traveling so often they could name the European airports with the best Admiral's Clubs from memory, or virtual jet-setters, observing and feeling connected to the far-flung reaches of the world from the comfort of their living rooms. No one cuisine dominates their kitchen because they eat from the world's table and are proud of it.

A third group, though, thought of themselves as religious global citizens. Faith was their membership card. Religious global citizenship has a lot in common with its political equivalent. In exchange for "obeying the law" and following the denominational rules, "paying taxes" by contributing dues, and participating in religious and social activities, members gain representation, protection, and access to resources and power. Pope Benedict XVI is their guide and benefactor, not George Bush or Irish president Mary McAleese. Their culinary choices are driven by what religion allows and prohibits—giving up meat or poultry during Lent to feast on lamb at Easter.

Understanding what's really going on in immigrant communities requires sorting out the different ways people situate themselves in the world. Claiming multiple memberships doesn't mean taking political citizenship any less seriously. It just means accepting that more and more people hold religious and global as well as national passports. And it means figuring out how to combine the rights and responsibilities of each.

National Responses to a Transnational Reality

The many immigrants who continue to embrace membership in a national community do so in different ways. National identities come in several varieties. There were some, like Bilal and Nadia below, who claimed an unadulterated tie to this country or to the country they came from. Others, like John Connelly, were emblematic ethnic Americans. They clung to much that had been brought over from their homelands—which in turn was transformed over time by its encounter with the United States. And finally, there were dual nationals, like Waldo Freitas, who participated actively in home country economics and politics while earning a living and supporting political candidates in the United States.

THE AMERICAN

Bilal Najam is the kind of immigrant many Americans would be glad to welcome. It takes a while to find the trailer he uses as an office at the subdivision he is building. First, you have to travel almost thirty miles from Boston to Route 495, the outermost highway surrounding the city. The 1990s' economic boom transformed this once no-man's-land into prime office park territory. The people who work in the area needed homes. So began the clear-cutting of hundreds of acres to build the twenty-first-century version of the "little boxes" about which Pete Seeger sang in the 1960s.

Although the market has since cooled down, you can still make a good living in real estate. Bilal is extremely successful. The new houses he was building on the early spring afternoon when I visited him looked a lot like the new homes in the subdivisions where the Bhagats have settled— aluminum siding, palladium windows, and glass chandeliers hanging in the entryway. A new, paved street had been added off a road in an older neighborhood. It wound slowly up a hill to reveal large homes, fledgling trees, and chemically induced lawns. There was an emptiness and an eerie stillness—not just because many of the houses were still vacant but also because many of the sites were only half complete. The trees and shrubs were still too young to soften the barren landscape.

Bilal was busy—answering his cell phone and dealing with one of his contractors before he could settle down to talk with me. He joked easily with the Irish electrician, who calls him Billy, and explained to me that they have worked together for years. Their good rapport became apparent as they consulted about the next day's work at another subdivision they were building together nearby.

When Bilal finally cleared his desk, I asked him to tell me his story. He came to the United States from Pakistan when he was nineteen years old. His father was an engineer who wanted his son to be educated in America. Bilal met and married his wife while in graduate school at the University of Massachusetts in Lowell. They have three teenage children.

When I asked Bilal who he is, he answered, without missing a beat, that he is unconditionally American. There is no hyphen in Bilal's experience—he is the pure American variety and believes that other immigrants should be the same.

> I came to this country when I was just a teenager and I have to say that I never looked back. Pakistan was only twenty years old then. What does that mean, then, to be a Pakistani? What can that offer me that America doesn't offer? By now, almost all of my family is here and I am very proud of what we have accomplished. I'm a successful builder. I am a staunch Republican. I helped establish our mosque in Worcester. My kids are going to college. What more can I ask for? I teach my kids about Pakistani values, that's important to me, but I don't need to go back to Pakistan to do that. We are here in America. We should feel and act like Americans. It's as simple as that.

Bilal's adopted home has given him everything he ever wished for. He worked hard and it paid off. He owns a beautiful house not far from the neighborhood he is building. Because his wife didn't have to work, she volunteered actively in their community. They entertained often and took great pride in treating their guests "royally," a practice for which they were widely admired. As his kids grew older, and he was no longer busy with their baseball and soccer, his interests turned to town politics. He is a loyal Republican and a firm believer that the Pakistani community specifically, but minorities in general, should get more involved to get ahead.

In all these years, Bilal has been back to Pakistan only twice. Eventually his parents and siblings joined him here. Only one sister and an uncle still live in Karachi. He doesn't feel any great responsibility to help his homeland. As he said, Pakistani nationalism is relatively new and weak. It is not potent enough to arouse strong patriotism. The country is corrupt, and its politics unpredictable. Why bank on a faltering ship when you can travel on a yacht? he asked.

Bilal typifies the immigrant who trades in his or her home country identity for an American one. Marise, a thirty-seven-year-old woman from Brazil who has been in this country for twelve years, feels the same way. Before leaving Brazil, she finished college and worked as an English teacher. When the opportunity to come to the United States and work as a nanny fell into her lap, she grabbed it. Her first marriage had just ended in divorce. She had nothing really tying her down. She already spoke English well. Marise also acknowledges that she doesn't look Brazilian. She inherited her light hair and blue eyes from her Italian grandmother. Why not try it, she thought, and see how it works out? She could always come home.

From the moment Marise arrived, she liked everything about this country and never thought about going back. A lovely family employed her. What's more, she fell in love with a Brazilian she met in the Miami airport who was also traveling to the United States for the first time. They eventually married, and three sons soon followed. Over the years, her husband built a successful landscaping company. She has also worked, from time to time, teaching English and counseling immigrant families. They now own their own home and a two family house that they rent to make extra income. About five years ago, they purchased four rental apartments in Brazil, to have something to fall back on, but now regret this decision, wishing they had invested the money here.

Like Bilal, Marise says she left Brazil without a second thought. "I feel more American than Brazilian now," she claims. "I don't know, I just feel like this is where I should be." Although she is in close touch with her family, she has been unable to return to Brazil because she doesn't have papers. Thoughts of Brazil evoke images of insecurity, corruption, and unpredictability as well as nostalgia. In America, she says, things work. People are not always trying to outsmart one another. A family can plan ahead. The Brazil she remembers is violent. Politicians are dishonest and government agencies unreliable. She had a career in Brazil that she is proud of, so she feels OK about not having had much of a professional life in the United States. "When you've been abroad," she observes, "you know another kind of reality that just makes it hard, I guess, to go back and start all over again."

It is not for lack of ethnic pride that she feels so American. Every week, she goes to the Portuguese Mass presided over by a priest from Brazil. Her closest friends are other Brazilian families also struggling to figure out how to raise their children in America. Despite all this, she and her husband live so much better than they would had they stayed in Brazil that any enduring homeland ties are quickly weakening.

Narendra Patel also feels American. He is on the board of directors of the Gujar Association.[1] He travels to India frequently on business where his contacts with old schoolmates make it easier for him to get things done. He says he contributes money to India as a way to give something back for the education he received there. But because he married an American woman, and isn't particularly religious, his family's social circle extends far beyond the Indian community. He does not speak Gujarati at home. "I don't think," he says, "that if I had an Indian wife I would feel any more attached to India. Now the kids might be, because she might have instilled a lot more religious things, or her beliefs and all that. I want them to respect their elders and to value education, but those aren't American or Indian values, those are just good values."

Bilal, Marise, and Narendra not only feel that their place is in America, they also feel it's not appropriate for them to play a role in homeland life. According to Prashant, a forty-five-year-old Gujarati migrant who shares their view,

> Our people have a tendency to talk about foreign policy quite a bit even though we don't know much about foreign policy. I strongly believe we don't have much to say or much to do with India because we have left that country, and this is our adopted home. My kids are going to grow up here, and their kids are going to be growing up here, and they go to the American school system and everything else so they are mainstream second-generation American. By talking about India, Pakistan, or Israel, or any other country, all the time, I mean our kids are getting mixed messages. If we really feel for the motherland that we left, for economic reasons or otherwise, we should try to influence American policy or foreign policy to be favorable toward those countries. And the way we should do that is to become part of the mainstream political system.

HOMELAND IDENTITY, OR "IT DOESN'T MATTER HOW MANY YEARS I LIVE IN THIS COUNTRY, I WILL ALWAYS BE (FILL IN THE BLANK)"

Then there is Nadia. She was born into an upper-middle-class family in Valadares but grew up in São Paulo, where she went to college and worked for IBM. She lived in a large, comfortable apartment in a pleasant neighborhood of the city. She thought that by coming to the United States, she would have some fun, improve her English, and then find a better job when she returned. Like Marise, she also came to work as a nanny. She was embraced by her "American family" to such an extent that she even started attending the English-language Mass with them. Nadia met her husband, got pregnant unexpectedly, and now has two children. The couple own their own home, and he is starting his own software business with partners he met at his last job.

Despite her husband's economic success, and the appearance of having put down roots in America, Nadia sees her life as having gone dramatically off course. Try as she might, there are too many factors working against her to get back on track. She knows that her husband, who studied management information systems at the University of Massachusetts in Boston, has many more opportunities here than he would in Brazil. She made the conscious decision to stick by his side, even though that meant sacrificing her own career. Still, she feels tremendous frustration at her inability to advance professionally. Furthermore, the lifestyle she enjoyed in Brazil, as a working woman from an upper-middle-class family, was far more comfortable than the life she leads now. "I was quite spoiled in Brazil," Nadia admits.

> I had a pedicure and haircut every month, and new clothes all the time. For me, this has been a very hard experience. I haven't adapted very well, and I know I left something much bigger back there and that I had a better life that I could go back to. Here I am making money, but it has been a lot of heartache. So it's like, am I doing the right thing? And here I have two children now who will not grow up with their families and knowing what it is to have close family. When I say we are going to grandpa and grandma's, they look at me and say, who are grandpa and grandma? My children belong here, but my husband and I don't feel that we belong here. And it's a very typical situation, because at the same time you want to see them grow up successfully, you also don't want to abandon your roots because that's what you are. So now, it's like we are really in a mess. I don't think it's worth it.

Nadia still considers herself Brazilian because she is deeply ambivalent about living in the United States. By her calculations, what she gave up far outweighs what she gained. But others, who have much more positive things to say about their experiences in the United States, also identify unambiguously with their homelands. Donal and Ian, the two young men from Inishowen in chapter 2, who are here for the experience, are still unquestionably Irish. But even their friends who have lived in this country for ten or fifteen years claim there is nothing American about them. "You know," remarks Mary, a thirty-seven-year-old migrant from Inishowen,

> my husband and I have been here for almost fifteen years, and we still feel as Irish as the day when we first arrived. I mean, our kids were born here and they started school here. But you don't change who you are just because you live in another country. You never forget the place you were born and brought up. I might take on some American airs and like some of things about this country, but I will always be Irish. We still care more about what goes on there then what goes on here. I mean, my husband can't wait to check the soccer scores in the morning. And even though we always say we will go back, and we're still here, I know someday we will. We've already started looking around for some land to buy where we can build a house.

"BEING ETHNIC IS WHAT IT MEANS TO BE AMERICAN"

John Connelly claims another kind of identity that most Americans would approve of. He grew up in South Boston where, he recalls, almost "99 percent of the residents were of Irish ancestry." All of his neighbors attended the same Catholic school, went to Mass at the same parish, and played on the same Little League teams. Being Irish American was such an integral part of daily life no one ever questioned what it would be like to be something different. Nor did they give much thought to what the Irish piece of being Irish American really meant.

John is a tried-and-true ethnic American. When asked who he is, he answers Irish American without taking a breath. He swears by this country. He is always right out in front at the Fourth of July parade. Although he left his Irish Catholic neighborhood when he went to college, his closest friends and associates share the same background as well as an allegiance to the Irish trinity: Irishness, Catholicism, and membership in the Democratic Party. "There's just something that happens when you meet a stranger and their people are from Ireland," he says. "It's a familiarity, a shared set of values that don't need to be explained, a memory of times when doors were closed to the Irish, and a deep pride in how far we've come." While he never questions his American-ness, it is an Americanness that is infused with Irish culture, humor, and family. And it is an Irishness that is made in America. It has little to do with what people live like or think about in Ireland, and much more to do with the experience of being Irish in the United States.

Fifty-seven-year-old Rajaram Shah also considers himself an ethnic American. Although his parents still live in Gujarat, and he travels there at least once a year, he calls himself an American with strong Gujarati roots.

> I like to think that I have a balance. I mean, because on the one hand I've spent more years in this country now than I have out-side, right, a majority of my life, and obviously been successful in adjusting to the American way of life. But at the same time, and I appreciate some of the things that you get here that you don't get other places, at the same time I'm very sort of aware and nurtur-ing of my Indian roots. My parents live there, which always helps, so I go back once a year. We're very involved, as you can tell, with the Gujarati community here, on a social, cultural, as well as a business level. And lastly, we are very careful about making sure that our kids stay very involved.

It upset him when his cousins opted not to teach their children Gu-jarati. "Language is a strong part of your cultural roots and identity," Rajaram says. "We speak Gujarati at home, and my kids speak English at school. So overall I'm pretty happy with the balance."

Becoming an ethnic American is a long and sometimes bumpy jour-ney. Paolo, a forty-year-old restaurant owner, is somewhat typical. He came to the United States with the intention of being a sojourner. He would stay for two years, make some money, and then return home. But he gradually realized that his plan was changing. Paolo started to like living in America. He realized it would be difficult for him to return to Brazil. If he went back, he says, simple things like getting a phone would be really expensive and time-consuming because there are so few phone lines available. "There is no way to compare the two. It's just so much more convenient here. Life here is easier."

It was a struggle at first. Although today he is fluent, he barely spoke English when he first arrived. The house, truck, and market he still owned in Valadares exerted a strong pull. He went back to test the waters. But Brazil, he was sadly reminded, is one of the most corrupt countries in the world. It's so difficult to plan for the future. "For a person with no political power like myself, who is not able to change anything, it is very difficult to get by. Who would I choose to be Brazilian president today amid such corruption? These are things that only bring unhappiness."

Paolo came back to the United States and ultimately decided to stay. He felt that his kids, who were born here, would have better opportunities in the United States. Although he is in the process of becoming a U.S. citizen, Paolo will never loose the Brazilian piece of who he is. "I know there are things that I do and ways that I think that are becoming very Americanized. But I will never stop being Brazilian. Since I decided to stay here, I set my mind on helping the Brazilian community. We need to be here and to be recognized. We should celebrate our Brazilian traditions and culture, but at the same time be part of the places where we live."

Adopting an American lifestyle and values while maintaining strong ethnic roots, according to forty-seven-year-old Tariq Khan, is what it means to be an American.

People have emotional attachments to where they came from, and this is an accepted practice in this country. We are all, not all but most of us are immigrant, hyphenated Americans—there are Greek Americans, there are Italian Americans, there are Irish Americans, there are Pakistani, Indian, or whatever Americans. And they have all of these hyphenated communities, they have some affiliation with where they came from, where their ancestors came from. Look what Ted Kennedy does. If something happens in Ireland, Ted Kennedy is the one who raises the flag and says, you know, we have to take care of that. I know a congressman, Marty Meehan, and he is like third- or fourth-generation Irish American, and he too speaks on behalf of Ireland. So what I'm saying is, that is the accepted practice. You are American, you live here, and you're not going to go anywhere, but you also care about the land where you and your ancestors came from. That's what I'm trying to say.

"MY COUNTRY—HERE *AND* THERE": THE DUAL NATIONAL

Waldo Freitas is a forty-eight-year-old from Valadares who arrived in this country in 1984. He came to Boston because his brothers were here. His eldest sibling was a busboy at a Holiday Inn, so two days after he arrived, Waldo was washing pots in the hotel's kitchen. He worked his way up to busboy and then waiter. In the 1990s, he even owned his own restaurant for a while, but it didn't work out. After that, he started his own housecleaning business. He now employs five other Brazilians, who each clean five houses a day.

Waldo is a leader in the Brazilian community. People know him as someone who helps newcomers find jobs and apartments. They often ask him to translate at medical appointments or in lawyer's offices. "I do it," he says, "because they need help. And if somebody later on were to have complications and die, I wouldn't feel good. It's the way I was brought up, the way my parents taught me to help people. You might be in a bad situation one day, who knows?" He never feels that anyone owes him anything in return. It's just their turn to help the next person who needs it. He also feels responsible for teaching people how to "act American." Drunk driving, for example, is something that people don't talk about in Brazil. There are no campaigns educating people about how dangerous it is. "So they come here," he explains, "and they drink and drive, and they don't realize how bad it can be. They don't realize that they really mean the laws here because in Brazil, there are laws but they don't really enforce them. It's a lot easier to get away with things."

Waldo is an example of someone who strongly identifies with the United States and his homeland at the same time. He travels to Brazil every year and stays for at least a month. He talks to his elderly mother and sister at least twice, if not three times, a week, and sends money to them on a regular basis. Waldo purchased a ranch in Brazil with the money that he earned in America, and his cousin and nephew manage it for him. He has quite a few friends, he says, who have ranches or small businesses run by their relatives. Although he knows the Partido dos Trabalhadores is active in Boston, he hasn't paid a lot of attention to what it does. Still, he voted during the last Brazilian presidential election and is happy to have dual citizenship. "If I don't vote," he maintains, "and Lula doesn't do the right thing, I don't really have anything to say about it."[2] It still matters more to him who the president of Brazil is than the president of the United States because "the people over there deserve something better."

Most Brazilians, he feels, don't care as much about the political parties or the government in Brazil as they do about the people. They express their ties to Brazil at church. Like Marise, Waldo goes to a Catholic church where a priest from Brazil officiates. Although the majority of migrants come from Valadares, their charitable efforts are "about helping Brazilian people wherever they come from." Last year, his church raised money to build a reservoir. He also became "godfather" to a Brazilian family, pledging to send them $20 each month. Waldo sees himself as someone who belongs to two nations. He has clearly made a successful home in America, but he also has a physical and emotional home in Brazil.

Although they have a lot in common, dual nationals differ from ethnic Americans in two crucial ways. The Irish or Indian side for the ethnic American is shaped by the experience of being Irish or Gujarati in America. It is no longer influenced by nor particularly interested in home country affairs. In contrast, dual nationals are still connected enough to the daily affairs of their home countries that they are strongly influenced by them. The Irish or Indian part of who they are is regularly reinfused and reinvigorated by home country influences. Dual nationality combines the experience of being Irish or Gujarati in the United States with the meaning and content of that identity in the homeland. How each group directs its energies differs as a result. Ethnic Americans are more likely to dedicate themselves to helping their immigrant community in the United States. Dual nationals are concerned about their immigrant community as well as their homeland one. They pursue homeland dreams and American dreams at the same time.

The Cosmopolitans

For Bilal, John, and Waldo, some kind of national identity comes first. They use the light pink, blue, and green national building blocks of the world map to construct who they are, be it Irish, American, or some combination. A second group makes the world their playground. They blur the black lines separating the pinks and greens of their mental atlas with their know-how and experience. They have studied, traveled, and worked abroad often enough to feel at home wherever they are. Their family members migrate between apartments in London, Nairobi, and Boston, but each living room has many of the trappings of the one back in Baroda and each kitchen is filled with the same smells. Where they were born, or their last address, is just another notch in the belt of these citizens of the world.

Today's cosmopolitans come in two varieties: people who are completely footloose and fancy-free, and people who create selective mental maps of the places that matter to them most. The first type of cosmopolitan is always at home. They are upper- and upper-middle-class Gujaratis and Pakistanis who are only weakly tied to one place or one nation because they have the money, education, and life experience to feel comfortable anywhere. To them, Karachi is a lot like Dubai, London, or New York, because the places where they shop, eat out, or lay down their heads in each city look a lot alike. They create parallel cultural organizations, organize comparable holiday celebrations, and entertain a constant stream of the same visitors. Home is portable and replicable when you have enough money and skills.

Cosmopolitans are *rule makers* rather than *rule takers*. Because they belong to their home country's ethnic or religious majority, they have the confidence and capabilities that come from setting terms that others follow. They can pick and choose what they incorporate from their lives in America, and what they want to hold on to from the other places they have lived. They're not afraid that contact with other groups will undermine their cultural core or make them forget their roots. In contrast, rule takers approach their new surroundings with less confidence. They are accustomed to living life on other people's terms, and this minority mentality carries over to their new home. They feel excluded from the mainstream conversation and reluctant to join it, because if they do, they may compromise their already weak sense of self.

Adil Khan is a cosmopolitan without roots.[3] He left Pakistan when he was barely seventeen to study in England. From there, he moved on to work as an engineer, first in Switzerland and then in Germany. He moved to this country because he thought his daughter, who suffers from mental illness, would get better care in the United States. A few months after he arrived, he started a company that manufactures medical imaging equipment. Although most of the production is done in Massachusetts, he outsources some new product development and marketing to Pakistan.

Location matters little to Adil. He claims he would be equally happy in Germany, England, or the United States, as long as he can live and work as he pleases. His identity is completely portable. How he sees himself professionally or religiously is separate from where he lives or works at any given time. He is a global actor who moves and settles easily in any setting. Global belonging, he says, comes with its own set of obligations—they are just not based on national loyalties. Instead, he participates in the religious or professional communities that matter to him most wherever he lives. In most places, he finds, his education and wealth allow him to be who he wants to be.

I don't feel a particular affinity to any country. I have lived and worked in so many places. It doesn't really matter to me where I am. We lived in England, and I liked it there. I worked in Switzerland and Germany. Now I am in the United States. As long as I can work and my family is happy, I can be anywhere. It really doesn't matter that much to me. . . . Yes, I am active in the Pakistani community. But that is because I have professional interests or religious commitments that I share with other people who happen to be Pakistani. Wherever I am, I find them, and I work hard for them, but not out of a sense of duty to Pakistan or the United States.

Aniya Patel, a forty-six-year-old Gujarati, is also a cosmopolitan without attachments. The way she sees it, people around the world might not always behave in the same way but their values are the same, making cultural and national differences superfluous. If she is in Baroda, she says, she goes to school, and she has friends, work colleagues, and relatives. This doesn't change when you move. You will still have classmates, neighbors, and a boss. All these relationships are guided by similar values. "If you are hardworking, ambitious, and you have certain goals in life," she explains, "then you make certain plans, you connect with these qualities in other people, and then it is irrelevant whether you are Gujarati, or American, or Irish. That's very common human behavior."

Ghazi Syed, a twenty-eight-year-old from Karachi, also identifies with the world community. He is keenly aware that he has different parts, and that on certain days, in certain situations, one part matters more than the others. He never completely identifies with any one group, though, because he always claims aspects of particular identities and rejects others. He attributes his ability to weave in and out to his upbringing. When asked, "Who are you?" he replies,

> The way I look at it is that I wear many cloaks, and not one is the primary one with everything else underneath. There is no one overcoat that I'm wearing, I'm just wearing many coats. At multiple times I have multiple interests, and those interests get aligned with certain groups, but never foolhardily, and completely and blindly. At times, I feel that I am very close to the Muslim community, but then there are elements in that community that I completely disagree with. I don't want to own them, and I don't want to be lumped into that one big pot—you guys are all the same. At times, I feel very close to Pakistanis. One day I may give money to a Muslim mosque here because I feel too Muslim, and another day I may save up that money and give it to a Pakistani charity because I feel very Pakistani.

Rubina Patel exemplifies a second type of cosmopolitanism. For this group, home has roots. The same background and money allow them to achieve a cosmopolitan lifestyle, but they selectively choose where to live it. Rather than being at home everywhere, their global playground is bounded by specific locales.

Most of the friends and neighbors that Rubina grew up with had family members living abroad. Like her peers, she went to England to study before settling in the United States. Her parents now live with her in Massachusetts, but her siblings are scattered in London, Mombasa, and Geneva. Like Adil, Aniya, and Ghazi, she also has the money, language abilities, and cultural capital to be at home anywhere, yet she uses them to reinscribe herself in India and assert her place in her adopted home.

I know that I could live in any city. We have the money, the education. We were brought up to do that. But I choose to live in India
and the United States. Some of the friends who we grew up with
don't care anymore about what country they are in, what group
they belong to. But I value the fact that I am a Patel, and that that
means I am a member of a community in India and a certain community here. I want my kids to know about that and enjoy that, because I think it is something of great value.

Rubina is a global actor who uses her social and cultural know-how
to embed herself in specific places. Her version of global membership
translates into a sense of belonging to a specific corner of India and the
United States.[4] The same is true with Dan Sullivan, a fiftyish-year-old
who is extremely active in Democratic Party politics. He considers himself someone who belongs to the world but has a strong affinity toward
America. He is convinced that global actors can be loyal to the countries
where they live and help the places they know the most about and to
which they have the strongest attachments. You can be American, Irish,
and a member of the world community at the same time. In fact, he
says, in this globally connected world, you have to.

Being a citizen of the world means that we are human beings and
that we care about people all across the world. But we have a certain emotional attachment to a certain part of the world and we
like to deliver something there. People on the street are the same
all over the world. They are concerned about poverty, they are concerned about education, they are concerned about how their kids
are going to grow up. Personally, I focus on Europe because that is
the area that I know the best. But I am also 100 percent committed
to this country. I'm totally committed to the political process, totally committed to the social process.

Different types of belonging, he claims, are not mutually exclusive.
"Being a better American and a better Irishman makes us better citizens of the world, and the other way around." In a world that is so
interconnected, you have to use your connections to particular places
to make the whole world better, Dan explains. It's not enough to be na-

tional citizens or global citizens. Today's world demands that you be both simultaneously.

Religious Global Citizens

Some people don't live according to an atlas, or at least not the kind most of us are used to. They think of themselves as living in a religious landscape, not carved up into nations or encompassing the entire world but delineated by the spiritual and the sacred. They are not nationals or cosmopolitans but members of communities of faith composed of fellow believers around the globe. Religious global citizenship entails rights and responsibilities that complement, supplement, and sometimes contradict other forms of belonging. But for this group, these rules matter most.

I purposefully use the term *citizenship*, although I know many will disagree. I recognize that citizenship, as it is legally defined, refers to a formal membership status in a self-governing political community, and that there are rights and obligations associated with that membership from which nonmembers are excluded. Living somewhere without documents involves serious economic and political limitations that religious citizenship cannot redress. Moreover, religious institutions do not command the same generalized authority and legitimacy as the state.

I insist on the citizenship metaphor, however, to drive home an important point. I am more interested here in migrants' subjective experiences than about how institutional arrangements constrain their ability to act on what they think and feel. The people who claimed religious citizenship understood it to work in a way that was similar to political citizenship. They used similar words and analogies to describe these two membership categories. In other words, the political limits to religious membership did not stop them from equating the two.

Conceptualizing the world as a global religious community changed the way people located themselves in space. Religious global citizens imagined themselves in global religious landscapes, dotted by religious buildings and shrines. It was not that they were oblivious to their surroundings or the salience of political borders. It was that they thought of themselves as living in an alternative topography, with residents, rules, and landmarks that mattered more to them than their secular equivalents. Sometimes, a person's religious geography fit neatly within

national boundaries. In other cases, religious space transcended its political counterpart, encompassing people and places across the world
and complementing, if not superseding, the nation in significance.

Some faith traditions already come with ideologies and organizations that resonate with a global religious identity. The Muslim umma
is an imagined religious community governed by Sharia. While the capital of global Catholicism is the Vatican, its boundaries encompass religious shrines, pilgrimage sites, and places where Marian apparitions
are said to have occurred around the globe. Members of Pentecostal
communities often place the culture of Christianity before secular culture because, as John Burdick argues, "it encourages believers to see
themselves as belonging to a transcendent worldwide brotherhood of
the saved."[5] Although the structures of transnational Hinduism are
newly emerging, as chapter 5 describes, they are well under construction. The Swaminarayan, Swadhyaya, and Bhagat communities that
Gujaratis belong to are its architectural building blocks. Individual
members appropriate these ideologies and structures to create customized religious maps.

Like political citizenship, religious global citizenship comes with
benefits and obligations. People interpret these differently. Some felt
their ties to coreligionists outweighed their ties to co-ethnics or co-
nationals, although these sometimes overlapped. They were responsible, above all, for the members of their religious group regardless of
their address. Their religious citizenship is exclusive. Others acted more
like religious cosmopolitans. They entered the human community
through the portal of their faith, which served as their guide for how to
act toward other members. Like other cosmopolitans, they felt an affinity to people around the world, but it was religion that motivated their
inclusive stance.

Eliana, a thirty-four-year-old Brazilian former Catholic who joined
an evangelical Christian church only after arriving in the United States,
is a global religious citizen. Being Christian, she says, means a lot to her.
It means being more separate from the world than she was before and
isolating herself from people who do not live a Christian life.

I used to go to parties and be around people who were drinking.
Life changes a lot when you decide to just leave that one side and
to follow the word of Christ. . . . I made difficult choices. Back

then, the transition to get out from one world to come to another, it was as hard for me as it was when I left Brazil and came to the United States. To come to the United States from Brazil, I left everybody and everything behind. A whole life. And I didn't even look back. Because if you look, you can go back some day, right? I never looked back. And I feel the same thing when I talk about the fact that I became an evangelical Christian. I left one world to go to another.

Eliana migrated once from Brazil to the United States, and then a second time from a secular space to a religious one. Her experience illustrates how people move between physical territories, and between real and imagined landscapes, and how religion helps them make these journeys. The religious terrain she describes shares many of the attributes of political territories. It has leaders. It has a government to which she appeals and voices her concerns. Being a member entails rights and duties. It gets her access to resources. She is represented and protected. And in exchange, she must serve and obey the laws.

Malik Zuberi and his wife, Diya, both middle-aged with two children, are also global religious citizens. They say that the most important thing about who they are and how they live as a family is that they are Muslim. It shapes how they act, who their friends are, how they conduct business, and where and when they contribute to charity. They firmly believe the injunction that Islam is a way of life influencing all aspects of daily experience. As Diya explains,

First and foremost, I am a Muslim. I want to teach my kids Muslim values—that is the most important thing I want to transmit to my kids. It is OK with me if the Pakistaniness is lost, just as long as they stay Muslim. It is not always easy. My daughter loves to play soccer. My husband has a fit when he sees her in that uniform. Her shorts have to be pulled down as far as they will go and her socks as far up as they will go so there is only a little bit of her knee showing. But she knows what is right and wrong. She is learning the rules, the traditions, the discipline.

For Malik and Diya, there is no such thing as dual citizenship or multiple membership because being a Muslim comes before anything else.

Others agreed, reminding me that when a Muslim child is born, the father or another male relative says the call to prayer, or Adhan, in its right ear.[6] They paraphrased the statement in the Koran that although Muslims are divided into tribes, the Prophet told them to stay together and "hold fast to the cable of Allah."[7] This, they said, means that you belong to the same community regardless of your nationality.

Religious global citizens want the right to live according to their interpretation of religious law. It's difficult to let your teenage daughter wear a gym uniform when you're concerned about modesty, as many parents are. Movies and television programs are filled with messages about sexuality, evolution, and lifestyle choices they adamantly disagree with. On the other hand, some think America is the best place to be a religious global citizen. Freedom of religion is guaranteed. Social programs like Medicaid and Social Security ensure that people's basic needs get met in the way that Christ or the Prophet intended. "America, you know," says Kudret, a Pakistani immigrant in her forties, "is the most Muslim country in the world. Everyone has enough to eat and a roof over their head. This is directly in line with Muslim teachings. You cannot say that about Pakistan where Muslim laws are broken every day because of the poverty."

Global religious citizens also have a clear sense of their responsibilities. Some define these narrowly, only in terms of the members of their own group. "My first duty," declares Eliana, "is to others in our congregation and then to other Baptists around the globe." That doesn't mean, she adds quickly, that she would refuse someone food or shelter, only that given the choice, she would rather help her own. "It doesn't matter if he is Brazilian or from Zambia, just as long as he is a Christian." Mohin Khan, who became a global Muslim in early adulthood, also changed his priorities.

> I fall more into the category of I am a Muslim first and then a Pakistani. Before I married, I never really went to the mosque, I wasn't interested in these issues. I didn't feel like the Palestinian-Israeli problem was any more important to me than the problem of Cubans in America. I really didn't care. But then I started going to the mosque more because [my] wife, who is American born, was converting and I had to explain things to her. I met people from all

over the world, and started to find out about what was going on and talking more about social issues.

The thing is, like, I was a member of PAGB [Pakistani Association of Greater Boston], but I am leaving that. Social and cultural events are important but I am more concerned now with helping Muslim people who need help. There is another organization called MCSS [Muslim Community Support Services]. It just happens to be that most of the people who are part of the board are Pakistani or South Asian, and we are helping Muslim refugees around the world. I am more interested in joining them and helping them out. Domestic violence, foster parents, those issues are more important to me than having some dance thing going on.

Others interpret religious global citizenship much more inclusively to mean they are responsible for all humankind. Mary McFee, a forty-five-year-old Inishowener, is a case in point. She describes herself as a devout Catholic. She is the first to volunteer for anything that needs to be done in the parish, always serving coffee or staffing the cash register at church fairs and tag sales. She learned this from her mother growing up in Malin Head. Her mother was stalwart in her faith. Nothing shook her belief that God would provide and that you served him in return. When she talked about this to her children, Mary recalls, she taught them not just to serve Catholics but to serve non-Catholics as well. Being Catholic means being part of humanity. God's grace is not limited to believers. He loves everyone, and so should we. Mary took this to mean everyone living around the globe.

> I know there are some people who feel we should only care about Irish Catholics. Or that maybe we should just care about other Catholics living around the world. But I have never thought that that was what my faith was about. I always believed it was about loving everyone and about making the world a better place for everyone, not just for people who believe the same things as me. It goes against Catholic teachings to be so narrow. Charity and love is for everyone, not just one particular group.

So says Vera, a twenty-nine-year-old Valadarense. She is a member of the Four Square Church, an evangelical religious community. Although she realizes that many people in her church disagree, she also feels strongly that being a Christian means belonging to a global community consisting of Christians and non-Christians alike. "I know there are a lot of people who would say that we should only care about other Christians. But I think that is the exact opposite of what Christ preached. He talked about universal, unconditional love that isn't given out by race or nationality. I think that means we are all connected to each other, no matter what we believe or what we look like. That's what living a Christian life is all about."

Rupa Patel, a fifty-four-year-old from Gujarat, arrived at a similar broad outlook, although by a slightly different route. She believes we all belong to the same family because we all have God within us. Her religious global citizenship is inspired by the humanity and godliness we all share.

> Dadaji is always talking about the in-dwelling God—that we all have God within us, and that is why we must treat every human being with love and respect. I don't think he means just other Hindus. I think he means that everyone has a bit of God within themselves, and that is why we need to take care of each other. That doesn't just mean other Swadhyayees. That means Muslims, Christians, and even other Hindus.

Can Religion a Humanitarian Make?

What would people like Alice and Florence say about exclusive religious global citizens like Eliana and Mohin? Globalization has many of us asking the same question. In a world where people are constantly on the move, will they still participate in the organizations we consider to be the cornerstones of democracy? What are the boundaries of the communities we belong to, and who gets to define the collective good? Two related conversations take up these questions: people concerned about cosmopolitanism and people who care about citizenship. Let me speak to each in turn.

Earlier portraits of cosmopolitans depicted them as members of a global society united by shared universal values. They went everywhere and belonged nowhere. Today's more subtle accounts recognize that local distinctions persist, and that everyone belongs to social groups, networks, and cultures, even though the hope is that they also feel an allegiance to humanity writ large. In other words, like most of the people here, every contemporary cosmopolitan is somehow rooted somewhere. Everyone cobbles together a unique combination of universal and particularistic ethnic, national, and religious elements.[8]

Thus, Kwame Anthony Appiah describes cosmopolitan patriots, whose concern for their homeland and "caring for lives nearer by" does not prevent their "loyalty to humankind." Appiah's patriots live in a world where their cultural practices are shaped by settings far away though their everyday lives are rooted in particular contexts.[9] Cosmopolitan patriotism gives them an umbrella that is broad enough to encompass their multiple political ideologies. Some are conservative and religious; others are secularizers of a socialist bent.

In contrast, Martha Nussbaum warns against putting particularistic loyalties first, and emphasizes the need for world citizens of the Stoic variety for whom the "accident of where one is born is just that . . . any human being might have been born in any nation."[10] The world community of justice and reason has to come before partisan loyalties and factions. Students "may continue to regard themselves as defined partly by their particular loves—their families, their religious, ethnic or racial communities, or even their country," but they must "also, and centrally, learn to recognize humanity wherever they encounter it."[11] Similarly, Amartya Sen argues that putting world citizenship first is the right thing to do because it makes us care about people not related to us by kinship, community, or nationality.[12] If one's fundamental allegiance is to humanity at large, *everyone* is included. Like Nussbaum, Sen acknowledges that multiple loyalties can (and will) exist, but that no one allegiance should take precedence over the other.

Noticeably absent from these debates is religion.[13] Faith communities have rarely been seen as instances of cosmopolitanism, or as inspiring their members to look beyond their own club. Religion is equated with parochialism and particularism. Nevertheless, history tells a different story. In their heydays, medieval and premedieval Arabic and Muslim empires brought together many peoples and cultures, producing thriving artistic, literary, and commercial communities. The streets of Cairo and Istanbul were well known for their pan-Islamic and Masonic enclaves of cafés, lodges, and salons.[14] And we don't have to look only to the history books. The Baha'i tradition is based entirely on cosmopolitan ideals, as are movements as disparate as the Jesuits and Swadhyaya.[15]

Despite this evidence, political theorists from John Stuart Mill to Ernest Gellner summarily concluded that religious allegiances would only lead to absolutism and intolerance. But if nationalism and patriotism sometimes function as springboards to a humanitarian embrace, why can't religion do the same?[16]

People like Florence, and the exclusive variety of religious global citizens, add fuel to Mill's and Gellner's arguments. But many others in these pages, including religious global citizens with more expansive views, are ready and waiting. Religion motivates them to engage with people beyond their neighbors and feel a sense of responsibility toward them. It inspires them to do the right thing no matter who the beneficiaries are. It teaches them their community is the world, even if it includes people with whom they disagree.[17] Its triumphalist messages can, and must, be offset by its more pluralistic, humane expressions.

Students of citizenship are also struggling to understand how people balance the competing demands of the multiple communities they belong to. They want to know how people claim rights in a public sphere that stretches beyond the nation-state.[18] They distinguish between liberal versus republican concepts of citizenship, or those based on status versus action. A status-based view sees citizenship as a legal position, or as full membership in a formal political community. The second, which I build on here, views practice-based civic-republican-style citizenship as a desirable activity; its scope and quality depend on how often individuals participate, and what they actually do.[19] Some argue against separating the two, emphasizing that participation and protection can only go so far without full, legal membership.[20] Again, my point is not that religious global citizenship replaces its political counterpart, or that it comes with the same power and possibility. It is to draw attention to a religious membership category that is salient to many individuals and that mimics many of the characteristics and outcomes of political citizenship.

When we talk about citizenship, we are also talking about identity. How people think of themselves racially, ethnically, or religiously strongly influences how they see themselves as citizens, how they perceive their rights and obligations, how they participate in the public sphere, and why.[21] Both the republican and liberal versions of citizenship locate it at the level of the nation-state.[22] But this view artificially separates citizenship and identity and assumes that each individual and group understands, experiences, and practices citizenship in the same way. Identity, though, is "an ensemble of subject positions" (such as female, Hindu, Gujarati, and Bhagat).[23] Its dimensions mutually shape each other such that Hindu women and evangelical Christian women understand being female differently. During a particular struggle, one dimension of identity prevails. Its other dimensions are defined in relation to that predominant position.[24]

Here again, religion needs to be brought more centrally into the citizenship conversation. Faith, directly or indirectly, permeates the lives of many people. For some, it is the sole basis around which they define who they are. For others, it is one thread among many that affects what they care about. Either way, religion influences what positions people take, what they decide to do about them, and who their potential partners are.

The next step in understanding how immigration changes the religious landscape is to take a closer look at the kind of faith immigrants actually bring with them. What do people really believe, and what do they think they are supposed to do about it? Is it really so different than the average American? Do they just do what their leaders tell them or do they talk back? For Alice and Luis as well as Florence, these questions conjure up images of women veiled from head to toe, twelve-headed Hindu Gods, and worshippers who speak in tongues as they thrash about on the floor. They assume, implicitly or explicitly, that imported faith comes in a one-size-fits-all package. As the next chapter reveals, they are sorely mistaken.

4

Values and Practices: "You Do Your Best and You Leave the Rest"

Luis, Alice, and Florence have only to attend an *iftar* at any of the universities in the Boston area to see that immigrant religion comes in many shapes and sizes.[1] Some of the women in the room would be wearing jeans while others would be dressed in long robes. Some men and women would sit separately during the meal following prayers and others would eat side by side. Some attendees would be Muslim born and others would be American-born converts.

After one iftar I attended, I spoke with Sara, a twenty-five-year-old graduate student from Pakistan. Did it bother her, I asked, that people take Islam to mean so many different things, and that people in the room practice it in so many different ways? "Not at all," she answered quickly.

When I first came to this country, I had a very different idea about my faith. I had no idea there could be so many different ways to interpret it, so many different ways of doing things. Because at home, it seems like, in our social circle at least, we pretty much all practice Islam in the same way. But here, I realized, you really have to make some choices. It's not given to you on a platter. Your parents are not here telling you what to do. So I've been experimenting. When I first got here, I always wore a veil. Now, I sort of feel like that isn't the most important sign of how faithful I am. We also never mixed much with our male classmates. Now, I'm not so sure that the Prophet meant that either. So I'm really in a stage of trying to figure out what this all means to me. And you know what? I think God has better things to do than to micromanage my faith. I think he would be happy that I am thinking, struggling, not just accepting things uncritically. It's more important that I'm trying than if I get everything right. You do your best and you leave the rest.

Not only is the faith immigrants bring with them not monolithic, its size and shape is very much a work-in-progress. Several different relationships to faith emerged during my conversations while writing these pages.[2] First off, hardly anyone called themselves "not religious." Even people who scholars might classify as "barely believers" claimed some kind of relationship to faith because from their point of view, many aspects of nationality, culture, and religion overlap. There was a small group who described a religion not open to debate, who believed that their way was right. But most people did not come to this country with a hermetically sealed set of beliefs written in stone. They did not simply accept what they had been told or do what they had always done. To varying degrees, their faith was open to negotiation. They actively wrestled with what they believed and how to practice it. They struggled with religion's public role in America because they knew it was different here than it was at home.

Alan Wolfe assures us that this is the nature of religion in America. "Democratic in their political instincts, geographically and economically mobile, attracted to popular culture more than to the written word, Americans from the earliest times have shaped religion to account for their personal needs."[3] The personalization of religion should come as no surprise in a country that places such a high premium on the individual.

But this story isn't just about what happens in America. Newcomers were already connected to the United States, socially and culturally, before they got here. They are exposed to U.S. culture every time they go to the movies or turn on their televisions. They come from places where the cult of the individual has also arrived, along with global values like self-esteem, gender equality, democracy, human rights, and good governance. Aspects of the religion they bring already resonate with what is here. What's more, immigrants' faith is constantly reshaped by its encounter with the American context.

To treat all Hindus, evangelical Christians, or Muslims as equal, or to imagine their faith as static and unyielding, is to make the same mistake as saying all Baptists and Catholics are the same because they are all Christians. It masks the diversity within and between groups and gives short shrift to the many voices included within them. It discounts the way in which all faiths evolve in response to changing cultural imperatives. Without listening closely to the diversity of voices out there, we'll never have a meaningful conversation, let alone have the opportunity to learn from the new perspectives immigrants introduce.

The Strict Faithful

The strict faithful are crystal clear about their beliefs. They subscribe to a well-established canon that is shared, accessible, and nonnegotiable. God is in charge, all-knowing, all-seeing, strict but beneficent. God can be reached directly, or through intermediary deities or saints. Leaders and teachers establish strict rules, and resolve any conflicts about how to follow them. The boundary between the acceptable and the forbidden, the believer and the nonbeliever, and the right and wrong way of doing things is clearly laid down in the sand, between both people of the same denomination and people of other faiths. Evangelical Christians, orthodox Jews, and conservative Muslims and Hindus probably have more in common with each other than with people of their own faith who they see as too permissive. They are also more likely to claim religious global citizenship.

Thirty-four-year-old Abrar Syed is a member of the strict faithful. When asked whether a good Muslim might drink alcohol or eat pork, he answers unconditionally no. There are certain things that are not open to debate. Men and women should not pray together because if God had wanted it that way, God would have said so. Abrar was not always a religious man. Ten years ago, he was kidnapped while on a business trip in rural Pakistan. His captors asked whether he wanted "wine or women" while he waited to be rescued. "The Koran," he answered, and swore to himself that if he returned alive, he would dedicate himself to his faith. Since then, he has become a self-styled mullah or teacher. He lives with his wife and their two children in a large apartment in a middle-class neighborhood of Karachi. Even inside the house, his wife, Kareema, wears a robe over her clothes and a veil when people visit. After his wife showed us into her drawing room, Abrar handed each of us a Koran while she set up their video camera to tape "our lesson."

The Koran, he explained, cannot be tampered with. Since God wrote it, and God is perfect, it cannot be changed. That is why the Koran is always read in Arabic, and why Muslim children have to learn it by heart. That way, the exact words of the Prophet remain intact. Any questions about what is written can only be answered by referring to other Koranic verses. Not even the Hadiths or Sunna (tradition of the Prophet) can be used. "There are certain things that you cannot change. Giving charity, you cannot change, fasting during the month of Ramadan, you cannot change. There are people who say beer is not a drink or that it is not hard liquor. I do not agree with that."

Daniel, born a Presbyterian, but now a member of a Maranatha church, also represents the strict faithful. He lives in Valadares, where he returned after fifteen years in Framingham. Daniel started as a dishwasher in a hotel, worked his way up, and eventually opened his own landscaping company. When he first arrived, he went to the Portuguese Catholic Mass because there were no Portuguese-speaking Presbyterian churches in the area. One day a pilgrim came to his door and invited him to a prayer group that the Maranathas were starting. He hadn't heard of them before, but he went because he was feeling unsatisfied by the Catholic Church experience. He and his wife liked it so much, they began attending twice a week. Eventually, the group opened its own church in a second-floor office overlooking Framingham's Main Street. Daniel was born-again soon after.

In addition to attending services, which he does on Tuesdays, Thursdays, and all day Sunday, he also prays regularly at home. He reads the Bible each day and discusses it with his children. Like Abrar, he says, "The word is the word." For answers, "all you need to do is look in the book." Daniel believes his fate is in God's hands since he accepted Christ as his savior. When he has a difficult decision to make or a challenge is thrown in his path, he simply prays and trusts that God will tell him what to do.

Part of being a Maranatha is spreading the word to others. And there is a certain way to do so. Teams, much like the one that landed on his doorstep, go out each weekend to Brazilian neighborhoods, personally inviting people to come and pray. Daniel spent many a Saturday knocking on doors. When he returned to Brazil, he was delighted to find that someone had been doing the same thing in Valadares and that a small congregation had been formed there. He became an active member, and has worked hard to build strong ties between his congregations in Framingham and Brazil.

Tall, impermeable boundaries separate the strict faithful from other members of the same faith and followers of other traditions. Their theology and practice is given. There is little to discuss because it comes directly from God. What it means to be a good person and a good person's responsibility to the larger community is set in stone. Right and wrong do not change with one's address.

The Questioning Faithful

Mehtab Rahman, in his thirties, professes a second kind of religiosity. He came to the United States from Pakistan to attend college, skipped graduate school, and is now running his second successful high-tech start-up. He and his wife married for love. Islam figures large in his life. He makes it his business to attend communal prayers every Friday. He eats only halal meat.[4] He fasts during the entire month of Ramadan, and the last time we met he told me proudly that the next day he would be getting up early with his eight-year-old son to accompany him during his first fast. His mother sets a high bar for religious practice. She fasts during most of the month prior to Ramadan so she gets used to going without food and can earn more blessings.

For Mehtab, being a good Muslim also means following the rules laid down by the Prophet. And he sees clear differences between Muslim rules and those professed by other faiths. But being a good Muslim also means understanding why you do what you do. It's not enough to pray and just do what you are told. You have to put those prayers and beliefs into practice, and know why. You need to study and ask questions. You need to actively engage with your faith.

> See, to me obviously the five pillars are important, but not important because you can just go check, check, check, I've done what I need to do, but because they form the basis for how you practice your faith. I think a lot of what is lost on not just the rest of the world but certainly on Muslims is putting these ideas into practice. So really sort of being good to your fellow human being is a very important part of Islam. Some people have said that 90 percent of your religion is how you act toward your fellow Muslims,

as well as your non-Muslims. You know, how kind you are to them, how helpful you are to them, how much you respect them and not do things like undermining them, all those sorts of things. Certainly the aspect of charity and community, you know, sort of what you give to God and all of those things, are obviously very important as well. I am not relegating prayers and the spiritual to a lesser level. I think those are, in my view, those are your private aspects. I think there's an overemphasis among Muslims, certainly in Pakistan, but even here to say, well, you know, how do you dress for prayers, or did you say your prayers at a certain time, those sorts of things. Or, for example, do you know the Koran by heart? Well, that's great, I know the Koran by heart, but do I understand it? I mean do you understand it, understanding what you're doing and why that's important. To me that's more important.

For Ghazi Ahmed, also in his thirties, the requirements of good faith are more up for grabs. No one can say what others should do or judge the sincerity of their beliefs. No one knows what is in another person's heart. Besides, it's not always clear how you're supposed to follow the rules in this day and age. Ghazi takes this as a sign that one has to question. People must go through their own personal struggles with their faith. They have to pick and choose what makes sense to them, understand why they choose what they choose, and then live their faith in the best way they know how.

Ghazi remembers being told the same story over and over again growing up. There was a war going on during the Prophet's time. One of Muhammad's good friends was fighting with a non-Muslim. The Prophet's friend was about to kill his opponent, who was down on the ground, when the man turned to him and said, "I believe in one God and Muhammad as a prophet of God."[5] The Prophet's friend did not believe him. He thought the man was just repeating the phrase to save his life. He killed him anyway and went back to tell the Prophet. Muhammad asked if he could really know what was in his opponent's heart. Ghazi recalls, "Muhammad was, like, did you open his heart and see if he was saying that truthfully, or how do you know? Who are you to say who is a Muslim and who is not? My parents always told me that religion is relativistic. People find different things in religion, but they're all trying to reach the same summit."

These questions don't just come up in America, where there is often no imam leading the religious community, but in Pakistan as well. Ghazi also told about the time his father visited a mosque in Karachi and got into an argument with someone who told him to cover his head. His father told the man that he was praying and "who the hell are you to tell me how to dress?" "To think," Ghazi continues, "that some guy sitting in Mecca or wherever thinks I am not a good Muslim, that's ridiculous. Do I care? No, I don't. I've gone beyond that. It's almost like saying do I care whether the president of a university thinks I am smart or not. I am my own man, and when I believe in something I follow it."

Ghazi and Mehtab exemplify the questioning faithful. They see clear boundaries between what they believe in and what others practice. They actively try to understand their faith and make it a meaningful part of their lives. They generally believe in prayer, and in a God who guides and protects them. They tend to do what their leaders say and, to a certain extent, see them as God's agents on earth. They know what they believe and what the basic tenets of their traditions are. But they also believe that traditions change and have to be adapted, and that it is OK and even good to do so. It turns out that what is actually in the Koran or the Bible, or what the pope or Pramukh Swami actually said, is often far less important than what people think has been said.[6]

The questioning faithful fall along a continuum with respect to how much they grapple with their faith and what aspects of it can be negotiated. They also differ over how much they value doctrine as opposed to ritual. At one end of the spectrum are people like Mehtab who understand their religion as a fairly preset menu with few choices and limited opportunities to change the recipe. What matters is to know what the recipes are and to follow the directions carefully. At the other end are people like Ghazi who see themselves as selecting from a smorgasbord of religious possibilities. Aside from remembering to eat from the five food groups, these individuals feel almost complete liberty to pick and choose what they like within the broad parameters of their faith.[7]

Most of the people I spoke with fell somewhere in between. They believe they have been given a clear framework, but one that they can alter so it makes sense in today's world. As Nana Islam, a twenty-six-year-old migrant, puts it, "You definitely engage with it. In any religion, no matter what it is, there is something beyond the human stuff. There's a divineness to it. For some it's God, for others it's something else. You interpret it yourself, of course, but at the same time there are certain rights that God has over you, so you cannot choose everything yourself."

When asked to describe the basic tenants of their faith, Nana, and many other Muslims I met, immediately mentioned the five pillars: pray five times a day, fast during the holy month of Ramadan, give to charity, refrain from eating pork, and go on hajj or to Mecca, if possible. The rest, many said, you have to figure out yourself.

As Malik, a fifty-year-old-migrant, explains,

> To think and debate, and to be enlightened rather than just follow things dogmatically, is to be a good Muslim. Some of the things in the book [the Koran] are very clear. Then over time, there were interpretations of Islam by imams, and you're supposed to follow one imam or the other. In fact, there are some people who don't even like it if you change between different imams. You have to pick one and follow him because then it's coherent. But at the end of the day, Islam is supposed to be for all times to come for all people. I absolutely believe in the fundamentals, and so on and so forth. But I didn't choose to be born in this century, in this day and age. But God brought me here, so I've got to live in the environment that I have. I can't really try to live in the environment that was thirteen hundred years ago. And I think that's where there may be digression between different people, some who want to go back and live exactly how it was in the Prophet's time, but that's really difficult.

Malik does his best to pray five times a day. When he sleeps late and misses his prayers, or he can't say his prayers in the afternoons because of business obligations, he makes them up later.[8] He is careful not to eat pork. Wherever he is, he tries to attend Friday prayers. Of course, this is easier to do when he is traveling in Pakistan, where there is a mosque in every neighborhood. But he also knows where all the mosques are in eastern Massachusetts, and tries to plan his day so he is near one at around noontime on Fridays. When he lived in Pakistan, he explains, he never had to think about what it meant to be a Muslim. It was simply a matter of living and breathing. Here, you have to think about not only how to make it work but what you are going to tell your children. "It's made me study and try to really understand things. It's also made me question. There are certain things that just don't make sense for today's world and that I will not do. But there are also certain things that you just have to go along with."

Malik sees himself as someone who would err on the side of the rules. Vineeta, a forty-five-year-old member of the ISSO, also has a clear notion of what she believes in. Every morning she rises and recites the same prayer, which she translates as "God is the one whole, who made us by little pieces of him. So when we die or whatever, our soul goes back to him and just recombines with him." God is not sitting on a throne in heaven, she says, but is inside all of us all the time.

According to Vineeta, Lord Swaminarayan was the incarnation of God on earth. The Shikshapatri, or book of his teachings, provides clear directions for how people should live. Lord Swaminarayan teaches us that your parents are your assets and you should always serve them, she explains. Your expenses should never exceed your income. A person's job should match his abilities. Not everyone is suited to do all things; societies need doctors as well as garbage collectors. But people must do their jobs as best they can and constantly try to improve. Religion is about self-control, discipline, and sacrifice. If people fast two times a month and give more to charity than they think they can afford, then they are on the right track. A woman's duty is to pass on her culture to her children and create a holy atmosphere at home. Lord Swaminarayan, she reasons, doesn't get angry as long as you are trying.

Erin Craig, a thirty-two-year-old from Inishowen, also struggles to be a good Catholic. She knows there are some basic ground rules and appreciates how they anchor her life. Erin believes "there is a higher power than anyone on this planet can offer," and that it comes first and foremost. She likes that the church emphasizes people's higher purpose in life—a point that gets lost in America, where there is so much materialism. She appreciates that the church is there for people who need counseling and services. Erin doesn't want to be Catholic alone and actively searched for a parish that was a good fit. But she also feels she has the right to pick and choose what is meaningful to her. That's how she deals with most things in life and it also works for religion.

I go to church, I try to kind of, I'm sort of, I think, by my nature and by my educational background, I sort of analyze and evaluate, and I just take away from the sermon what I think is relevant to me. A lot of times, it's not relevant to me, because it's not like they're catering to people who are single and in their thirties. So sometimes I'll go to another parish where they do sort of cater to more of a student crowd, more philosophical, the philosophy of the religion as opposed to the rules and regulations of the religion. . . . That's sort of the way I am with everything. I just sort of take what is relevant to me, what I can use, as opposed to say, oh I'm just going to wholesale adopt what that priest just said, I'm going to give a tenth of my income to the church right now. Like, personally, I'm not in a financial position to do that, plus, I'm not sure I truly agree with that, so I sort of go through all sorts of thought processes. A lot of people might call that tailoring the church to myself, but that's the way I am, that's what it means to me.

People like Erin, Vineeta, and Ghazi are fairly comfortable making it up as they go along. Religion is an important part of their lives. They actively identify with their faith, but feel that what falls under its broad umbrella is negotiable. The boundaries that differentiate what the questioning faithful believe in and the beliefs of others are lower and more easily permeated. They select a personalized, changing package of what belongs inside while still associating strongly with their religious label.

The Golden Rule Faithful

Maria is an example of the golden rule faithful.[9] She moved to the United States after she divorced, accompanied by her teenage daughter, and left two grown children in Brazil. Before migrating, she worked as a teacher, but she has worked cleaning houses ever since. She has been quite successful; last year she finally had enough money saved to buy her own condominium.

Maria grew up in an observant Catholic family. When she first came to the United States, she went regularly to the Catholic Mass. She helped organize social events for the Brazilian community and made sure there was a Confraternity of Christian Doctrine class in Portuguese. But she gradually became disenchanted. The community became so large that it lost its intimate feel. Her favorite priest went back to Brazil, and the priest sent to replace him was not her cup of tea. When a friend invited her to a Baptist service, she liked it, and decided to switch congregations. She liked the smaller size and the pastor, who was easy to talk to. She liked how the church members helped each other out when someone got sick or couldn't pay their rent.

The truth is, it doesn't really matter to her that much where she worships. She has come to believe that all faiths are pretty much the same. If you look closely, she says, they preach the same things and support the same kinds of values.

> You know, everywhere in the world, there are human beings and they all have the same fundamental rights. They deserve a good life, they deserve opportunities, they deserve peace. The basic thing I believe, and I have studied all the religions, is that they all teach the same thing. I don't think there are real major differences between any of these religions. You may have a certain way that you preach or that you pray. But the fundamental message of all religions is the same. So why should I talk about this religion or that religion? Why can't I just respect what they all say about being peaceful, respecting others, being helpful and caring for people, praying to God?

In contrast to the strict and questioning faithful, the golden rule faithful do not see significant differences between their faith and what others believe in. They are not particularly knowledgeable about official doctrine nor do they feel any pressing need to learn more. They are proud to belong to their faith community and identify unequivocally with it, but they are not inclined to convince others of their truth. They feel they are fine Christians or Muslims, and strongly disagree with anyone who says otherwise. It is where their faith leads them that makes them different. They do not hear it as a call to turn inward or draw impervious boundaries but rather to recognize the similarities between all human beings, regardless of their creed.

The golden rule faithful are sure they have the basic idea. Over and over, when asked to describe the most important principles of their faith, they gave strikingly similar responses. All religions teach the same things. A good person is someone who does not lie, cheat, or break the law. It is a person who feeds the hungry and clothes the naked. It is someone who pays taxes and contributes to the community. Why make such a big fuss over religious differences if these are things on which we all agree?

The golden rule faithful are not particularly concerned about practice. They sometimes go to worship services or they sometimes do things at home. How much or how often is not a measure of their faith, nor is it anyone else's business. Like the questioning faithful who operate according to a varied menu, they also feel entitled to be selective about how and when they express their beliefs. By doing so, they are not so much asserting ties to their coreligionists as expressing membership in an inclusive community with broad humanitarian goals. They may do things only from within their own traditions, or they may include rituals and symbols from other faiths. Paula, a Valadarense of fifty-nine, wears a gold chain bearing a cross, a star of David, and the om symbol, all at the same time. Twenty-nine-year-old Rupa has a statue of Saraswati, the goddess of knowledge, and a picture of the Vírgen de Guadalupe, patron saint of Mexico, on her desk to get "as much help as possible" from as many sources.

The Symbolic Faithful

Herbert Gans called people symbolically ethnic when they used ethnic symbols but did not participate in ethnic organizations or take part in ethnic culture on a regular basis.[10] He later proposed the parallel term "symbolic religiosity" to describe people who used religious symbols to express feelings of religiosity and identification, without participating regularly in religious culture or celebrations.[11] When nonobservant Jews celebrated Hanukkah once a year so that their children would feel Jewish, they were being symbolically religious. Symbolically faithful people collect religious artifacts; are proud of civic leaders, entertainers, and celebrities who share their faith; listen to religious programs; or do "religious tourism" while hardly ever participating in religious rituals or thinking a great deal about religious teachings or values.

Breda Sullivan, a fifty-five-year-old migrant, exemplifies this variety of faith. Her home is filled with pictures of saints and the Sacred Heart. She wears a cross around her neck. But when you ask her what it is that she believes in, she answers quite frankly,

Not much. For me, these are decorations, like some people have pictures of landscapes on their walls. In our house, we always had religious pictures. So when I got married and I was decorating my own home, I wanted to surround myself with what was familiar. I suppose if I didn't feel something toward Catholicism, I wouldn't want these things here. I mean, at the end of the day, I probably do believe in God, and when things get tough, He's the first person I turn to. But, day to day, it's not part of my life. . . . Having this stuff around also means that I'm Irish. I mean you can't wear a Claddagh ring, without people thinking that you must be from over there.

I met many others like Breda in Inishowen. Since Catholicism is in the air that Inishoweners live and breathe, the symbolic is never purely symbolic nor is the secular ever totally devoid of faith. They didn't go to church, nor were they great fans of the parish priest. They attended the religious part of any town fair or community celebration begrudgingly. But they were interested in Saint Clement's role in Ireland's history or in visiting a sacred well because it was part of their family's tradition.

Avanti Patel also fits this bill. A middle-aged woman who has lived in the United States for the past twenty-five years, Avanti recalled that the last time she went to a temple was to make an offering before her daughter went to college. Her house is decorated with religious art because she just happens to like that style and because it reminds her of India. When something good happens, she doesn't attribute it to God or to karma but to the fact that she was in the right place at the right time. While most of her friends are Gujaratis, she doesn't get together with them to study or pray. Still, she believes in what she calls the Hindu philosophy and way of life. For her, that means recognizing the importance of parents and teachers, and "to do good stuff, the neighborly stuff, the general citizen values."

Salal Qidwai, a thirty-one-year-old physicist, sees a similar phenomenon in the Pakistani community. There are many people who show up once in a while at the mosque who treat it like a social center. They are not interested in coming to lectures or study groups. They might do good works, but they're not particularly concerned about whether they benefit other Muslims or not. When it comes to Eid ul-Fitr or Eid ul-Adha, however, they are the first to sign up. They want their children to meet other Muslims and to associate their religion with having fun.

The Self-Help Faithful

For Omar Mirza, a young Pakistani in his thirties, religion is about becoming more disciplined. It is not about selflessness or sacrifice but about achieving personal happiness and success. He changes the restrictions he imposes on himself all the time so he is continuously challenged.

> I believe that humans have remarkable control over what they do and what they say. You have to discipline your life. Now whether you have to pray five times a day or three times a day, whether you drink alcohol or you don't, or whether you have premarital sex or not, whether you go to Mecca or not, these are ways that society disciplines itself. These can be taken as a given and just adhered to, or every person can say, you know what? I'm not a lesser person if I pray three times a day versus five times a day, or if I give to God 2 rather than 2.5 percent of my income. It's more a matter of you setting a limit for yourself and then adhering to it.
>
> I'll give you an example. When I came to this country for three years, I was vegetarian because halal meat was not available where I was living. Why? Because it was a way for me to discipline myself. I didn't drink, and I didn't eat pork, and I didn't eat meat. In Michigan at that time, it was very hard to find halal meat. And that taught me to control myself. It was almost like working out. You practice until you can tell yourself I can do this. And [when] I came to Boston, I realized I could just go down to the corner and get halal meat. It wasn't that difficult anymore. So there was no longer this thing about control anymore. Not eating meat was something I was doing for the heck of it. So I stopped it. I eat meat now and I don't just eat halal meat, because to me eating halal meat was not just about halal meat per se. It was about my disciplining myself. . . . Now that I am working, it's tougher for me to take five minutes out to pray than it used to be. Every day I do that, I feel like this "oomph factor," I was able to do something. So now it's prayer. Later, it could be something else. I don't drink alcohol

not because I think I will go to hell but because when I don't in my particular professional circle, I feel like I can take the social pressure. I can deal with that. In my kind of job, it's very hard not to be a social drinker. It's something that makes me special. I have an added value in some ways.

In their well-known book *Habits of the Heart*, Robert Bellah and his colleagues made famous Sheila, a young nurse very much like Omar, who said that faith was about being loving and gentle with oneself. People like Sheila feel that religion is essentially a private matter, and that they are not beholden to any requirements established by their historic church, the Bible, or tradition.[12] But religion as self-help doesn't just happen in the United States. People in South Asia, Ireland, and Brazil also described their faith as something in their personal service rather than the other way around. They tended to be younger and to have spent time living abroad. They believed that self-satisfaction was a universal goal—the current recipe served up by all global media outlets. It was part and parcel of the global values package that everyone around the world now subscribes to.

Self-actualizers like Omar consider themselves religious. There is no question in their minds that they are committed Hindus or Baptists. At the same time, their list of mandatory beliefs is quite short. They feel entitled to select, from a long menu, what brings them the most fulfillment. In many ways, they resemble their symbolic and golden rule counterparts. The basic difference is that they "do religion" primarily to further their own growth and satisfaction. They structure their faith as if it were their own twelve-step program for personal betterment.

Malika Shah, a thirty-year-old living in Pakistan, acknowledges that Islam teaches her to care for others, but she also considers it to be a kind of therapy that helps her feel better about herself. She tries to follow what she thinks are "the rules," but she can change them to suit her needs.

I try to pray five times a day, but I have to say, I don't always do it. I pray when I feel like it and I make up prayers. If it's nighttime and I've been out all day, I do make-up prayers. It depends on my schedule and my mood that day. Some people call me a cheater but

that's what I do. Sometimes, if I am traveling, they also have ab-
breviated prayers. You are allowed to spend less time praying. I
love that. I love the shortcuts.

Being a good Muslim, she says, is good for your health. It helps you cope
with the stresses of everyday life and deal with the challenges God
sends you.

Narendra Patel, a forty-year-old engineer in Gujarat, sees God as his
personal partner. He has to give his best effort, but God is the difference
between being able or not being able to get something done. He describes the essence of his faith as

> the need to have in your head that there is somebody who's really
> taking care of you in the world. And that thing is God. Believing
> in that is the most important thing. The second most important
> thing is believing in yourself and learning to be content with
> yourself, and that basically you can do what you really want to do.
> I want to do that and God wants me to do that. They go hand in
> hand.

God, he explains, does not just drop us off and leave us. He is our partner. Narendra feels this when he faces a particularly hard puzzle at
work. He might be going around and around about it in his head for several days, and be unable to come up with a solution. Then, all of a sud-
den, something happens, and he gets a new thought or idea. That is
God. "That won't happen unless I put my full-fledged effort in, but if I
do, he will help."

Catherine Grey, a young Irish woman in her twenties, was drawn
back to Catholicism for that very reason. She hadn't been to church for
years but during a particularly hard period of her life, she thought she
would give God another try. She didn't start by going to Mass or talking
to the priest. She just started talking to her friends about how they
thought about their faith. They didn't talk about a God who got angry
or whom they were afraid of. They talked about a God who was their
cheerleader—who wanted them to be happy and satisfied. The sin, they
told her, was to let your own lack of confidence hold you back, to live a
life in which your potential was unfulfilled.

Wow, she thought. This is really different. She began speaking to

God in a different way. And you know what? He answered. She didn't even need a priest to tell her the phone number. God helped her to figure out what to do.

> I still don't go to Mass or even celebrate any holidays other than Christmas. But I consider myself to be a very religious person. Because, for me, being a good Catholic means being the best person I can be. If I don't do something because I am too shy or I'm afraid I'll fail, then I am not doing what God wants. I talk to him all the time. And he helps me conquer my fears. I've had a lot of personal breakthroughs since I found God again.

Religion as Mixing and Matching

One thing that people of all religious varieties shared, although much less among the strict faithful, was their willingness to mix and match from different traditions. Syncreticism, both within and between faiths, was the norm rather than the outlier. In fact, in some cases, syncreticism is something of a misnomer because the original practice and what is being incorporated become indistinguishable over time.

Mixing and matching comes naturally to Valadarenses; migrating between Catholicism and Protestantism is fairly common, and popular Catholicism has always included African and indigenous influences. In Gujarat and Pakistan, where Muslims and Hindus have lived side by side for centuries, there has also been a good deal of slippage between faiths, even if people don't want to admit it.

So while people at the stricter end of questioning faithfulness disapproved, others openly embraced elements from different faiths. Why not cover all bases, they asked? It doesn't diminish my love for the Prophet to have a statue of Ganesh on my mantel. True, there were people who expressed some embarrassment about this, like Giselda, a forty-five-year-old Valadarense, who seemed to feel, deep down inside, that she was doing something wrong.

> I still go to Mass on Sunday. I light candles to the saints and go to the procession when they do the Stations of the Cross during Holy Week, but I've also started going to services at the Assemblies of

God Church during the week. I haven't told my family. I know they wouldn't approve, but I just feel like there is something missing that I get when I go there. I know this is wrong, but doesn't God want me to find him any way I can? I don't think he really cares if it's at a Catholic church or a Protestant one, as long as I am there.

But those among the golden rule faithful needed no excuses. Since all religions are the same, it doesn't matter what route you take to your destination. It just matters that faith is in the driver's seat. They believed, as did Ahmed, a thirty-five-year-old return migrant in Karachi who informed me that Islam and Hinduism on the subcontinent have much more in common than most people think.

Muslims have their own kind of caste system. They also have arranged marriages. These aren't just Hindu things. They are part of living in South Asia. After so many centuries of being neighbors, we are a lot more similar and do a lot more things the same way than anyone wants to admit. Islam in Pakistan has been Hinduized. That's why it is so different than the Islam of the Middle East.

Similarly, self-helpers also argue for "the more, the merrier." If doing things from other traditions helps them achieve their goal, why not? "When I first came to Dorchester," explains Conner, a twenty-five-year-old Inishowener,

I was working in construction. On one job, we were working with these guys from Vietnam. Most of them couldn't speak English but there was one guy who I got to talking to. He told me about the town he came from and all the things he had been through to get here. Well, this guy had seen so much and lost so many family members, he was very religious. And when my sister passed away, he talked to me about his faith. He gave me this little Buddha. And I always carry it around in my pocket. Even today, I don't feel right if I've left it at home. It doesn't mean that I'm not Catholic. It just means that I don't have all my eggs in one basket, you know what I mean? We can all use a little more help, you know.

The Possibilities for Partnership

Let's take Florence and Alice's worst-case scenario: that all transnational religious actors are related to Osama bin Laden and that they will all try to make us think the way they do. This may be true for people who count themselves among the strict faithful, who are convinced there is a single truth. But the other people in this story clearly feel differently. They are actively grappling with what their faith means—it is their right and responsibility. They don't just take things for granted but question, combine, and reject. They mix and match from faith traditions. Some people do so to make the world a better place; others do it to be happier people. The faiths that immigrants bring to America, then, are not static, monolithic packages. Islam, Hinduism, evangelical Christianity, and Catholicism come in many shapes and colors. They echo the gamut of religious expressions found among the native born. What better conversation partners could Florence or Alice wish for?

5

A New Religious Architecture

Jagdish Chandra Maharaj, the leader of the Bhagat community, is visiting his followers. He left Elizabeth, New Jersey, at the crack of dawn to drive to his cousin's home in Chelmsford, Massachusetts. There he will meet for lunch and prayers with a small group of his closest associates before he leads a Janmashtami celebration for the entire Bhagat community in honor of Lord Krishna's birthday.

The past few years have not been easy for the Maharaj. I first visited him at his home in Punyiad, a small town about thirty kilometers from Baroda, in 1998. The condition of the road leading there was my first clue that all was not well. Once we turned off the highway, it took nearly half an hour to travel the less-than-two-mile stretch because the track was in such bad condition. When we got there, we were ushered into a spacious entrance hall, almost empty, except for a large, flat swing where the Maharaj receives visitors, and a few wooden sofas and chairs arranged near it. The building's dark coolness was a welcome respite from the midday sun.

The Maharaj is a slight, soft-spoken man with thinning gray hair. He appears more diminutive than he is because of his modest, unassuming manner and impish smile. After his wife served us lunch, we went into a back room, where he and I talked with help from a translator, while his son and advisers listened. No, he said, the Bhagats who go to America do not change. They continue to live according to Indian values. They come back to visit him each time they return to India. Still, he clearly realized that changes were happening and that he needed to stay in better touch with his followers. He showed me a copy of a mimeographed, four-page magazine he had put together that he mailed to

Bhagats around the world. The last page even included a message to the children of immigrants, written in broken English by his son and heir apparent, telling them how much the community needed them and urging them to stay within its fold.

During my second visit, it was clear that the Maharaj's troubles had only gotten worse. I met more and more Bhagats who spent much more time being Swadhyayees or Swaminarayan than they did in their own community. They complained that the Maharaj was weak. He refused to put on the stole of the guru, the ceremony that makes him the official head of their group, preferring instead to think of himself as doing social service. The community was in flux, they said, and his *kirtens* or lectures did not offer them much helpful advice.

Yet people continued to support the Bhagat samaj because "they were disappointed in Jagdish, not in their community." In Bodeli, we visited a new marriage hall covered with plaques honoring donors in the United States and the United Kingdom. During my next trip in 2001, we visited a school construction site that included a special English-language classroom to prepare kids to emigrate. The Maharaj knew about these efforts and gave his blessing, but he did not supervise them directly. Chapters of the Udah Bhagat Society, which includes Bhagats living in other districts near Baroda as well as Bodeli, had each formed their own trusts or charitable foundations, so they could collect and administer their own funds.

Loyalty was at a low point. When I asked the Maharaj if this "walk-out" bothered him, he responded confidently that it did not as long as his followers came back to him when they died. Even Bhagats who have been Swadhyayees during their lives, he said, will come back to be buried according to Bhagat traditions. He felt no need to proselytize. He was interested in quality not quantity. When you have the best product, he asserted, the customers come to you.

Many of his followers apparently felt otherwise. In addition to their dissatisfaction with his leadership, they also had concerns about money management. They disagreed with his refusal to officiate at intermarriages between Bhagats and people from outside the community, or at the thread ceremonies of their children. Times were changing, they said. They needed a visionary who could go with the flow and teach them what their tradition had to say about living in today's world. They still wanted to participate in Bhagat rituals, but more and more they wanted to do so without this Maharaj at the helm.

Leadership in the Bhagat Samaj is a family affair. The top decision makers in India and the United States are all related. It's a matter of trust. The leader of the community in the United States, who officiates at all formal celebrations, is the Maharaj's first cousin. Another first cousin, who lives in Baroda, also travels between India and the United States. More distant relatives also direct local chapters up and down the eastern seaboard. On his way back to New Jersey, the Maharaj would stop in Danbury and Stamford, where there were other Bhagat communities. He also planned to visit followers in Chicago, Florida, and Washington.

The house where the Maharaj lunched was very much like Pratik and Dipa's new home. Outside, young children and teenagers dressed in their best Indian clothing played in the driveway. As I entered, a group of women scurried to finish the meal they were preparing for the thirty-odd guests. The Maharaj was sitting in the living room with his wife. We ate lunch sitting on the floor and then, as in Punyiad, a small group of men accompanied the Maharaj into another room where we could talk.

He decided to visit America, he said, because he needed to be in closer contact with his followers. He was losing his grip and had to do something about it. He showed me a four-color booklet he brought with him explaining the teachings of Ram Kabir, written in Gujarati and translated into difficult-to-understand English. He hoped that by giving these out and meeting his followers, they would return to him.

The Janmashtami celebration was supposed to begin at 3:30 p.m. at an elementary school in Lowell. At 3:15, we were still in Chelmsford discussing the Bhagat community's future. The school was located about half an hour away. I left to go over and was greeted by what had become a familiar scene at many Gujarati celebrations. A small group rushed around frantically, trying to set up the audiovisual equipment before the guest of honor arrived. Others stood outside chatting in the parking lot. The children entertained themselves by running back and forth in the auditorium. Two sections of chairs, where men and women sit separately, had been arranged in rows facing the stage. The women not busy preparing the communal meal sat on their side, talking quietly together and admiring each other's children. Since some families came from far away and many are distantly related to each other, religious and cultural celebrations double as family reunions.

The word that comes to mind to describe how the Bhagats greeted their leader is "lukewarm." When his caravan finally arrived, everyone went out to the parking lot. He and his wife walked between two lines of chanting followers who showered flower petals on them. But the Maharaj's shyness and his followers' ambivalence were painfully apparent. The procession moved on to the auditorium stage, where a green carpet, strewn with flowers, had been laid out. The men gathered, sitting cross-legged, around the Maharaj. Some of the women also joined them on the stage and sat behind them. Various percussion instruments were distributed. The next hour was spent singing *Bhajans* or devotional hymns. The Maharaj was supposed to lead these, but again he was more than happy to pass the microphone to anyone who offered. When he did lead, his mumbling was barely audible.

Still, the group's prayers were spirited. People closed their eyes and swayed to the music. By the end of the day, the Maharaj had accomplished what he came for. By sharing prayers and a meal with his followers, he helped reaffirm their ties to the Bhagat community. The next day, he would be off doing similar damage control in Connecticut, in the hope that by the time he returned, the Bhagat Samaj would remain intact despite the widespread dispersion of its members.

The Maharaj's problem is not unique. Lots of religious communities have members around the world who are struggling to figure out how to belong to several places at once. Sending and receiving country political and cultural groups compete for their loyalties. The Maharaj is doing what many communities do: constructing a new religious architecture and way of working that responds better to the reality of members' everyday lives. Religion already comes equipped with messages and rituals that help followers negotiate the many layers of the global experience. Religious organizations are also changing to reflect that reality, creating dense, intricate webs linking local, regional, and national players. In the process, they invent new structures, job descriptions, and membership requirements, and reorder the organizational chart.

When you go to your local candy store to buy a Nestlé Crunch bar, you know that even if you just walked across the street to make your purchase, what you bought was probably manufactured hundreds of miles away. Not only that, global production and distribution networks make the same candy bar available in Mexico, Milan, or Manila. The McDonaldization of the world is old news.

Similarly, if you walk down the street in any immigrant neighborhood, you're likely to find homeland political party offices. The Dominican Revolutionary Party and the Party of Dominican Liberation, for example, organize their immigrant supporters into local chapters, citywide zones, regional sections, and national organizations that take orders from the national headquarters in Santo Domingo. Each party also belongs to an international network of like-minded groups. In the Dominican Revolutionary Party's case, the Socialist International—an umbrella for 161 social democratic, socialist, and labor political parties and organizations—supports its efforts and is supported by them. The Indian Bharatiya Janata Party and the Brazilian Worker's Party function in a similar way. Domestic politics, then, is not just produced inside the nation. It is also produced outside it by members of the diaspora who vote, lobby, and finance election campaigns as well as by international political organizations.

Increasingly, religious organizations are taking their place alongside these global corporate and political actors. Worldwide production and distribution networks also manufacture religious goods. The local mosque or church is just one brick in this extensive global religious architecture. Some structures simply connect immigrants with people in their homelands. Others link them to fellow believers around the world. As a result, like politics and economics, domestic religion is both transnationally and nationally produced.

The Transnational Religious Corporation: The Catholic Variety

Every Sunday morning, groups of families in Governador Valadares gather in their living rooms to watch the Catholic Mass broadcast on their local television. But this Mass is not taking place in Valadares or any other Brazilian city. It is a recording of the Portuguese Mass held at Saint Joseph's Church in Somerville, Massachusetts, where many Brazilian immigrants worship. People in Brazil watch, hoping to see their relatives.

These worshippers belong to one kind of transnational religious organization: a transnational religious corporation. Transnational religious corporations are eminently familiar. The Catholic Church is the "jewel in their crown." Workers around the world, at all levels of the organization, take orders from the same chief executive officer in Rome. The organizational chart and lines of authority are clear.[1] Workers fulfill similar functions and abide by the same employee manual. Worshippers in Valadares and Massachusetts use the same weekly prayer supplements. When parishes in Brazil earmark their collections for the homeless, parishioners in Boston mount a better neighborhood campaign so that congregations everywhere work on similar problems.

When migrants circulate in and out of parishes in the United States, Ireland, or Brazil, they are extending and customizing this powerful, well-established corporate structure. In each case, migration makes some aspects of organizational life transnational while others remain inside national borders. How the national and the transnational combine varies by organizational level. Local sending and receiving country parishes in Brazil and Boston may work together, but the Brazilian and U.S. National Catholic Conferences may not. Likewise, migrants from Valadares sometimes participate in homeland activities, not because they feel loyal to their sending parishes, but because they still want to be part of the Brazilian national church.

This was the case of Inishowen. The big church in Carndonough sits high above the town on a big, flat, open hilltop. Father Charles has served in the parish for over twenty years. Yes, he says, he knew many people had migrated to Boston. It was true there was a long tradition of that. But it didn't make much difference for the everyday life of the parish. "A couple of years ago, some fellows in Boston raised money to help replace the cupola, but that was about it." Instead, unlike many Latin American migrants who become the principal patrons of their sending community churches, the Irish church engaged in cross-border activities designed to reinforce migrants' ties to the national church as a whole.[2]

The New York City archdiocese knew it needed help when the "new Irish" arrived en masse in the early 1980s. It turned to the Irish Episcopal Commission on Emigrants in Dublin, charged with caring for Irish emigrants around the world. The commission responded by loaning priests to New York. As more immigrants fanned out along the East Coast and to the Midwest, more priests followed.

That is how Father Patrick and Father Mike came to Boston. There were just too many Irish singles and newly married couples with young children who needed care. It was too much for Sister Lynn and Father Matthew, the team already working for the Boston archdiocese. Oddly enough, Patrick and Mike landed at Saint Brendan's because there were extra rooms at the rectory, not because migrants from Inishowen have been worshipping there for decades.

Father Mike said he decided to come to Boston because the Catholic Church is "a global organization and we are supposed to take care of Catholics everywhere." Father Patrick came because those abroad "still belong to the Irish family." Just as families do not abandon their relatives who move away, neither should churches or governments.

I don't know if you are a mother or not, but a mother doesn't say she is no longer responsible if her children go away. You want to know that if something happens, someone will be there who is attuned to their needs and can help them. You want to know that if something goes wrong, you can phone up and someone will watch out for them. A mother doesn't act like that, and neither should churches or the government. Irish emigrants show they still want to remain part of Ireland by the investments they make, the new homes they build, and the skills and ideas they import. It would be foolish of us to abandon our sons and daughters just because they no longer live among us. They still contribute so much to our lives.

The two priests set about getting to know the community by going to Gaelic football games and visiting the bars along Dorchester Avenue. Pretty soon, they set up a support group for new mothers, Irish-language classes, and a social club for singles, all under the umbrella of the new Irish Pastoral Center. They also filled in at christenings and funerals because the parish was short staffed.

It became clear to them early on that some people "had one foot in Ireland," so their programs should as well. "We talked about it and we decided that we needed to be where the people were," said Father Patrick. "If they wanted to be part of the parishes where they lived, we needed to help them. If they wanted to stay part of Ireland, we needed to help them do that too." At the premarital classes he offered, which you have to take if you want to be married in the church, he discussed how to get a mortgage or open a bank account in Boston and Ireland. He talked about getting a job and paying for college in both places. And because so many people actually go back to Ireland to tie the knot, the Pastoral Center assigned someone to help them complete the paperwork before they leave.

The Boston archdiocese and the Irish Catholic Church split the cost of the priests' living expenses. The priests report to superiors in both countries. The Pastoral Center is also part of the Irish Apostolate/USA, a national umbrella group of programs for immigrants. Father Chris, an Irish priest working in Washington, DC, had to get permission to create it from the Irish Episcopal Commission on Emigrants and the National Council of Catholic Bishops. In the early 1990s, he went to Ireland to talk to people in the government about his concerns. "The people in America are not American citizens," he told the officials he met with. "They still need help. Without citizenship or a green card, they are very vulnerable. If the church does not help them, they will be in bad shape." From his point of view, the priests over in America don't work for the U.S. government or the church but for their Irish equivalents.

By 2001, the Irish Apostolate/USA was running programs up and down the East Coast as well as in Chicago, Milwaukee, and San Diego. During the summer, it sent chaplains to places like Ocean City, Maryland, where Irish students found seasonal work. Since Father Chris worked for the National Council's Office of Migrant and Refugee Services, if someone had a problem in a place where there was no specific official working with immigrants, he picked up the phone, called the local priest, and asked for help. In 1999, the Irish government supported these activities with a yearly grant of $300,000. In 2002, the amount grew to $453,000.[3] The National Council, private foundations, and "Irish Americans who have made good" also make occasional contributions. Each year, Father Chris sends reports to the Irish government about what he has accomplished.

The Catholic Church is a transnational corporation with discrete national units that function independently and as part of the larger operation at the same time. In the Inishowen case, the corporate structure broadened and deepened in response to migrants' cross-border lives. The Irish Pastoral Center's funding, leadership, and in part its services all operate across borders. Migrants express broad national and religious identities through their church membership. Belonging to a particular community or congregation mattered less to them than belonging to the Irish Catholic nation as a whole. As such, membership reaffirms Irishness and Irish ethnicity in America while also integrating migrants into the Catholic community worldwide.

The Transnational Corporate Model: The Protestant Experience

Transnational religious corporations also come in a Protestant variety. Pastor Carlos is the leader of the Church of the Good Shepherd, a large Baptist congregation in Valadares affiliated with the Southern Baptist Convention. He said that more than eighty of his members had joined "sister" congregations in Newark, New Jersey. When they leave Brazil, he gives them a *carta de transferência*, or a letter of introduction, to the Baptist Church where they are moving; if they don't come back to Valadares within three months, he tells them to switch their membership to their new congregation. While some colleagues allow people to be members of two churches at once, he thinks people need to decide which community they live in.

His church belongs to a national network that also links it to churches of the same denomination around the world. The Valadares statewide association includes congregations from over forty cities. The state group belongs to the national Convención Bautista Brasilera, started by the Southern Baptist Convention over a hundred years ago. The Southern Baptists maintain three offices in Rio, and until recently built, funded, and staffed many of its own churches. New congregations are now independent, though affiliated with the convention; they receive support for special missions. If Pastor Carlos needs help on a project, for example, he requests it from the Rio office, which then finds him a partner church in the United States. The national churches also send representatives to the World Baptist Alliance, a transnational governing body.[4]

Scattered on the end tables in the waiting room at the Convención Bautista Brasilera office in Rio are copies of the monthly Portuguese-language magazine *O Jornal Batista*, filled with articles about the activities of congregations in Brazil, Florida, New Jersey, and Massachusetts. Churches advertise to attract new members. Convención staff encourage congregations in Brazil and overseas to coordinate more closely with each other. You can't force congregations to work together, they explained, but you can strongly suggest that they do their homework so they don't end up duplicating efforts by working in the same place. Back in Valadares, Pastor Carlos admitted he is building relationships beyond his denomination because so many of his members now belong to other Baptist denominations in the Northeast. "What's the difference between the Southern and the Northern?" he asked. "The doctrine is the same, it's just how we do things that is different."

National Groups That Work Transnationally

Groups like the ISSO and Swadhyaya are national religious corporations whose financing, leadership, and structures operate transnationally. They are globally managed with clear chains of command. As Gujaratis moved to the United Kingdom, South Africa, and the United States, they expanded their operations to serve their migrant clientele. The organizations they established reinforce members' ties to Indians around the world and the homeland in general.

Groups in the United States and the United Kingdom operate like chapters or franchises of their Indian headquarters. Franchises are firmly controlled and partially directed by homeland leaders who make most of the important decisions, to preserve the brand. Religious chapters, on the other hand, enjoy greater flexibility. While they are part of the corporate structure, they have more control over decision making and leadership. Everyday religious life grows out of an interactive conversation between leaders in India and the United States rather than a series of nonnegotiable directives.

Compared to their counterparts in the United Kingdom, the U.S. branches of these groups are relatively new.[5] Devesh was a founder of the ISSO in Lowell. When he first moved to the area, he traveled to New Jersey to go to temple. He remembers the day he realized enough people lived in Massachusetts that they could form their own group. At first, they met at someone's house and rented halls on holidays. When their leader visited in the mid-1980s, he gave them permission to build their own temple. Satsangees or Swaminarayan followers in Houston and Chicago were also building temples at that time. To help each other out, they created a revolving loan fund. Each group contributed funds toward the temple in Houston. When it was completed, they set their sights on Chicago. "We helped each other," Devesh recalls, "not just with money, but with expertise. When we were buying land, the guys in Houston understood the real estate market and all that stuff." In fact, similar resource sharing enabled the Boston ISSO to build a new, much-larger headquarters, in a former Goodwill Industries warehouse that they converted into a temple complex in August 2006.

The ISSO leader, Acharya Shri Koshalendraprasadji, a direct descendant of Lord Swaminarayan, is considered God's incarnation on earth. According to Sandeep Dave, who supervises the group's overseas activities from Ahmedabad, "There is just one type of worship, one way of living, and one type of social action." But as people spread out more, "we felt the need for a structure that would protect Lord Swaminarayan's moral teachings." Each local group has a president, a vice president, and a secretary. Sadhus or sages are sent to areas where there are large communities. They offer guidance, enforce discipline, and set broad policy. In places where there is no sadhu in residence, local leaders move ahead on small things, but consult leaders back in Ahmedabad about big decisions. People in the United States are in constant contact with India and each other. They travel regularly to participate in temple inaugurations, celebrations, and national meetings. They often meet informally because they have become each other's closest friends and advisers.

The devotees of Bochasanwasi Shree Akshar Purushottam Swaminarayan Sanstha (BAPS), the other Swaminarayan denomination in the Northeast, reject the idea that Lord Swaminarayan has a representative on earth. They believe he lives through his saints. Pramukh Swami is their current leader. Maintaining their message as Satsangees moved around the world also concerned BAPS leaders, who created a world-wide organization in response.[6] Temples in the United States and the United Kingdom are integral pieces in their organizational chart. Initially, laypeople ran the BAPS temple in Massachusetts, but they answered to the sadhu in Flushing, New York. Now, the community has grown large enough to support its own *Pujari* or priest.

The ISSO and BAPS also organize their members into special-interest groups. People belong to the national and international organization through their membership in their local temple as well as their membership in smaller age- and gender-specific groups, which have

national and international networks of their own.[7] The women's wing
of BAPS, established in 1954, has chapters at each local temple, which
in turn belong to the National and International Women's Wing. The
idea, according to one of its directors, is to reinforce members' relationship to the organization in a variety of ways and reach out to them at
specific stages of their lives. The same person who belonged to the
youth group as a teenager participates in the Women's Wing as a young
mother.[8]

Flexible Specialization

The clothing manufacturer Benetton was the company célèbre in the
late 1980s. It abandoned its central warehouse and one-size-fits-all
product and distributed its operations among several locations to be able
to respond quickly and with agility to slight changes in the market. If
the most popular color in the new spring line turned out to be yellow,
Benetton could switch its production to yellow in a matter of days.
Economists hailed this flexible specialization as a way to remain competitive in a global market no longer driven by local tastes.

Flexible specialization represents a radical departure from assembly
lines and their strict division of labor.[9] Multiskilled, adaptable workers
use flexible manufacturing techniques to produce goods for relatively
small, segmented markets. Loose, fluid partnerships between different
parts of the supply chain arise organically rather than being imposed
from above. Such groups function like Manuel Castells's network society.[10] Just as decentralized, adaptive modes of production are better
suited to the challenges of the global economy, so the flexible production and dissemination of religious goods may be better suited to meeting the needs of people of faith living in a global world.[11]

A second set of transnational religious organizations resembles this
model. They are horizontally managed, loosely coupled changing sets
of partnerships. Their organization is impermanent and unsystematic,
arising in response to a particular moment's opportunities and needs.
Decision making and power is decentralized, allowing actors to cus-
tomize, downsize, or otherwise alter the way they do things to meet
members' demands. Like their corporate counterparts, there are both
transnational and national aspects to what they do.

One example of religious flexible specialization is the International

Church of the Four Square Gospel (ICFSG). Aimee Semple McPherson founded the church in Los Angeles in 1924. It sent its first missionaries to Minas Gerais and São Paulo in 1951. Though a relatively small denomination in the United States, the ICFSG spread rapidly in Brazil. By 2001, there were an estimated ten thousand churches throughout the country, located primarily in Minas Gerais, Parana, Guarana, and São Paulo. Brazilian migration to the Northeast, and the American ICFSG's decision to focus on evangelization in the region, produced a reverse missionary movement to New England.

When I spoke to Pastor Gabriel, an ICFSG leader in Valadares, he estimated there were twenty-one churches in the city, each with at least a third of their members in the United States. These local groups formed part of an extensive national architecture. A six-member director's council runs his 3,500-member church. Ten local churches make a regional church, and regional churches are organized into state federations, belonging to the National Council in São Paulo. The Secretario Nacional de Missionario, operating in more than twenty countries, oversees the ICFSG's missionary activities.

Several types and layers of relationships produced the web of transnational ties connecting Boston and Brazil. For one thing, a number of migrants still belonged to their congregations in Valadares and continued to tithe there. Even people who transferred their membership to the United States still sent money back now and then in response to what Pastor Gabriel called their "diplomatic linkages." They sent him letters about what they were doing in America. He got calls all the time asking him to pray for people who had emigrated. And, he said, migrants continued to be present because their relatives still attended church every Sunday.

Relations between leaders in the United States and Brazil produced another layer of connection. Pastor Luis, who was responsible for much of the ICFSG's work with Brazilians in New England, keeps in close touch with his colleagues at home, including Pastor Gabriel in Valadares, leaders from his former church in São Paulo, and members of the ICFSG national board, on which he served before emigrating. He has two sets of pastoral credentials: one from the United States and one from the Brazilian national church.

Pastor Luis's networks and activities speak to the informal, flexible character of these arrangements. He had to get permission from the

Brazilian national governing board to work in the United States. He got start-up funds from the U.S. ICFSG and a onetime $500 grant from his church in São Paulo to support his efforts. In 2000, he got additional funds from the Secretario Nacional de Missionario in Brazil, in part because the director is a personal friend. Mostly, he supports himself with income he earns from investments in Brazil.

Although Pastor Luis is no longer officially a leader in Brazil, he recognizes the importance of maintaining good relations with his homeland colleagues. He visits at least once a year and often invites pastors to preach in Massachusetts. He makes sure they know about his church-planting activities. He knows he will probably go back to Brazil someday, and in the meantime he can always count on his fellow pastors if he needs to.

Brazil-to-U.S.-oriented and U.S.-to-Brazil-oriented missions form another layer of connection. In 1994, the American ICFSG president began actively encouraging cooperation between national churches to heighten members' sense of belonging to a worldwide community. What started out as flexible specialization may turn into a transnational corporation. According to an American-born former missionary, who now has his own congregation in Massachusetts,

> Last year, the American president invited all the missions departments around the world to meet with him. I think he is trying to encourage us all to feel, whether we are Brazilian, Panamanian, or American, that we are all part of an international church with various national parts that work together. He is trying to bring about greater coordination in the mission activities, so that we don't duplicate our efforts. All of the countries are independent, equal members of the worldwide assembly that meets once a year, but this is an effort to strengthen our international church community.

The Transnational Supply Chain

Many religious groups operate primarily in the United States. They are only transnational in that they depend on inputs from abroad. Some are informal communities that meet every so often for prayers and religious education. Their members want to be connected to their culture and faith in some way, but they are not strongly attached to a particular version. They want to improvise, cobbling together a mix of religious practices that still have some roots in their homeland.

Growing up, Hetal Patel, a seventeen-year-old high school student, attended such a Satsang school, where he learned about Indian holidays as well as how to read and write in Gujarati.[12] Most of the other families did not consider themselves very religious. They didn't pray at home and were satisfied with the monthly meetings and holiday get-togethers the Satsang had to offer. There was no official leader—someone always took charge when something needed to get done.

They depended, though, on a steady supply of goods from India. The pictures and statues they put up when they prayed were all imported. So were the oils they used to care for the Gods, the CDs of prayers and chants they listened to, and the educational materials they used with the children. They often invited teachers from India to spend a week with them. These events were open to the public and were frequently well attended by native-born Americans interested in meditation and spirituality.

The Islamic Center of Hopkinton, which is loosely affiliated with the Ithna Ashari tradition within Shia Islam, is a second example of a group that relies on a transnational supply chain. The Shia are a minority in Pakistan as well as in Boston. While Sunni Muslims have no central organization or leader, and each mosque operates on its own, the Shia community has a federated administrative structure and imam.[13] While the Islamic Center functions autonomously, it is tied to other Shia groups in several ways. Its members look to imams from overseas when questions arise over ritual and practice. It regularly hosts preachers from around the world because the community cannot afford a full-time imam of its own. The community members import circular clay disks, made from soil from Karabala, Iraq, on which they rest their heads while praying, because the Prophet prayed with his head on the earth.[14]

The Interior Design of New Religious Architectures

When Nike manufactures sneakers with parts made in Asia and Latin America, it's not just the production process that is worldwide. The entire corporate operation goes global. The company's strategic planning, financing, and human resources manual must change to reflect its new circumstances. Managers have to be schooled in cross-cultural management. Those who oversee corporate giving have to rethink their approach to reflect the changing boundaries of the communities they serve.

The same is true for global religious groups. The religious organizational architecture changes and so does what goes on inside it. Many members live aspects of their religious lives via long distance. To keep them satisfied and supervised, religious groups have to invent new ways of operating. Global religiosity requires different kinds of leaders. It demands new production processes. It requires different ways of communicating with followers, and new technologies for doing so. It means revising the membership requirements so people can still fulfill them in their new homes. It means figuring out how to educate the next generation. All of this adds up to major changes in business as usual.

When members emigrate, religious communities can't depend on face-to-face contact between leaders and followers anymore. Groups develop long-distance leadership techniques, rescripting authority and who can assume it. Members who were unable to be leaders before can now step up to the plate.

Since many groups aren't large enough to support full-time clerics, those who are most knowledgeable generally take charge. Women, in particular, play more central roles. And because many mosques double as social centers and schools, women lead prayers, serve on boards of directors, and also run educational programs. Leila, a thirty-eight-year-old Pakistani migrant, is clear that

> women are the obvious answer. And they are ready and willing to step in. We pray separately, and there is still a tendency during social occasions for men and women to mingle among themselves. But I've been on the board several times in the past ten, eleven years in different positions and never felt sort of kept at the back, oh, she's a woman. I've become more vocal about my rights than I ever was. We are not going to let men tell us what to do. And, you know, they wouldn't try because they need us too much.

Female members of the ISSO and BAPS were particularly pleased by the enhanced opportunities emigration brought them. They are not allowed to speak directly to a sadhu; a "brother" or male member of the community must intervene on their behalf. While critics claim this is proof that the Swaminarayan faith treats women like second-class citizens, and that Hindu values are being used to justify keeping patriarchy intact, both immigrants and members in India adamantly rejected this view. They run the Women's Wing without men interfering, they said, so they have all the freedom they need. They have even more power now that their activities have expanded to serve members in England and the United States.

The relationship between leaders and their flocks also changes in transnational religious organizations. Like international aid workers and corporate executives, a cadre of religious leaders circulates around the world. The boundaries of the communities they serve and how familiar they are with their daily life contrasts markedly with religious leaders in the past who often served the same community for decades.

Ulf Hannerz makes the same argument about how globalization changed journalism. He jettisons the idea that the media is a single tribe, or that classic categories like staff correspondent, freelancer/stringer, or parachutist still hold. He reclassifies reporters as "spiralers" or "long-timers," depending on how they move through the globalized news landscape. The global networks and institutions these correspondents relate to may influence their work just as strongly as the foreign locality that is their beat. As such, foreign correspondents are crucial catalysts for the globalization of consciousness, or for driving the very same shared package of values of individualism, consumerism, self-actualization, and democracy that some of the people in chapter 4 subscribed to.[15]

Globalization also changes the way religious leaders relate to their territories. Their knowledge about and involvement in members' daily lives varies considerably. Some are firmly integrated into the local scene while others are themselves tourists. Some work for the same organization for many years while others change jobs and denominations frequently. What leaders experience in their last position strongly influences what they do in their next one. They are like pied pipers, accumulating opinions and strategies with each new encounter, which they then add to an ever-expanding repertoire. As such, like reporters, they drive the globalization of religious consciousness by carrying ideas and values from post to post.

Father Patrick, one of the Irish priests working with Inishoweners in Boston, is intimately acquainted with the people in his community and quite skilled at relating to people outside it. He interacts with parishioners in much the same way as the old-time parish priest who guided generations through the sacraments. The only difference is that Father Patrick's parish extends to Ireland. By joining the church's expatriate priest corps, he became part of a professional religious class, which also includes missionaries and other types of leaders, who circulate from one congregation to another.[16] They bring the lessons learned in their last post to the challenges of their new position, thereby spreading global religious consciousness.

Pastor Martin carries ideas and skills from one religious organization to another. He came to Boston to work with a Baptist colleague who wanted to start a Portuguese-speaking congregation. When things didn't work out, Martin found work in a Presbyterian church. Being in the United States changed his views. He now believes you can "rewrite the book, within reason," rather than taking it literally. "Sometimes," he notes, "you just have to look around you and see that what you have always done doesn't work anymore." He recently returned to Valadares, where he started a nondenominational church mixing various denominational styles. He feels that it's OK to combine anything as long as it brings people closer to God. He does not rule out "migrating again" to the United States or another denomination. Like Father Patrick, each time he does, he integrates new tools into his kit.

These religious leaders come in contact with people outside the communities they directly serve, albeit superficially. They know enough about what happens on the other side of their church's walls that they can help their members deal with it. In contrast, the sadhu at the ISSO temple relates to his followers completely differently. He knows little English. He cannot speak to women. He doesn't go out of the temple unless someone accompanies him. While he can advise them about life in India, he doesn't have a lot to say about life in the United States. His devotees are his guide, rather than the other way around. He is like an English-speaking business consultant working in a country where he doesn't know the language. By day he is the expert, but by night he becomes totally dependent on his hosts.

Pastor Elton also exemplifies this second type of leader, although not for lack of trying. He came from Brazil to lead a new Pentecostal congregation. He speaks little English and also relies heavily on his congregants to tell him what to do. His limits frustrate him deeply. "I have no time to learn English or to learn about the United States. The needs of my community are so great. But what kind of a leader can I be if I know so little about the world outside my church's doors?"

A third group of leaders parachutes in and out of the immigrant community before returning to their home base. They are like the business professionals who organize a one-day seminar yet aren't involved with the participants on an ongoing basis, nor are they expected to. Jagdish Chandra Maharaj and Didiji are parachuters. They make quick, symbolic visits to their followers and then move on. While members generally have little, if any, direct contact with them, they still feel as if they have a personal relationship with their leader. The leaders' short visits, whether they involve close physical proximity or a brief sighting from the other side of a packed football stadium, reinforce these bonds.

Religious organizations have to renegotiate the membership requirements when members change their address. They have to modify what they expect from their faithful, and what they are willing and able to give in return. They have to invent new ways to communicate and revise the messages they transmit. To ensure quality control, or that the message remains intact, and to make sure they are systematically disseminated to potential members, they have to tightly script their recruitment activities so that anyone, with little supervision, can perform them.

For example, Swadhyaya, BAPS, and the ISSO each have specific ways they spread "the word." An interchangeable, global cadre of religious workers efficiently follows this recipe. In India, Swadhyayees do Bhakti Pheri—visiting the same village every two weeks and talking to people about Dadaji's teachings. After months of repeated visits and getting to know people over time, some residents join the group. But members can't be expected to devote the same time and energy to Bhakti Pheri in the United States, where they barely have time to visit their own families. The new religious architecture's interior design has to be modified to reflect their changing circumstances.

Bhakti Pheri has been reinvented in America. People make monthly

visits to communities where Indian families are living. They look in the
phone book for addresses of Patels and knock on their doors. Since hospitality is a deeply held value, most people invite them in. Four weeks
later, they drive up again, revisit the same families, and visit a few new
ones. Eventually they create a new *parivar*, thus beginning the system-
atic replication of Swadhyaya throughout the region. Recently, members in Massachusetts have been visiting families in suburban New
York, and Fiji and Trinidad, where they are reaching out to Gujaratis
who have been living there for generations.

Swadhyayees also do Yogeshwar Krishi—devoting time to money-
making activities and then giving away the profits to the poor. In Gujarat, commercial fishermen spend one or two days a month working on
a fishing collective, or farmers dedicate time to a communal farm. In
the United States, the function, if not the form, of Yogeshwar Krishi
has been replicated. In Boston, Swadhyayees earned money assembling
circuit boards for local computer companies. In Chicago, they made ink
refills for pens.

Another example of changing religious production comes from the
encounter between a Brazilian church and its American hosts, although
in this case, what was imported was combined with established practice
to produce something new. When he first came to Boston, Pastor Luis of
the ICFSG said that planting churches was a high priority. The only
problem was that his ideas about how that should be done differed
markedly from his American superiors. The native-born pastors "took
months," surveying the population, doing needs assessments, and
checking out the competition. They were, in his words, "slower than
molasses," and let far too many opportunities go by. "I understand that
you have to be smart about these things. That you can't go around wast-
ing resources. But I also know that there are people just waiting to accept God's word, and that someone will get to them if we don't get there
first."

His strategy was to bring people together, convince them of God's
truth, and, presto, a church is planted. And you do that any way you can.
One time he rented a bus and invited a group of Brazilians to go with
him to Connecticut to watch a soccer game. On the way down and back,
he talked, evangelized, told stories about the Bible, and, by the time
they got home, five new churches were created. When he told his

American supervisors about it, they stared in amazement. But when he had started five churches for every one of theirs, they began to see the light. Now he does what he pleases and is considered a role model for others in the region. They, too, have become much more bold and creative in their outreach approach.

Technological innovations also enable people to continue to be full-fledged, long-distance members of their faith traditions. Religious communities have become quite skilled at using technology to further their cause. They change how people "attend" religious services and what happens once they are there. The Valadarenses described earlier in this chapter, who went to Mass in Boston by watching it on television in Brazil, are a case in point. The women seated at the back of Pramukh Swami's birthday celebration, who participate by watching the proceedings projected onto large video screens flanking the stage, get a much more "up close and personal view" of him than they would if they simply sat in the back of the ten-thousand-plus crowd. Swadhyayees spend most of their time together watching videotapes of the *pravachans* or lectures Dadaji delivered each week in Bombay before he passed away.[17] Some videos now even come with English subtitles so that the second generation in America and the United Kingdom can understand them. Technology makes it possible for Dadaji to replicate himself and reach millions. It also makes it possible to control his message and make sure it doesn't get watered down.

Finally, not just the practice of religion changes when it is enacted transnationally but also how it is passed down to children. To stay viable among expatriates, groups have to figure out how to reproduce themselves and be meaningful to a second generation raised where different rules apply. In places like India or Pakistan, religion pervades every institution and interaction. Children generally receive some sort of religious education at school; their homes and neighborhoods are also living classrooms.

But in the United States, religious communities have to be much more purposeful. In response, Hindus and Muslims create their own versions of the ubiquitous Sunday schools and vacation Bible schools we are all familiar with. On any given Sunday, the mosque is filled with students of all ages, from kindergarten to high school, taught by parent volunteers. While adult Swadhyayees watch videos of Dadaji's lectures, their children are down the hall also discussing his message. Each summer, kids go away to Swadhyaya or Swaminarayan camp—an especially formative experience for youngsters growing up with few Indian neighbors.

What's particularly interesting is that many groups have created special homeland schools where children are sent for cultural immersion. Swadhyayees can enroll their children in a one-year post–high school "cultural education" course in Bombay. BAPS brings twenty-plus girls of high school age to live at the temple complex in Ahmedabad each summer. It also opened a high school for nonresident Indians. The idea came from a Satsangee living in London who, the story goes, visited Pramukh Swami and placed a bag of money at his feet. He was fed up, he said, with how his children were growing up in England. Because Swaminarayans are such a minuscule minority, it's impossible to maintain their culture. "The kids can answer multiple choice questions," he complained, "but they can't write an essay about who they are." He donated money to build a school for girls that now has 350 students. Fifteen percent of the students are nonresident Indians; most come from the United States, but there are also students from the United Kingdom, Dubai, and Africa. Indian residents pay about $1,150; nonresident Indian families $1,800. You don't have to be Swaminarayan to attend.

It's not just Nike, Coca-Cola, or Benetton, for that matter, who are producing and distributing their products globally. Religious communities are also structured and operating across borders. They channel flows of ideas, rituals, and values. They bring people and practices from different places together under the same umbrella. The resulting encounters alter the fabric of everyday religious life. Moreover, they provide members with strong, intricate, multilayered webs of connections that are perfect platforms from which to live globally. They offer a haven in every port, be it London, Boston, or Bombay. They speak to the challenges of life in the neighborhood, the nation, and the universal human experience. They offer solutions to ideational and cultural clashes that reflect the transnational reality of migrants' lives. And because faith traditions respond so powerfully to globalization and have adopted so well to it, their architectures are likely to broaden and thicken.

"That's terrifying," Alice and Florence say. Al-Qaeda and Hezbollah are transnational religious organizations, and look where they have gotten us. Luis would agree, if he would just wake up to what is going on around him. And there is no doubt some truth to what they say. There are too many religious groups that want to make the world over as they see fit and use violence to do so. But again, they represent religion at the margins. We don't yet know what the people in the religious middle say about putting their religious beliefs into practice.

6

Getting to the Other Side of the Rainbow with Faith as the Car

The United States is gripped by debates over morality, liberty, and identity.[1] In its most dramatic telling, those on the Right of the fault line
want to let religion loose in the workplace, school, and political arena.
People on the Left want to lock religion up and throw away the key. But
these debates have yet to acknowledge the shifts in the ground beneath
our feet. Antagonists on both sides are operating according to assump
tions that do not accurately reflect the world we live in. The major
structural changes in the religious architecture detailed in the previous
chapter take place below most people's radar. The majority of Americans think that once immigrants arrive, they abandon their ties to their
homelands, or at least that they should. Most people have limited experience with Muslims, Hindus, or evangelicals who don't speak English.
They automatically assume these people are terrorists, fundamental-
ists, or that they hold such different beliefs they will either destroy the
American fabric or shift it too far to the right.

Weary of hearing so much said about immigrants, I decided to listen
to what they actually had to say about these debates. After all, migrants
and their religious lives lie at the heart of these conversations. They are
both the subject of these discussions and inform them, with the decid-
edly different political and cultural assumptions they bring to the table.
How America responds to newcomers says a lot about who we are as a
nation. When we look in the mirror, do we include those darker-
skinned, non-Christian faces or do we still see our reflection the way it
was before 1965, when this new wave of immigration began? Do we
recognize that what gets reflected back is shaped by connections to far-
away places or do we still assume it is only made in the U.S.A.? Septem-

ber 11 and the heightened xenophobia it generated make it particularly important to listen closely to what immigrants say about the kind of society they aspire to and their role in bringing it about. It's not just that their dreams might clash with the American dream but that many people routinely assume they do. Against this backdrop, the cultural impact of immigration is far greater than its numbers might suggest because so many people automatically fear the person who looks and speaks differently living next door.

My conversations revolved around several related questions. I first asked people about their assumptions about interethnic and interfaith relations, the relationship between church and state, and their expectations about politics in general, based on their experiences in their homelands. I then asked them to talk about how they envisioned a good society and how we should go about creating one. What constitutes good citizenship? What does it mean to be an American? What did they think the appropriate role of religion in public life should be? Next, our conversations turned to the relationship between politics and religion. How did religion help incorporate them into the political and civic life of the United States and their homelands? How did their faith shape their political views and choices?

What I heard rarely conformed to the daily headlines. It should reassure people who worry that American values and immigrant values don't mix. It should make people who automatically give immigrants a terrorist or extremist face consider giving that face a makeover. Newcomers do come from countries where ideas about how to manage diversity and expectations about intergroup relations differ from those in the United States. They do bring different notions about the relationship between church and state. They have strong, mostly negative, opinions about politics.

But in the end, what they wanted to do about it was not that different from most of the people already living here. Their vision of a good society and their practice of faith within it had a lot in common with many Americans. There were both extreme conservatives and extreme liberals. Most people fell somewhere in between. There were people who Florence could embrace, and people who Alice and Luis would love to talk to. That's not to say that hot-button issues like abortion or the death penalty don't inspire passionate debates, in the same way that they do among the native born. It is to say that most people were much more concerned about the same bread-and-butter issues, such as health care, jobs, and education, that we all care about. What is over the rainbow for immigrants and Americans looks a lot alike.[2]

Managing Diversity: What People Said about Living Side by Side, Church and State, and Politics

To understand how people define the collective good and their part in creating it, we have to look at the mental maps they use to make sense of the world. The religious and professional organizations, social movements, and even the generations people belong to influence the ideas they take in and how they make sense of them.[3]

People's mental maps are a product of how they think as individuals and how they think as members of groups. Their interpretations also depend on their preexisting beliefs, prejudices, and assumptions. A Muslim uses a Muslim set of file folders to organize new information about religion and public life in the United States. A Gujarati brings a Hindu set of cognitive categories to the same challenge. Both are exposed to the same information, but what they assimilate and how they interpret it depends on the assumptions and cognitive tools they bring to bear. When people live lives that cross borders, they belong to communities influenced by several cultural contexts at the same time. In some cases, what they leave behind and what they encounter fits into the same drawer; in others, it's a case of a round peg in a square hole.

What people take in also depends on whether they are the rule makers, or in the majority in their homelands, or among the rule takers, or the minority. Rule makers, having always been in charge, can't imagine what it feels like to have another group set the terms of the status quo or how this might weaken their own position. They are not worried, for example, that having a Christmas tree in their homes will undermine their children's religious identities. In fact, they see that as a way to demonstrate they are American. Their Hinduness, Catholicism, or Muslimness is untouchable because they come from places where most of the people they interacted with each day shared their beliefs. Brazilian Protestants, on the other hand, are more defensive, coming from a country with a Catholic majority. They are more careful about what they take in or what they introduce their children to.

Immigrants' presumptions about public life, and the mental file cabinets they use to organize them, are also shaped by the "philosophies of integration" in place where they come from. Adrian Favell compared how such differing philosophical outlooks in England and France framed debates about race, immigration, and citizenship.[4] France, he argued, characterized ethnic relations in terms of republican ideas of *citoyenneté* and *intégration*. The British discussed similar issues in terms of managing race relations and fostering multiculturalism. These differences were rooted in distinct national "philosophies of integration," based on different understandings of citizenship, nationality, and pluralism. Each country has its own "public philosophy" that emerges from this shared set of ideas and linguistic terms.

The migrants in this story move from countries with very different philosophies of integration than those in place in the United States. Different expectations about relations between "us" and "them," and about how much newcomers or minorities can ultimately become part of "us," are also at play. Their homelands were not founded by immigrants. Their national story has not been about incorporating newcomers. Nor is it about living somewhere where there is no official church. They have not been brought up to assume that some kind of cultural mixing and social integration was automatically a good thing. Their *personal* philosophies of integration reflected these experiences.

In fact, Inishoweners, Gujaratis, and Pakistanis come from places where ethnic and religious distinctions rule the day.[5] Furthermore, most people had had little contact with people unlike themselves. Everyone knew there were Protestant families living "over in Buncrana," but they generally kept to themselves. In Baroda, most people equated being Hindu with being Indian without a second thought, even though that meant leaving out nearly 15 percent of the population.[6] They lived in villages or neighborhoods strictly segregated by caste and religion. They couldn't remember any government attempt to improve Hindu-Muslim relations.

Immigrants also came from countries with very different understandings about the relationship between church and state. In Pakistan, India, Ireland, and Brazil, religion plays an active role in politics, and the state routinely manages aspects of religious life. Islam, for example, is the state religion in the Islamic Republic of Pakistan. The country's president and prime minister must be Muslim and pledge allegiance to the "Islamic ideology." In the early 1980s, Pakistan even briefly experimented with making Friday, the day of communal prayer, its national day of rest, although it quickly changed back since, as one gentleman reminded me, "the rest of world was open for business on Fridays." While officially a secular model of government, the state actively regulates religious life, in no small part because Islamist parties favoring the creation of a theocratic state have gained power in the last decade. *Islamiyyat* or Islamic studies are compulsory for all Muslim students in state schools. The government recently attempted to register and standardize the curriculum in the thousands of privately run madrassas or Islamic schools throughout the country, although it met with limited success.[7]

Even in officially secular states, such as India and Brazil, religion is alive and well in the political arena. During the 2002 Brazilian presidential election, the third-place candidate, Anthony Garotinho, was an evangelical preacher and popular governor from Rio de Janeiro, just one of many Pentecostals claiming a place in Brazilian politics since the fall of the military dictatorship in 1988. At that time, 32 lawmakers in the 513-member Chamber of Deputies made up the so-called evangelical bench.[8] By 2005, there were 62 evangelical deputies and 3 senators.[9] When the new constitution was drafted in 1988, Protestants actively opposed giving Catholics a disproportionate influence over the national calendar, philanthropic laws, or use of public space.

The ascension to power of India's Bharatiya Janata Party (BJP) beginning in 1998 also signaled a shrinking of secular space, as L.K. Advani, the former deputy prime minister and party president, indicated when he described the party as "the chosen instrument of the divine."[10] In the last decade, Gujarat has witnessed some of the worst communal violence in its history. Over a hundred thousand Muslims have been displaced. Independent human rights advocates have accused the BJP of purposefully failing to bring the perpetrators to justice. In fact, the U.S. government denied Chief Minister Modi a visa in 2005 because of his alleged support of terrorist activities.[11] Some people see groups like the ISSO, BAPS, and Swadhyaya as fueling this fundamentalist neo-Hindu agenda.

In general, the people I talked with deeply distrusted politics, whether or not it was accompanied by a stiff dose of religion. You shouldn't, they warned me, come near a politician with a ten-foot pole.

They used phrases like "useless," "inefficient," and "rotten to the core," over and over, to describe their governments. If the state couldn't provide basic services like health and education, how could it run fair elections? And why did it care so much about them now, when it never paid any attention to them before they migrated? Many people thought it was a complete waste of time to participate in homeland politics; they were not so sure about U.S. politics either. "Brazilians have become inoculated against politicians' promises," Gilberto in Valadares told me. "Why should we vote, when each government is worse then the next?" To believe in the political system, and feel that political participation was worth their while, would be an uphill battle.

Religiously Informed Politics and Politically Informed Religion

Given this background, immigrants might be expected to import worldviews antithetical to those in the United States. Florence may be right when she predicts that newcomers will only fuel the cultural fires. But when I talked with people about what they wanted for themselves and their children, and what their rights and responsibilities were, these differences largely disappeared. While they recognized that they used different file drawers in their home countries, most people felt it was their responsibility to adjust to those they encountered in the United States. It turns out that homeland dreams and American dreams were not that far apart. In fact, in many cases, they were transnational dreams.

International public opinion surveys like the World Values Survey and the Pew Global Attitudes Survey have measured people's beliefs about things like religion, politics, and globalization for over twenty-five years.[12] Regardless of the data, the conclusions are the same: there are few differences in moral values throughout the globe. There is much more consistency across civilizations than within them.[13] In particular, political attitudes are remarkably consistent; a desire for religious and personal freedom as well as democratic ideals predominates, even if they are not realized in one's own country.[14] A worldview commonly associated with the "Protestant ethic," for example, which embraces trust, respect, hard work, and determination, is prevalent throughout the East and West.[15]

My conversations corroborated these findings. Immigrants from around the world, and from different faith traditions, expressed remarkably similar ideas about what constitutes a good society. In such a world, no one lacks food, clothing, or shelter. Neighbors care for each other. Basic decency rules the day—people tell the truth, they treat each other with respect, and they obey the rules. They give generously to causes that don't benefit them directly. Freedom of religion and speech are guaranteed. Moreover, in an ideal society, the institutions work. People obey the law, and the law protects them in return. It treats individuals equally regardless of what they think about God or how much money they make. You rely on the police rather than fear them. Schools educate, hospitals cure, and politicians represent the interests of their constituents.

It is not a society in which everyone is equal, however. Most people claimed that racial and class differences were inevitable. Certain people are natural achievers. They do more so they get more. "Even five children of the same parents are not equal," Didiji told me. "You can feel emotional oneness, but you cannot expect intellectual or economic equality." Most people were not particularly concerned that some people do better than others. It's one thing if a group is extremely disadvantaged but it is just the way things are when one group gets a better deal than the rest.

CREATING GOOD SOCIETIES: WHAT'S RELIGION GOT TO DO WITH IT?

People from different backgrounds were deeply concerned about what makes a good society and the proper role of faith in getting us there. Many said that to create good societies, you need good citizens. For John Doherty, born in Inishowen and now in his seventies in the United States, being a good citizen is about neighborliness. "How can you have a good community if people don't know each other and watch out for each other?" he asked. For Rosemary Houghton, also in her seventies, good citizens have some kind of faith. "I think a good American should have some religion. I don't care whether it's Catholic or Protestant, long as you are good in your own faith, what you believe, higher power, whatever you believe." Father John, her cousin, in his sixties, stressed responsibility. When asked to describe a good citizen, he answered, "Do you have a couple of hours?"

There was a Jewish psychologist, who had been, I'm not too sure, in one of the prison camps, Dachau or whatever, Erich Fromm. He spent a number of years in this country after World War II and he was interviewed as he was leaving New York City. One of the points he made in that talk was that corresponding to the Statue of Liberty there should be a Statue of Responsibility in San Francisco Bay. Because you don't have real freedom without responsibility. He said the stress, the accentuation that freedom receives is good. But it needs to be counterbalanced with its counterpart responsibility. Today, people try to get off, claiming guilt or anything simply because they do not want to own up to the fact that they're responsible for their actions. . . . Being a citizen is an honor and a privilege. It gives me rights but it also gives me duties. I'm not too sure people think about citizenship that way, that it's a privilege, it's an honor to be an American, and it's an honor to contribute to making it a better country and making all of us a better people.

Most people believed religion had a role to play in making a good society a reality, even if it hadn't always done so in their ancestral homes. Their views also echoed those expressed by respondents in the World Values Survey. Authors Pippa Norris and Ronald Inglehart propose a "cultural axiom"—religion's role remains strong, even as societies grow more secular in other ways, such as declining church attendance. Most people think that religious leaders wield a positive influence.[16] In fact, Norris and Inglehart question the actual feasibility of a cultural separation of church and state. "The distinctive worldviews that were originally linked with religious traditions," they write "have shaped the cultures of each nation in an enduring fashion; today, these distinctive values are transmitted to the citizens even if they never set foot in a church, temple or mosque."[17] Indeed, in the United States, the separation of "church and state" has not, despite two hundred years, led to a decisive split between religion and politics. According to a 2004 survey, only 18 percent of Americans would remove the Ten Commandments from public buildings, a solid majority (59 percent) favor teaching creationism in schools, and nearly one-third support making Christianity the official religion of the United States.[18]

My conversations also revealed a desire to bring religious values into the public square. If you don't have religion, many people asked, how do you know what is right and true? It is the ethical baseline in a world where, too often, selfishness and greed rule the day. Religious differences are a natural, inevitable part of human nature. But most people realize there is no absolute truth. They are willing to discuss things. They try to treat others with respect. "Most people," said Ashu, in his thirties,

> are not like Chief Minister Modi or even like President Bush. We believe. We pray. We try to live our lives the way we think God would want us to. And not just our personal lives but our lives in our communities. But that doesn't mean we have to force what we believe down other people's throats. It doesn't mean that we are going to strap bombs to our backs and kill other people. I feel so sad that the people who do this have spoiled it for the rest of us. Those of us who are trying to live a moral, religious life have a difficult time raising these views in public because the way the world is today, people think we're just naive.

Cathleen, a migrant from Inishowen in her forties, agrees:

> I'm a pretty religious person but I tend to keep it to myself. I don't feel like I have to advertise in public how important my faith is to me in my daily life. But it is. I would say that I try to think about God in everything I do, every time I open my mouth. If people think I'm a good person and that I give back to my community, they don't realize it's because of my faith. I'm not trying to make everyone else believe what I believe. I'm just centering my own life based on my own beliefs. So, you see, you can be religious and not make everyone else be. You can live out your beliefs and not make everyone else follow.

Giving religion free reign, people admitted, was not without problems. Politicians often misuse faith for their own purposes, and it's hard to argue with people who claim that God is on their side. They misrepresent God's words to achieve their own ends. Thirty-five-year-old Malika, for example, remembers the Pakistan of her youth as a religious country, but one where religion didn't really influence everyday life. There were folks who wanted to obey the Koran strictly, but they didn't expect everyone else to. Now things are different. The religious genie is out of the bottle and out of control. Powerful people in powerful places are distorting faith and using it to pursue what she sees as "unfaithful" goals.

> When I left the country, religion was a side issue. And that's how my family lived, and really the whole country lived like that. And now when you go back, although I know it's just a small percentage, religion dominates the place so much that everybody, it's not everybody, but the aura is like, it's become a religious state, and that bothers me a lot.

Gabriela, a forty-five-year-old from Valadares, also has no inherent problem with religion. She just wants it to stay within certain limits.

> I really don't have a problem with religion. It's the imposition of religion that is bothersome. And I'm beginning to see that a lot. So wearing the hijab, there's nothing wrong if you wear it by choice. It's when France tries to stop it that it bothers me. At the same time when I see little girls bogged down by those long robes in parts of the Middle East, and the boys are wearing shorts and running around, I say you are handicapping that girl to begin with. Her role in life is defined. So that doesn't feel fair to me either.

You also have to distinguish between the public politics of a religious community and its individual members' beliefs. This was especially important to Gujaratis who worried about the people who think nonresident Indians are responsible for increased religious fundamentalism in India.[19] Most people adamantly opposed such projects, however. It didn't mean that they were particularly fond of Muslims. Old prejudices and hurts die hard. But that was not the reason they were Swaminarayan or Swadhyaya, and this was not what their faith was intended for. As Raj Bhatt, a forty-six-year-old Gujarati immigrant, explains,

> I know that a lot of people think that Pramukh Swami and Dadaji are good friends with the RSS. There are a lot of rumors about the tons of money nonresident Indians send back to India to help these groups. I don't know if this is true or not. There is probably something to it. But that's not why I am here. In fact, I hate that my religious community has that reputation. It seems to me the

worst kind of perversion. Do I wish that Indian society did a better job of living up to Hindu values? Yes. But does that mean that I want to kick all the Muslims out of our country? No. But we can't always control what our leaders do or what the public thinks about us. We can only stay true to our own faith.

AMERICANNESS: WHAT IS UNIQUE ABOUT THE U.S. RAINBOW?

Given that people bring very different mental maps to the immigrant experience, how do they ultimately make sense of what they encounter? What does being American mean to them, and how does it differ from other identities? I was surprised that most people had a ready answer to my question. They didn't always agree with all the values they found here, or unconditionally adopt the entire package, but they respected America. They also felt it was their job to get with the American program rather than the other way around.

Almost everyone equated being American with being tolerant and knowing how to get along in a pluralistic society. It meant being liberated from the watchful and demanding eyes of your relatives and neighbors, and being able to determine autonomously who you are and what you really believe. "What is American about me," said Narendra, a Gujarati in his twenties, "is probably the ability to challenge everything. I only believe certain things very deeply that I have thought through for myself. The ability to make a choice and the power that comes from that. I think that's probably American."

Being American meant being able to be an individual. According to Najiba, a forty-four-year-old migrant, Americanness is a state of mind. "I am very American but so was my mother, and my mother never came to this country until she got cancer and was ready to die." In response to my question "So what is American?" Najiba replied,

To be yourself. You know there is beauty in being a nobody, when nobody looks at you, nobody cares, you can be walking around in your pajamas and nobody would care. . . . My mother was not the least concerned about physical appearances or social strata or anything. She was a physician. She was very strong. She was the major breadwinner in our household. She was a feminist. She called the shots, how we lived, where we went to school.

"Why is that American?" I asked. "Because she claimed the right to exist," answered Najiba. "I think being American is that you can do what you want to do. You have the right to determine what you want to do. For anybody. In Pakistan, there are all these constraints."

Americanness was big enough to encompass good Hinduness and good Muslimness. For example, America honors Muslim values more than most places. It is wealthy enough that the Prophet's teachings can actually be put into practice. Imram, a thirty-eight-year-old migrant, said,

> I always tell people from Muslim countries, none of you have ever really tested Islam in the way in which is it meant to be tested—as a pluralistic religion that is tolerant of everyone and accepts everybody for what they are. I tell people that America is probably the most Islamic country in the world even though it is not a Muslim country. Because in theory, it has all the same principles that an Islamic state is supposed to have. So freedom of expression, of thought, the freedom to associate, religious tolerance, the fact that everyone can practice their religion and no one can tell you otherwise. Now these are all the things that are in an Islamic state. . . . I would say the word tolerance, and I would even go beyond that because tolerance, in my mind, means that you can just bear to have someone there, you tolerate them, but it goes far beyond that. It is really acceptance and brotherhood. That is really its essence.

People tended to associate the positive aspects of Americanness with their workplace or the social institutions with which they interacted. That was, in part, because that was where they had the most contact with the native born. Work and school were also two of the few places immigrants inhabited where American values predominated.[20] And Americanness received high marks. You moved up because of your ability, not your connections. The rules were written to be followed, not just disregarded every time the boss disagreed. It's not that America isn't corrupt, they said, but it is nothing compared to India or Brazil.

Americanness, though, comes with a price. Francisco, from Valadares, in his early thirties, clearly recognized the trade-offs. Because America is more individualistic, people care more about themselves. They have less time for others. Family life, particularly the relationship between adult children and their elderly parents, suffers. People claimed Americanness when they acted like workaholics. They were Americans when they put performance before people, sacrificing their humanity to get ahead. But this is what you need to do in this country to succeed, as Dilip, a Gujarati financial planner in his thirties, described:

> In many ways, the biggest thing I had to learn was not to call everyone "Mister." At work, I treated everyone with respect, no matter who they were. I was told that, you know, you're being way too nice, just cut it off, you have to take authority. I have a mentor, a senior mentor, here at work, and he teaches me, like, psychology, like, what I have to do, what I don't have to do. I don't have to say, oh, thank you for meeting with me, he says, I should say I appreciate meeting you. Little things like that that make a difference. Ever since we were little we treated everybody with the same respect, especially elders, teachers. Normally in our religion it's the teachers are up there, parents are up there, and then your neighbors are up there [gestures at a high level with his hand]. And people don't tend to do that here. With teachers especially they don't do that. You can't treat your boss like that or he won't take you seriously.

For that reason, Zariad, also in his thirties, avoided hiring other Pakistanis. They are highly technically skilled, he said, but they can't think outside the box. They're afraid to challenge authority. It takes the "FOBs," or those who are "fresh off the boat," forever to realize that they don't have to stand up when the boss comes into the room and that they don't have to call him "sir." "This," he remarked, "goes against the grain of capitalism."

Americanness also meant being more concerned about the material than the spiritual. In exchange for individual autonomy, you get moral leniency. Parents and children grow distant. Boys and girls interact from a young age in ways that made many people uncomfortable. There is too much sex, too much alcohol, and too much freedom in general.

Finally, Americanness also signified a certain ignorance about the rest of the world. The United States is so big and powerful that people don't have to pay attention to what goes on outside it. Even the humblest worker in Pakistan or Brazil has to know what's happening because they come from places too poor and powerless to afford to isolate themselves.

> Unlike Pakistan, in the United States you don't care about anything, you are living on this huge island, which has everything, which has every wonderful thing God could create. If there could be an Eden in the world, it would be the United States, and I am not talking about the people. It is vast, the skies are bluer, the trees are greener, the mountains are there, the rivers are there, what more could you want? I mean this is the most gorgeous land of all lands. It's not overpopulated. You have the ultimate life, and you have created this wonderful existence in which the individual can strive and succeed. And what is going on in the rest of the world is hunger, poverty, man on man, the trees are dying, people don't care. It is true even for Muslims who have moved here or the Pakistanis who have moved here, we become selfish. We are all about creating our own Eden. We don't care what is happening back there because we have the perfect existence. Now take people in Europe or in Asia or in Africa. In those countries, the world is very small, they are more aware of what is happening in other countries. But if you talk to a blue-collar worker here, he doesn't care, he just wants to know what he is doing Friday, what game the Patriots are winning. In Pakistan, you go to any fruit seller or newspaper seller on the street, and he will involve you in a long discussion about how to interpret events in Ethiopia.

Even with its individualism and moral laxity, however, the overwhelming majority appreciated the United States. They were grateful for the opportunities this country afforded them, claiming emphatically that they would not have achieved so much if they had stayed home. What's more, the beauty of America is that you don't have to agree with everything, you just have to accept the basic contours. When you live in Rome, you should live basically like Romans. It's incumbent on immigrants to adjust and adapt, not the other way around. "Islam teaches us to obey the laws of the land where we are living," twenty-five-year-old Nazli told me. "If there is a conflict between the national law and Islamic law, it's the national law that prevails."

RELIGION AS A PATH TO POLITICS

Most people, therefore, admired American culture and embraced aspects of it selectively. They wanted to be part of this country's civic life, and religion was often the path they followed to get there. Faith communities come equipped with powerful resources and tools that encourage civic activism and shape its outcomes. They bring people into contact with fellow believers who don't all come from the same country. Sometimes they even find themselves sitting in the same pew as the native born. Migrants hear sermons and attend programs that influence how they think about changing the world. Their experiences in religious communities influence how they put these into practice. In some cases, like the Irish and Brazilian Catholics here, it also integrates them into influential, well-endowed institutions with a great deal of clout. Rather than being mutually exclusive domains, then, religion and politics speak clearly and often to one another.

When people interact with each other, in their neighborhoods, at work, or when they drink coffee after worship, they create "social capital"—or the various enabling and empowering resources generated by social relations, including trust, norms, and reciprocity.[21] Connections created by faith are powerful social capital generators. "Faith communities in which people worship together are arguably the single most important repository of social capital in America," Robert Putnam asserts. He cites statistics that show that nearly half the associational memberships in America are church related, half of all personal philanthropy is religious in character, and half of all volunteering occurs in religious contexts.[22]

But as Putnam and others warn, not all social capital is created equal.[23] Certain forms of "bonding" social capital, or that which works within groups, can keep marginalized groups isolated. People develop norms of reciprocity and trust with others in their network, but that doesn't necessarily translate into bridge building to the mainstream.[24] Thus, the age-old story about immigrant churches helping members acclimate to the United States and stay connected to their homelands (in other words, providing "bridging" social capital) is sometimes incomplete.[25] There has to be enough inward bonding and outward bridging social capital for these relations to develop.

Indeed, religious membership was a potent social capital source for the people I talked with, though it often remained within their own communities. For one thing, belonging to religious communities taught them political skills. Even when religious institutions don't have explicit political agendas, people learn about fund-raising, organizing, and leadership by participating, and they then apply these skills to other settings.[26] Information is disseminated and opinions are formed. What happens at the church or mosque strongly influences how people distribute their time and money between home and host country issues.

People belonging to communities where they interact regularly with native-born coreligionists get a crash course in civics. Inishoweners, for example, attended Mass in English alongside native-born parishioners led by native and foreign-born priests. Unlike non–English speakers, who often form their own ethnic parish councils, they participated directly in parish governance. They could rattle off a list of things they did at church, like signing petitions or attending a "Meet the Candidates Night," that they had never done in Inishowen. Worshipping next to people from other countries was also an eye-opening experience. Brendan, a thirty-seven-year-old migrant, put it this way:

> You know in Malin everyone is Catholic. Irish and Catholic are synonymous. But here, at St. Michael's, there are Vietnamese Catholics, and Polish Catholics, and Dominican Catholics. They all come with their own idea about how to worship, and what is right and wrong. It really made me think for the first time, well, maybe the way we do it at home isn't the only way. It's been good for us to learn from these other groups and to realize that Catholicism comes in a lot of different flavors.

It hadn't occurred to most people to think about church as a place to find a job or an apartment. "In Ireland," according to Dan, a thirty-five-year-old return migrant in Buncrana, "we go to church for forty-five minutes and that's it until next week. The church and the state are so intertwined, the priests would never say anything against the government. Over in Boston, the priest used to say things and I didn't always agree. But you had to hand it to him for not being afraid to speak up."

In addition to providing services, some religious groups actively encourage political participation. The Irish Apostolate/USA, for instance, has become something of an advocacy group, working for migrants in the United States and Ireland. In 2000, it joined with a coalition of Irish immigration centers across the country to promote immigrant rights. The Irish government stays in touch with the emigrant community through the apostolate. "When they need to know what is going on," said Father Mike, "they ask a priest."

> The minister of foreign affairs came here three years ago, and the minister for social welfare came last year. Any time a president comes, like Mary Robinson or Mary McAleese, they come and talk to us. Mary Robinson came and talked to us at lunch, and asked us about the different issues we confront. We also visit Irish prisoners here, and we keep the government informed about whether they are being treated properly, what their sentences are, whether they can be sent back home. We are the voice of the immigrant community for the Irish government.

The apostolate's priests also see their job as keeping emigrants on the Irish public's radar screen. Father Ronald, who directs its activities from Dublin, worries that people will forget emigrants because by leaving, they call into question the strength of the Celtic Tiger. "But no matter why they leave," he said, "we still have to look out for them."

Valadarenses' religious political socialization keeps them firmly tied to Brazil. Both Protestants and Catholics usually attended services led by a Brazilian-born leader, conducted in Portuguese. Many congregants still sent contributions to the churches they attended before migrating. They remained on the rolls as dues-paying or tithing members. They contributed to projects and campaigns to help Brazilian causes. They discussed Brazilian politics over coffee following Mass.

Members of foreign-born-led congregations hosted by native-born churches receive an intermediary education in U.S. politics. When they interact with other members, during interethnic services or all-church events, they learn about the issues facing their communities and how to address them. The greater the contact, the more skilled they become. In contrast, members of stand-alone congregations, with few U.S. ties, are on their own. They have no one to tell them about the lay of the land, or to guide their initial forays into it. They gain few political tools by participating in faith communities because they do not know who to reach out to, and few outsiders reach out to them. Cristina, a forty-five-year-old from Valadares, remembered,

> When they were going to tear down the stores on the block where our church was located, we didn't even know about it because most of us couldn't speak English. But one Sunday, Sister Flor came in and she told us what was happening. We had no idea what to do, what our rights were, who we should talk to at town hall. Luckily, someone worked with another person from Brazil who had been in Framingham for a long time. He came by and talked to our pastor about what our options were. He helped us deal with the landlord and to find another home for our church.

RELIGIOUS VERSUS POLITICAL RAINBOWS

A big questions remains. Once people decide what they think about religion and politics, and acquire skills by participating in faith communities, what do they want to do about it? Their answers reflect not only how they think you get over the rainbow or achieve social change but who comes along for the ride. They also reflect how people locate the real and imagined landscapes they inhabit—their personal accounting of the relative weight of the political and the sacred, and where they stand in relation to each other. The immigrant who cares more about holy sites and shrines makes different kinds of political choices than the person who puts the national flag first and foremost.

A small group of people saw themselves living above all in a religious landscape where religious institutions prevailed over the political. They tended to be religious global citizens, though there were also those among them who embraced ethnicity or cosmopolitanism as the predominant force shaping who they are. Pastor Wilson, from the ICFSG, is an example of someone who puts the religious landscape first. He believes that the world would be a better place if everyone was a religious global citizen. He doesn't believe it's his responsibility to convince the members of his congregation to participate in U.S. or Brazilian politics. He wants them to feel that they belong to Christ's kingdom, where they are accountable to God and subject to his laws and teachings. It's not that political citizenship is unimportant. It's that when people are good Christians, they will be good citizens too.

So when we teach them to be consistent in their faith, they will be, at the same time, good people, good husbands, because they will try to help others, try to make a difference in their neighborhoods. They will be concerned about other's well-being. So it's not necessary to become legal and become naturalized and so forth. But in the Bible itself, in the way that Christians should be, it would be enough for them to be good citizens. . . . There are ways of being in the world that have nothing to do with whether you are Brazilian or whether you are from the United States, but that have more to do with faith in Christ. I teach my followers that they have a responsibility to all mankind, but especially to their fellow Christians. We live in a world where Christ is the king, not George Bush or Fernando Collor.

For these residents of God's kingdom, the power of the Prophet, Christ, or Pramukh Swami far outweighs that of any elected official. It's not hard to decide where to put your loyalty or energy because God always wins. As Vikram, a forty-five-year-old migrant, maintains,

If I had to choose, I would say that I try to live my life as if I lived in Swadhyaya country. By that I mean, Dadaji teaches us a whole wonderful set of lessons about how we should conduct ourselves. And I try to really live up to them. I mean, can you really tell me that Prime Minister Singh is a better leader, a more moral person than God? Even Gandhi can't compete. So, yes, I live in between India and the United States, and I try to give back to each country, but it's because I follow God.

People like Pastor Luis and Vikram see themselves as living in a religious space and responsible to a religious polity. Their political choices and how they act on them reflect this stance. Zara, a thirty-seven-year-old woman from Gujarat, agrees:

I know that some people turn to politicians when they have a problem. Well, I turn to Pramukh Swami. I don't need politics because I have the Swaminarayan community. I don't know anyone in our community who has gone to a government office when they couldn't pay the doctor or they lost their job. Here or in Gujarat, we turn to each other. Now, if you are not a member in good standing, people are not going to help you. But if you come regularly, contribute, and volunteer, then you have the right to get help. If you are a good citizen of our community, then you will be treated that way.

The protagonists on all sides of our alleged culture wars fear this kind of individual. They are too religious for people on the Left, who fear they will undermine the secular. People on the Right probably admire their religious fervor but dislike that it's Hindu or Muslim flavored, or even made in Brazil.

But this group is largely outnumbered. For most people I talked with, it was not nearly that simple. They want to live in imagined religious landscapes *and* real political ones. They want to change the world in confessionals and ballot boxes everywhere. Their responses to my questions about how they wanted to translate their faith into action fell into three broad categories: they wanted to put religion first yet use it as a platform to help all humankind; they wanted to pursue both religious and political solutions; or they wanted to keep religion out of it. Sound familiar?

There were people like Pastor Wilson or Vikram who also put religion before politics, but who heard that as a call to help people inside and outside their communities. This is the politics of inclusive religious global citizens. Their faith also matters more to them than the nation or the ethnic group, and it colors how they vote, give to charity, or volunteer. But their theologies of change are all-encompassing. They are about making the world better for everyone, not just people who look or think like they do.

Take twenty-eight-year-old Samina, who migrated from Pakistan. She is firmly rooted in a religious map, although her politics extend way beyond those who share the territory. The point, she says, is to interact with other people, and to get to know what they think and feel. You change the world by setting a good example.

As an adult, being a Muslim has always mattered more to me than being from Pakistan. And Muslims believe in the umma, the idea of a worldwide political community. So it's not a stretch for many of us to feel more connected to Muslims around the world than those who say that they are Pakistanis or Malaysians first. But for me belonging to the umma means working outside it. By that I mean, that is where I start from but not where I finish. Because I am a Muslim first, I have to care about others. When we help anyone, besides just our own, we set an example of how to change the world.

Forty-year-old Teresa, from Valadares, feels the same way. She says you make the world better by getting to know people, sharing with them, changing them and changing in response. She belonged to a congregation in Framingham, hosted by a Congregationalist church with many gay and lesbian members. She recalled many difficult conversations among the members of her church about how they should interact with their hosts. Some members rejected the idea out of hand of praying alongside homosexuals. They declined invitations to attend bilingual services and left to join other congregations. At first, the pastor agreed. But as he got to know his hosts better, he changed his mind.

> I remember the day he gave a sermon on just that topic. He said Christ taught us about unconditional love, and that means unconditional. We might change someone by getting close to them or we might be changed ourselves. That was a very difficult thing for me because we had always been taught, and taught others for that matter, that homosexuality was the ultimate sin. But I decided to go. What he said made sense to me. Besides they were reaching out to us, they wanted to love us. It would have been unchristian not to respond. And once homosexuality had a human face, I couldn't really hate them anymore. I might not agree with how they lived their lives but they were fine, honest people. Some of our members left our church. They couldn't get used to the idea. But many of us stayed and became very close friends. I was very sad to leave that church when I came back here.

She finally realized that she changed as much as she did the changing, and that was the point. Her faith, she said, inspired her to reach out beyond her "comfort zone," and God rewarded her with this unexpected gift.

A second group wants to change the world through religion and politics. The two realms coexist and sometimes even complement each other. They're not inherently contradictory or in competition. Your political views naturally inform the kind of religion you practice, and your religious beliefs naturally inform your politics. You can choose to put religion first, but always in accordance with secular law, or you can put the political landscape before its religious counterpart. It's not always easy, but you can work it out.

For Ali, a thirty-five-year-old from Karachi, religion and politics are like two tools in the toolbox. Some problems demand religious responses while others are best addressed through political means.

I guess I see myself as a card-carrying member of two communities. I am American and I am a Muslim. As a member of both groups, I have certain obligations and I can expect certain things in return. We have all been worried, after September 11, about Pakistan and about the Muslim community here. Some of us wrote to our congressman. Some of us gave talks at the local high school. Some of us thought that to defend Muslim rights we should work as Muslims. The mosque became a place where we could organize ourselves and reach out to the broader community. I chose to work from a religious base because I think that religious problems need religious solutions. But others disagree and do it their own way. Everything helps because we are ultimately all fighting for the same cause.

Twenty-eight-year-old Annie from Inishowen believes religious and political citizenship are perfect complements. Why not, "excuse the expression, try killing the bird with several stones?" she asks. Religion and politics work together. When you raise your voice in several places at the same time, you're more likely to be heard.

First and foremost, I am a Catholic. That is the community that matters most to me and that I try to give the most back to. But why not get politicians to help you along the way? Last year, at our church, we worked a lot on school vouchers. A lot of families wanted to be able to send their kids to parochial schools. We organized activities at the church and with the archdiocese, but we also contacted our local representatives. There's a long history of that in Boston, you know, of Irishness and Catholicness being the same thing.

For Tayibba, in her forties, you can't separate religion from politics because Islam is a way of life.

> Islam is not just a religion and a belief. It's a way of life. It affects everything that you do every single day. How you eat, how you talk, how you behave, and not just with fellow Muslims but with everybody else. Understanding everybody else's ways, the politeness and the fairness, the justice. So for us it's really about humanity. You cannot separate religious from secular law. You have to find a way to obey Muslim laws and secular laws wherever you live.

Admittedly, tensions arise when you try to be true to your faith in a secular society. Anna, a sixty-four-year-old Valadarense, takes time off from work to prepare herself spiritually for Easter because you have to work during Holy Week in the United States. Ahmed, in his forties, asked his boss to let him pray in an empty office and take breaks during prayer times. When his former boss wouldn't agree, he quit. Others reasoned away the conflict between the secular and the religious. They acknowledged the inconsistencies but sought ways to resolve them. Time and time again in my conversations, people brought up Muslim adultery laws as an example of beliefs that have been tragically misunderstood.[27] Samir Nasrullah, a thirty-five-year-old Pakistani, described it as follows:

> You know, we talk about having the right to this and the right to that. In Islam it is the reverse. Before you get rights, the first thing is duty. So, for example, you have a duty to protect people from harm. If you see someone being oppressed, whether it's a Christian or another Muslim, it is your job to protect the person and allow him to practice his religion. People talk a lot about this issue of adultery, and they say Islam is such a barbaric religion because if someone is an adulterer you stone them to death. But you have to remember that this is also tied to a burden of proof that is so heavy, it can never be met. You have to have four witnesses who ac-

tually witnessed the sexual act. The only way that something like
that would happen is that you either invite people into your house
or you are doing it in the street like a prostitute. So the issue is
what you do in the privacy of your home is nobody's business.
But the moment you start to do something in public, it affects the
entire community. And because in Islam, things like adultery
are considered to be sinful acts that have a great consequence, the
level of punishment is very severe, but then on the other hand, the
burden of proof is so severe. It is a system of checks and balances.

From people like forty-year-old Aisha's point of view, the tension between religion and politics is vastly overblown because we all believe in
pretty much the same thing. The religious and the secular are not that
different because we're all listening to similar channels.

I mean we all believe in one God. A lot of people don't know this
but Prophet Muhammad also taught us that Jesus Christ is also
our prophet. We totally believe that Moses was a prophet too. Most
of the principles are common. So the principles of humanity, you
know, taking care of other people and human rights, it's the same.
To me, these are fundamental human issues that are not necessarily Islamic alone. We should all follow them.

Likewise, Claire, a sixty-plus Inishowener, says,

I think no matter what religion you are, it's the same, if you're a
Baptist, Protestant, Presbyterian, or Catholic. Oh God, I just hope
you have some religion. I think we're all the same as long as you
believe in God. Religion is really about how you treat others more
than how many times you get down on your knees and pray. It's
much more important to help people than to say the rosary every
night.

Finally, some people, the religious and the barely believing among
them, want to keep religion out of politics. One part of this group asserts unconditionally that religion does not define who they are. They
admit that some of their traditions have religious roots, but they prefer

to think of them as cultural. They realize that religion permeates the air in the places they come from. That's why they're so happy it's not that way in the United States. "I was glad to leave Ireland," explains twenty-eight-year-old Brian.

> I mean, Ireland is a lot less religious than it used to be. The church doesn't have the same kind of power that it had, say, even ten years ago. But even so, so much of what we do is influenced by Catholicism. How men and women relate to each other, how we think about sexuality, how we think about sin. These roots run very deep and they will take generations to go away. And you see it in politics. A politician can't go too much against the church or he'll have no chance at all. It's hard to be pro-abortion or pro–gay rights. I think that limits my personal freedom and it limits Ireland. I think that's one of the reasons why America is farther ahead.

"Pakistan," Ismael, in his early fifties, observes,

> has become so religious, you can't go anywhere without bumping into it. Well, I'm not a very religious person. And I don't really want anyone telling me what do. Not the president or an imam. Pakistan would be better off and make more progress if it went back to the other side of the pendulum and became more secular again. It's OK for people to be very religious, but they should just live and let live.

Brian and Ismael, like Alice and Luis, are the first to reel off a long list of the historical ills religion is responsible for. The world would be a better place, they say, if religion would just stay out of it.

But there are others, like Priya from Gujarat and Ronaldo from Valadares, who call themselves believers and yet still want faith to remain outside the political fray. When they talk about their lives and what matters to them, religion looms large. They just don't feel the need to wear it on their sleeves or advertise it to everyone. In fact, they think it's better for people to keep their beliefs to themselves. If your faith influences how you vote or the kinds of community projects you're involved in, that's OK, but everyone else doesn't need to know about it. As Ronaldo, a thirty-nine-year-old migrant from Valadares, relates,

I consider myself to be a very religious person. I mean, I spend
three, four nights a week at my church. It is the center of our
family's life. But I still think that religion and politics should be
separate. If I choose to live according to my faith, that is one thing.
But if the government tries to make me do that, it's another. That's
where we run into problems. Religion should play a minimal role
in politics. It certainly needs to be kept under control.

Priya says that even though she has become more observant since she
came to the United States, it hasn't changed her mind about the need to
keep religion and politics separate. "Look at Gujarat," she remarks, "so
much bloodshed between Hindus and Muslims. That is not what God
intended. I don't want a group of swamis telling the rest of us how to
live our lives. That totally distorts my faith for political purposes."

What does all this add up to? Right now, perceptions about immigrants play a much greater role in the culture wars than the actual facts
about them do. Many people fear non-Christian newcomers without
ever having talked to them. But if we listen to immigrant voices, what
do we actually hear? Do they exacerbate or assuage these conflicts?

If the voices expressed here are any indication, incorporating immigrants into the national conversation is not likely to shift civil society
debates considerably in either direction. People from all four faith traditions articulated views spanning the political spectrum, from the very
liberal to the very conservative. Their contributions echoed the range of
opinions expressed by native-born Americans. Americans' general beliefs and values, as well as their views on controversial moral issues such
as abortion, the death penalty, gays and lesbians, and gender equality, do
not vary significantly based on birthplace.[28] Factors such as age, how
often you attend church, and your level of religious commitment have a
much greater impact on beliefs and values than ethnic or religious divisions. A higher percentage of committed individuals believe "churches
should express views on political matters" (73 versus 59 percent), for instance, than the differences between Catholics and mainline Protestants (46 versus 43 percent), or whites and Hispanics (50 versus 53
percent). In fact, practicing Protestants' views are strikingly similar to
those of Catholics.[29] The newcomers in this story, then, are potential
partners on all sides of these debates.

So the people who want us all to believe as they do are in good company among the native born. And those who want religion to dominate public life also find strong support from some native-born corners. But there were many others, even among those who hold faith dear, who clearly respect other people's choices. They want to live a certain way, but they don't expect everyone else to. Rather than having their minds made up before the conversation begins, they are struggling to figure out what they want to say and what they want to do about it. Hot-button issues like homosexuality or abortion evoke heated responses on either side. Yet most people were much more concerned about education, health, and responsible government in this country and the places they come from. Their vision of a good society looks a lot like the picture painted by people in California and Kalamazoo.

Conclusion: Tolerance in the Face of Terrorism

> Brazilian values and U.S. values are not so different. And if you mix, it can get better. Everything mix, get better. Like we say, like if you eat the egg when it is raw, it's terrible. If you eat the flour, it's terrible. You can drink the milk, OK, it's fine. Right? If you eat the yeast, it's not good for you, you're going to get sick. But mix all this stuff, you can make a nice cake.
>
> —Jose Carlos, forty-two-year-old migrant,
> Marlboro, Massachusetts

July 7, 2005, the morning of the London subway bombings, was also the day after my son's birthday. My parents were visiting to celebrate, and I gave my father some chapters from this book to read during his stay. When I came back from my run that morning, I told him the news. Later, he asked me how I could write what I was writing given the day's events. Despite the stories in the preceding pages, many readers will undoubtedly agree. People like Alice were already sure religion was up to no good before they opened the cover, and they are not likely to change their minds any time soon. The Luises of the world may have been convinced of religion's salience, but they probably remain skeptical that it can ever be a positive force. People like Florence welcome religion's public face, but they want it to be a certain kind of religion acting in a particular way. And people like Wasim, and my father for that matter, are baffled. They know religion is out there and that sometimes it causes trouble, and that sometimes it is a force for good, but that it should not and cannot be ignored.

The history books are filled with reasons why we should be worried. People might agree on the golden rule, but they don't always practice what they preach. And if they are intolerant locally and nationally, how can we expect them to be tolerant across borders?

I am not an apologist for religion. I know that it is frequently hijacked by conservative, if not extremist, voices. If the nation-state passport gives people license to batten down the hatches based on territorial divides, a "religious passport" sanctions similar exclusiveness based on faith. But I also know that I talked to dozens of people while writing this book who know this is wrong and want to do something about it. They don't always agree with their neighbors, yet their faith teaches them to find common ground. These people want to take religion back from those they feel are abusing it. They want to speak "tolerance to terrorism"—to use faith to arrive at a shared vision and then get to work making that vision a reality. They know this is a hard sell given the current headlines, but that now, more than ever, precisely because of those headlines, this is what needs to be done. They need help being heard, and if and when they are, they will provide a much-needed counterpoint to extremist religious voices.

What is it that we really need to listen to?

Seeing Religion Transnationally

Despite predictions to the contrary, religion has not retreated to the private sphere.[1] Neither, as Nancy Ammerman writes, "do our religious nor our political institutions require that religious traditions remain outside everyday public life, only that they enter those public domains with a due humility."[2] Religion is clearly front and center on the public stage; it's the humility we have to work on.

Christians in the United States will always outnumber people who profess other faiths. But even though the numbers who belong to non-Christian faiths are small, their influence is growing. Moreover, migrants are changing Christian denominations to reflect the increasing ethnic and cultural diversity of their membership. And the changes they prompt are not just a response to what happens in the United States but also to what happens in India, Pakistan, Brazil, and Ireland. Just as the faith traditions in this story were transformed by their encounter with Christianity, so Christianity in the United States is slowly and subtly transformed by its encounters with Hinduism, Islam, and its own reimported self. True religious pluralism, then, happens transnationally and nationally.

These trends are not confined to America. In Europe, migrants also live lives that cross borders by belonging to religious communities. Some sending country governments actively facilitate these linkages. The Paris Mosque, for instance, with its many member mosques, is run by the government of Algeria. The National Federation of Muslims, one of the largest Muslim organizations in France, is run by the Moroccan government. The Turkish-Islamic Union for the Institution of Religion maintains foreign branches that act as the government's "caretaker" of Turks abroad and supports the community's many Turkish-Islamic cultural organizations.[3] In this way, it indirectly controls nearly half of all Turkish mosques (about 1,100) in Europe; 870 are in Germany alone.[4] With partners from Austria and Holland, the union opened the European Union and Religion Project in Brussels. Its goal is to become the EU's sole interlocutor around Islamic issues on the continent and to make sure that EU law becomes more responsive to Muslim concerns.[5] These developments do not indicate that religious organizations are taking over European governments. Rather, states are actively encouraging the creation of centralized, umbrella organizations (like the Turkish-Islamic Union) to meet the challenges posed by transnational religions.[6] They are slowly accepting the fact that religion is important not only to migrants but to the second and third generation, who increasingly claim their "inherited religion" as their primary source of identity.[7]

To expand the parameters of pluralism in the United States, Christian Americans have to be willing to share some of their privilege. While Protestant cultural templates laid the foundation for religious tolerance, a legacy that should be neither discounted nor abandoned, our current national reality demands a broader model. It needs to make room for those it has always included and those it has marginalized—for points of view long acknowledged and those that are continuously overlooked. If not, we run the risk of taking for granted meanings and values that increasing segments of the population do not share.

In particular, this means acknowledging that not all religious life consists of a church community that repeats the same liturgy together every Sunday. The experiences of the migrants in this story are clearly otherwise. They also enact their religious lives in their living rooms and on street corners. The boundary between the secular and the sacred is blurred. Migrants do not always agree on one official canon. Male leaders do not always stand up in front of the sanctuary and tell them what to do. They mix and match elements from different faiths rather than observe strict boundaries between traditions. As a result, migrants are miles ahead of most of us. They no longer expect a world characterized by Catholic versus Protestant, or American versus Brazilian, but recognize instead that mestizaje is in the cards that the future holds for all of us.[8]

Moving toward a deeper religious pluralism also means letting go of the expectation that cultures are coherent wholes. Cultures are not made of a single, tightly woven fabric, but rather cloths of diverse, changing threads. "Cultural wholists" predict civilizational clashes because they expect the cultures that migrants import to collide automatically with those already in place.[9] But for every person in this book who was strictly faithful, there were others who made up the religious script as they went along. For every exclusive religious global citizen, there were those who were inclusive. Just as putting all of Christianity into one basket masks the diversity within groups, so treating all Muslims and Hindus as if they were equal ignores who they actually are, and makes collaboration and cooperation less likely. To build bridges and identify possible partners, the variety in place in each of these communities has to be brought into sharper relief.

And as I said in the introduction, promoting diversity means simply acknowledging difference. It means being willing to live and let live, without being willing to change and be changed. Pluralists take the next step. They go beyond "separate but equal," interacting with others and inventing something new. Pluralism means not just letting individuals speak but letting them shape the collective narrative so they recognize their voice within it. In a multicultural world, argues Charles Taylor, people are ethically obligated to extend a "moral cognizance" to those whose perspectives differ sharply from their own. Intercultural understanding is an obligation, not an option. This extends to religious understanding as well.[10]

Seeing Migration Transnationally

Florence and others like her criticize migrants for their transnational lifestyles. They say the income, skills, and charitable contributions migrants accumulate in the United States should remain here. Being loyal to two homelands is like polygamy—it just doesn't work. Critics in sending countries say that emigrants should have little say in their affairs because they've abandoned ship and are out of touch with the everyday reality. It's not right for governments to grant them special privileges. The limited resources of sending states should be spent on those at home.

But people who live transnationally are the face of the future. They drive home that homeland and host country poverty and community development are not separate issues. Both the national and the transnational are produced by forces inside and outside our borders. When a small group participates on a regular basis and a larger group participates periodically, their activities add up, challenging established values and behaviors in the United States and around the globe. Some migrants are not just Americans or ethnic Americans but transnational Americans.

Moreover, it's not necessarily the case, as Florence worries, that transnational migrants care so much about their homelands that they don't have time to become part of the United States. People can, and do, exercise rights and fulfill responsibilities in several communities. Their multiple memberships can reinforce rather than detract from each other—they don't necessarily add up to a zero-sum game. Here again, history is filled with examples of how this has been badly managed in the past. Catholics' transnational loyalty to Rome is just one case in which strong religious ties have been taken as a sign of national disloyalty in the United States and throughout Europe and used to justify laws and public policies denying them privileges.

It doesn't have to be this way.[11] People who know how to function across borders, who are bicultural and bilingual, have the best résumé for today's world. They have the capacity to transmit as well as translate, serving as intermediaries between parties who desperately need to understand each other. Take the Pakistani business owners who act as go-betweens for potential partners in the United States and Karachi.

Take the Valadarenses who tell people back home about good government, but who are also at the forefront of efforts to politically integrate Brazilians in Framingham. Take the Gujaratis and the Pakistanis who are helping to create and re-create Islam and Hinduism in this country as well as their homelands. Granted, some send back a version that is even more conservative than the one they came with, but others introduce a more moderate vision that challenges the status quo. Contrary to what Florence thinks, transnational migrants are good for this country and their homelands.

So rather than seeing remittances as a drain on America's bank account, we can see them as rectifying years of uneven global economic development. Instead of perceiving transnational political groups as suspect, we can help them strengthen homeland political institutions and foster political integration into the United States. Rather than viewing transnational entrepreneurs as contributing to brain drain, we can create mechanisms enhancing their contribution to brain gain.[12] The question is not whether transnational lives are good or bad but, given that they are here to stay, how can the people who lead them best be protected and represented, and what should we expect of them in return?

And this works both ways. How people fulfill their rights and responsibilities is as much a function of what immigrants do as how native-born Americans receive them. Even though many in this story wanted to participate actively in the United States, they felt real limits to how American they could become. They acknowledged this with deep sadness. They talked about how much they loved America and how grateful they were for what they had accomplished here. They said that homeland ties notwithstanding, they were part of this country and had every intention of remaining so. The roadblocks they encountered along the way profoundly disappointed them. Particularly after September 11, the United States had withdrawn its welcome mat. What they had perceived as unconditional acceptance turned out to be only a temporary membership card.

Both Gujaratis and Pakistanis felt this particularly strongly. Even people who said that they never experienced discrimination before the World Trade Center bombing now said that Muslims in particular, but South Asians in general, were treated with suspicion. Everyone had a story to tell about someone who immigration or customs officials had treated badly. These stories spread like wildfire, passing from living room to living room in Massachusetts, Karachi, and Gujarat, so that regardless of the actual numbers everyone was seen as affected. They contribute to widespread anti-Americanism.

Speaking Tolerance to Terrorism

Many of the people I talked with while writing this book saw themselves as living in a religious world influenced by people, ideas, and organizations from around the globe. The religion they described and what they wanted to do about it was the religion of the middle, not of the margins. Some people wanted to impose their views on others or convince them of the error of their ways; many more separated their personal views from those they thought should dominate the public square. The official party line of their religious communities differed from their personal accounts. Just as the pope's views on birth control or ordaining women are not shared by many practicing Catholics, not all Swaminarayan or Swadhyaya members want to make India into a Hindu state.

So why does it feel like radical, intolerant religious voices dominate the airwaves? Why do we forget that the history books are also filled with examples of people whose faith motivated them to become abolitionists or civil rights leaders? Why does it feel as if religion at the margins, all over the world, is slowly but surely shrinking that common, middle ground? Why doesn't the silent majority talk back? And if it did, what would it say?

This is an age-old problem. What we are witnessing is simply the latest cast of characters acting out the conflict against a new backdrop. Reinhold Niebuhr had a good answer for religious triumphalism over sixty years ago. We can either try to empty out religion from culture, he said, which was unlikely, or pose a *religious* solution to the problem of religious diversity.

Such a solution, wrote Niebuhr,

> makes religious and cultural diversity possible within the presuppositions of a free society, without destroying the religious depth of culture. The solution requires a very high form of religious commitment. It demands that each religion, or each version of a

single faith, seek to proclaim its highest insights while yet preserving a humble and contrite recognition of the fact that all actual expressions of religious faith are subject to historical contingency and relativity. Such recognition creates a spirit of tolerance and makes any religious or cultural movement hesitant to claim official validity for its form of religion or to demand an official monopoly for its cult.[13]

Niebuhr believed people could bring their religious commitments to public debates and speak from that platform. If they were true to the "highest" teachings of their faith, they would act with humility. He envisioned a kind of religious diplomacy that many in this book, in the United States and elsewhere, are ready to sign on to. They want to prove that Alice, Luis, and Florence are wrong, and show Wasim that this kind of dialogue is possible. Furthermore, given world events, they're in a hurry. As Ian Buruma argues, we need religious diplomacy among moderate actors who can speak tolerance to any kind of intolerance, be it "intolerance-light" or terrorism.[14] The stakes are not generally as high as the standoff between George Bush, Osama bin Laden, or Mahmoud Ahmadinejad. That they are usually about schools, workplaces, or health care systems makes them no less important.

These discussions bring to mind debates about U.S. foreign policy toward human rights in China in the late 1970s. While one side felt we should isolate China, thereby forcing it to change its stance, the other argued that engaging with the Chinese was the best way to encourage reforms. An analogous choice confronts political moderates and progressives. They can either pretend that religion will go away and ignore those who articulate a kind of faith they don't agree with. Or they can engage with people who bring their religion to the table. The Right already does this, and a strong and powerful group of allies supports it as a result. The Left can stubbornly continue to take no notice of what is already there or it too can find partners among members of faith communities. It won't always work. There will surely be conflicts. But there will also be issues, like health care, education, the environment, and jobs, around which cooperation is possible.

People who live transnational lives are uniquely suited to contribute to such dialogues. Who better to translate than those who know how to successfully negotiate multiple worlds? Transnational actors are natural

religious diplomats, as Arjun, a middle-aged Gujarati man living outside Boston, articulated:

> I know that some people think the United States should be very
> homogeneous and that there are people talking of building walls.
> Well, it's not going to happen and it shouldn't. With today's tech-
> nology and economy we're way beyond that. We live in an inte-
> grated labor economy. The people who complain about jobs going
> overseas are the same ones who don't have any problem patroniz-
> ing Wal-Mart and buying all this cheap stuff that's produced in
> China. So if you will, the cat is out of the bag. Now the only appro-
> priate way, I think, is for everybody to start thinking in global
> terms. And if I think about India a lot, that's because I spent
> twenty years of my life there. I understand that reality well. To
> me, any kind of isolation is not of any help to us. Instead, people
> like me, who have one foot in both doors, so to speak, are the wave
> of the future because we can function here and there, and build
> bridges between them. It's not a question of taking the U.S. model
> and just trying to follow it in India. You've got to blend it with
> local conditions. And who can do that better than someone
> like me?

In a global world, loyalty and energy are not finite commodities.
There is enough to go around. "I can be, above all, a Muslim," Simeen,
a fifty-year-old Pakistani, told me, "but it doesn't mean I belong any
less to Pakistan or America. It just means that what motivates and ori-
ents me are religious principles. To try to keep those parts separate, or to
force me to choose which one matters most, would be stupid. They are
all key parts of who I am."

It's time to stop expecting people to have one stable, nationally defined identity and to abandon the assumption that social worlds fit
neatly within national boxes. Instead of turning back the clock, it
makes more sense to embrace the fact that many individuals and organizations already operate across cultures, and to ameliorate the costs and
reap the benefits. It's smarter to recognize that religion is alive and well
on street corners, in hospitals, and in legal aid clinics, and that it doesn't
come in a hermetically sealed box but that it evolves over time. People
claiming any kind of faith, therefore, may find they have more in com-

mon than they first assume. The more they come into contact and interact with one another, the greater the chance there is for a robust pluralism to emerge. "Who gets to say what the American dream is?" asks
Ahmed, a thirty-five-year-old in Boston.

> I think if anything, it embellishes America to have somebody who
> came with a background and gave what I did to this country, and
> now that I've learned from this country I might be able to give to
> some other countries, if that ever happens. I think that, to me, is
> the American, my version of the American dream. So I don't think
> that George Bush and Newt Gingrich can define the American
> dream. I was at one of those community conversations that every-
> one was organizing after 9/11 not too long ago and one of the
> women basically said, well, I don't think you can truly understand
> us because you're not born American. I said no, I think you can't
> appreciate this enough, because I'm an American by choice, you
> are an accident of birth. So I had options of going to, I had schol-
> arships for Japan, for Belgium, for France, but I chose America.
> That was where I wanted to be because I believe in this country. So
> I create my own American dream. And it is a dream not just made
> in America.

Appendix

Demographic Characteristics and Transnational Ties: Similarities and Differences

My book is based on nearly ten years of research among Pakistanis, Gujaratis, Irish, and Brazilian immigrants. It is unique in its comparison across four cases, its focus on religion, and in that it is based on fieldwork in each sending country and the United States. Here, I review some demographic data—collected by my research team and the U.S. Bureau of the Census—that underlie many of the conclusions in the preceding pages.

I conducted interviews with 247 first-generation migrants from Ireland (52), Brazil (70), India (64), and Pakistan (61).[1] After each interview, we completed a small survey that collected information about respondents' socioeconomic characteristics; participation in homeland and U.S. social, religious, and political organizations; and homeland contacts. I talked with slightly more men (52 percent) than women (48 percent). Roughly one-third were in their thirties (33 percent); approximately 20 percent each were in their twenties, forties, or fifties and older, and 3.7 percent were in their teens.

The majority arrived in the United States when they were in their twenties (61 percent) or their teens (24 percent). Because nearly three-quarters of the sample was at least thirty years old, a significant number have been in the United States for some time—about two-thirds for at least ten years. This is especially true among the migrants from Pakistan and India. In contrast, 23 percent of the Irish and 34 percent of the Brazilians have been here five years or less.

Most people were married or in some form of committed union (70 percent), or had been married at some point in their lives (5.2 percent were divorced and 0.9 percent were separated). The people who were

Table 1. Demographic Characteristics of Study Sample

		Brazil	India	Ireland	Pakistan	Total
Subject sex	Female	41.4%	57.8%	40.4%	50.8%	47.8%
	Male	58.6%	42.2%	59.6%	49.2%	52.2%
Subject age	10–19	1.4%	13.3%	0%	0%	3.7%
	20–29	21.4%	21.7%	26.9%	18.0%	21.8%
	30–39	45.7%	18.3%	40.4%	24.6%	32.5%
	40–49	21.4%	23.3%	7.7%	24.6%	19.8%
	50+	10%	23.3%	25%	32.8%	22.2%
Marital status	Married	62.9%	83.3%	61.5%	70.5%	68.8%
	Single	20%	12.5%	34.6%	27.9%	23.8%
	Divorced	12.9%	4.2%	0%	1.6%	5.2%
	In union	2.9%	0%	1.9%	0%	1.3%
	Separated	1.4%	0%	1.9%	0%	.9%
Birthplace of children	Homeland	76.9%	13.5%	0%	9.8%	30.2%
	U.S.	19.2%	62.2%	100%	75.6%	59.3%
	Both	3.8%	24.3%	0%	9.8%	9.3%
	Abroad, not homeland	0%	0%	0%	4.9%	1.2%

unmarried were more likely to be in their teens or twenties; by age thirty to thirty-nine, only 16.6 percent were single or divorced. Most of the single respondents were from Ireland (35 percent) and Pakistan (28 percent), with the smallest numbers from India (11 percent).

The most common occupation in the homeland prior to migration was being a student (28 percent).[2] Among those who worked, substantial numbers came with a managerial or professional background (20 percent), especially among people from Pakistan, India, and Brazil. In addition, a similar proportion (22 percent) had worked in either production (for example, construction workers or artisans) or agriculture, service, or operations (for instance, factory workers or laborers). Nearly two-thirds of the people from Ireland had worked in these low-skilled fields, mainly agriculture and production, before they came to the United States. Nearly one-third of the Brazilians had worked in technical, sales, or administrative support. Finally, there was a small group of approximately 6 percent who owned their own businesses in the homeland, and they were almost exclusively from Gujarat.

Table 2. Occupation in Homeland and United States (Study Sample)

		Brazil	India	Ireland	Pakistan	Total
Occupation in homeland	Unemployed*	20%	13.3%	3.8%	4.9%	11%
	Managerial/professional	22.9%	22.2%	3.8%	29.5%	20.2%
	Technical, sales, administrative support	32.9%	4.4%	11.5%	1.6%	14.0%
	Service	0%	2.2%	3.8%	0%	1.3%
	Farm, forestry, fishing	0%	6.7%	23.1%	0%	6.6%
	Production, precision, craft, repair	2.9%	2.2%	32.7%	1.6%	9.2%
	Operators, fabricators, laborers	8.6%	2.2%	5.8%	0%	4.4%
	Own business	0%	22.2%	1.9%	3.3%	5.7%
	Student	12.9%	24.4%	13.5%	59%	27.6%
Occupation in the U.S.	Unemployed*	24.3%	6.8%	0%	0%	8.8%
	Managerial/professional	34.3%	47.7%	9.6%	60.7%	38.3%
	Technical, sales, administrative support	18.6%	9.1%	9.6%	6.6%	11.5%
	Service	10%	2.3%	15.4%	0%	7%
	Farm, forestry, fishing	1.4%	0%	0%	0%	.4%
	Production, precision, craft, repair	1.4%	0%	38.5%	1.6%	9.7%
	Operators, fabricators, laborers	2.9%	13.6%	9.6%	0%	5.7%
	Own business	5.7%	20.5%	5.8%	21.3%	12.8%
	Student	0%	0%	0%	1.6%	.4%
	Housewife/raising kids	1.4%	0%	11.5%	8.2%	5.3%

*This category also includes some students.

How did the occupational picture shift once people came to the United States? The Pakistanis who had been students were now overwhelmingly managers or professionals (61 percent). A substantial number also started their own businesses (21 percent), primarily in the information technology and financial sectors. Most of the Irish remained in production (39 percent), with small numbers shifting into

Table 3. Education in Homeland and the United States (Study Sample)

		Brazil	India	Ireland	Pakistan	Total
Education in homeland	Primary	15.7%	14.6%	21.2%	1.7%	13%
	High school	55.7%	31.3%	48.1%	20%	39.6%
	Trade school	7.1%	2.1%	17.3%	0%	6.5%
	College	20%	37.5%	5.8%	56.7%	30%
	Graduate school	1.4%	14.6%	0%	21.7%	9.1%
	Some college	0%	0%	7.7%	0%	1.7%
Education in the U.S.	None	61.4%	34.1%	80.8%	15.8%	48.9%
	Primary	0%	2.3%	0%	0%	.4%
	High school	15.7%	6.8%	0%	0%	6.3%
	Trade school	2.9%	6.8%	13.5%	3.5%	6.3%
	College	12.9%	18.2%	3.8%	14%	12.1%
	Graduate school	7.1%	29.5%	0%	66.7%	25.1%
	Some college	0%	2.3%	1.9%	0%	.9%

the service sector (15 percent) or managerial/professional (10 percent) roles. About 21 percent of the Indian community continued as business owners, but their ranks doubled among managerial/professionals (48 versus 22 percent in the homeland). Valadarenses and Inishoweners have not experienced the same upward mobility as Gujaratis and Pakistanis. For example, while the numbers of Valadarenses in managerial or professional jobs did increase (plus eleven points), those in technical, sales, and administrative support positions dropped considerably (minus fourteen points), and many are now within the lower end of the job scale, particularly in the service sector (plus ten points), where they work as housecleaners and restaurant workers. About 6 percent each of the Irish and the Brazilians are business owners.

With the exception of Inishoweners, all groups have enjoyed considerable gains with respect to education. Migrants from Pakistan were already well educated. The majority had at least a college degree as well as some graduate school under their belts. But both Pakistanis and Gujaratis have become even more educated since they arrived in the United States—quite a few obtained a college degree (18 percent from

India and 14 percent from Pakistan). Even more attended graduate school, including 30 percent of those from India and 67 percent of those from Pakistan. People from Valadares also improved their educational profile. Almost two-thirds arrived with a high school or trade school diploma and more than a fifth with a college degree. Subsequently, in the United States, many completed high school (16 percent) or trade school (3 percent), and another 20 percent went on to college and/or graduate school. In contrast, while two-thirds of Inishoweners came with a high school or trade school diploma, no additional high school education was reported, and only 14 percent went through trade school. Only a handful pursued a college education.

What follows is a broader profile of each group, based primarily on U.S. Census data from 2000 for Massachusetts and other scholarly work. In the next section, I focus on the socioeconomic characteristics of migrants in the United States. I then use data collected specifically for this study to examine migrants' continued homeland ties. A final section asks why transnational involvements arise when and where they do. It spells out cultural and structural differences in transnational social fields that encourage or thwart the emergence of cross-border activism.

Census Profiles: The Big Picture

BRAZILIANS

Brazilian immigrants in the United States, and in particular in Boston, have been well studied.[3] According to the 2000 Census, there were slightly more Brazilian men (51 percent) than women living in Massachusetts. They were young, with a median age of just twenty-nine compared to thirty-seven for the state as a whole. Of those who are twenty-five and over, 67 percent were high school graduates, and only 14 percent had a bachelor's degree or higher. Many Brazilians who entered the United States had already achieved some level of higher education in their homeland, however. Teresa Sales found that 47 percent of the people she studied in Boston had attended college.[4] New York's Brazilians exhibited similar numbers; 46 percent had attended a university and 31 percent had graduated.[5] Educational attainment differed by gender. The number of Brazilian women who completed either a high school or university-level degree was about 5 percent higher than that of men.

In 2000, just over three-quarters of Brazilians in Massachusetts were reported to be in the labor force. The majority were employed in service occupations (48 percent), followed by production, transportation, and moving (16 percent), and then sales or office (14 percent). While the vast majority were salaried or government workers (85 percent), another 15 percent were self-employed in a business that was not their own. The median household income was considerably less than that of the general statewide population—$37,231 compared to $50,502. The poverty status of Brazilians was 19 percent (compared to 9.3 percent overall in Massachusetts). Sixty-four percent of Brazilians spoke English less than "very well."[6]

Nearly 84 percent of the Brazilian population in Massachusetts was foreign born, and just under 11 percent were naturalized citizens. These figures, however, increase dramatically for those who entered the United States in the 1980s and before (28 and 53 percent, respectively). Citizenship is correlated with poverty status—only 11.4 percent of the people who were citizens lived below the poverty line compared to 21 percent among those who were not naturalized. Currently, Brazilians are second only to Mexicans in the numbers coming to the United States without documents. All told, more than thirty-one thousand Brazilians were apprehended trying to cross the United States–Mexico border in fiscal year 2005–2006.[7] Even when they make it across, living in fear is an everyday reality, not unwarranted, since crackdowns and deportations have increased significantly since 2004. And while the incidence of actual violence in MetroWest Boston between native- and foreign-born residents is minimal, there is constant tension, exacerbated of late by the emergence of strong, vocal anti-immigrant organizations.[8]

INDIANS

An unofficial estimate of the total number of people of Indian origin living outside India is about 22 million people. There were just under 44,000 individuals in Massachusetts who identified as "Asian Indian alone" on the 2000 U.S. Census.[9] Just over three-quarters were foreign born (76.1 percent). In addition to Gujarat, they came from many parts of India, including Punjab, Kerala, and the southern regions. Seventy-five percent lived in the metro Boston area. These individuals have been coming for several decades. About 60 percent came in the 1990s, another 25 percent arrived in the 1980s, and 15 percent came prior to 1980. Just over 90 percent came directly from Asia; the remainder came by way of Latin America, Africa, Europe, and Canada. Only a small percentage of the newest arrivals are U.S. citizens (9.2 percent of 1990–2000 migrants). As with the other groups, though, naturalization increases sharply with time in the United States. Fifty-five percent of those who came in the 1980s are now citizens and 86 percent of those who arrived prior to 1980 are citizens. The foreign born among the state's Asian Indians are less likely to be poor than the foreign-born Brazilians, Irish, or Pakistanis in Massachusetts (8.3 percent). Their poverty rates are also lower than the overall state (9.3 percent) and national (12.4 percent) poverty levels.

The statewide census data for the Indian and Pakistani communities paint a somewhat different picture than the data we collected for this study. According to the census, the median household income for Asian Indians was the highest among the four groups—in fact, substantially higher than that of the entire state population ($71,265 versus $50,502). (In contrast, while we did not ask about income directly in our survey, I estimate that Pakistani respondents had the highest annual income of the groups in the study.) There were more Asian Indian men (54 percent) than women (46 percent). Over 90 percent had at least a high school diploma, and over three-quarters (79 percent) had a bachelor's degree or higher. Nearly half (48 percent) had graduate or professional degrees. Sixty-one percent of the men and 67 percent of the women, fifteen years and older, were married.

Just over 70 percent of Asian Indians in Massachusetts over the age of sixteen were in the labor force. The vast majority were employed in management, professional, and related occupations (72 percent), followed by sales and office occupations (14 percent), with small numbers in service (6 percent) or production, transportation, and construction (8 percent). Nearly all worked for a wage or salary, with private employers (91 percent) or the government (7 percent). Few were self-employed in their own businesses (2.3 percent). Employment was much lower among women. Nearly two-thirds of the Asian Indians in Massachusetts over sixteen years old who were in the labor force were men, and

Table 4. General Profiles from the U.S. Census (Massachusetts), Part 1*

	Massa-chusetts Overall	Brazil (Ancestry)	India (Race)	Ireland (Ancestry)	Pakistan (Race)
Total Population	6,349,097	30,583	43,801	1,426,453	2,356
Nativity Total population					
Native	88%	16%	24%	98%	22%
Foreign born	12%	84%	76%	2.0%	78%
Naturalized citizens	44%	11%	32%	59%	29%
Period of Entry Foreign-born population					
Entered 1990 to March 2000	40%	79%	60%	26%	63%
Entered 1980 to 1989	26%	18%	25%	19%	27%
Entered prior to 1980s	34%	3.2%	15%	55%	10%
Gender Total population					
Male	48%	51%	54%	46%	56%
Female	52%	49%	46%	54%	44%
Median Age	37	29	29	55	27
Marital Status[†] Population 15 years and up					
Never married	31%	35%	32%	22%	40%
Now married, except separated	52%	55%	64%	58%	55%
Separated	2.0%	3.2%	0.5%	1.4%	1.0%
Widowed	7.0%	1.4%	1.9%	13%	1.3%
Divorced	8.3%	5.9%	1.8%	5.9%	2.8%
Educational Attainment[†] Population 25 years and up					
Less than 9th grade	5.8%	17%	4%	8.3%	5.8%
9th to 12th grade, no diploma	9.4%	16%	3.5%	13%	13%
High school graduate (includes equivalency)	27%	36%	5.5%	30%	14%
Some college, no degree	17%	13%	4.3%	18%	7.8%
Associate degree	7.2%	4.0%	2.5%	6.0%	1.4%
Bachelor's degree	20%	10%	32%	13%	27%
Graduate or professional degree	14%	4.0%	48%	11%	31%
Percent high school graduate or higher	85%	67%	92%	78%	81%
Percent bachelor's degree or higher	33%	14%	79%	24%	58%

† Figures for Ireland on this variable not available for Massachusetts only; stated percentages are based on the U.S. foreign-born population from Ireland.

* The U.S. Census utilizes both "ethnic" and "racial" categories. People who identify with a country — for example, Brazil or Ireland — are categorized as belonging to Brazilian and Irish "ancestry groups." However, individuals from countries of birth or communities associated with a "race," i.e. Asian, black, Hispanic, or Native American, are categorized racially, rather than according to ethnicity. One cannot choose Pakistani "ancestry"; he or she can choose to be of the Asian "race": and then a subcategory by country. Thus, in this study, we have two ancestry groups and two race groups. To complicate matters further, beginning with the 2000 Decennial Census, individuals can choose more than one race, but only about 2 percent do so.

Table 4. General Profiles from the U.S. Census (Massachusetts), Part 2 *
(All figures represent percentages of the total)

	Massa-chusetts overall	Brazil (Ancestry)	India (Race)	Ireland (Ancestry)	Pakistan (Race)
Median Household Income					
In 1999†	$50,502	$37,231	$71,625	$49,780	$45,087
Poverty Rate Total population					
Individuals	9.3%	19%	9.4%	5.1%	23%
Families†	6.7%	14%	5.4%	3%	21%
Foreign born					
Individuals	14%	20%	8.3%	5.8%	24%
Home Ownership†					
Owner-occupied housing units	62%	13%	40%	64%	34%
Renter-occupied housing units	38%	87%	60%	36%	66%
Occupation† Employed civilian population 16 years and up in labor force	66%	76%	72%	55%	62%
Management, professional, and related	41%	11%	72%	41%	45%
Service	14%	48%	6%	16%	8%
Sales and office	26%	14%	14%	22%	40%
Farming, fishing, construction, maintenance	8%	11%	1%	14%	1%
Production, transportation, and material moving	11%	16%	7%	7%	6%
Language Spoken at Home Population 5 years and up					
English only	81%	6.3%	20%	89%	5.7%
Language other than English	19%	94%	80%	11%	94%
Speak English less than "very well"	7.7%	64%	19%	1.3%	28%

*The U.S. Census utilizes both "ethnic" and "racial" categories. People who identify with a country — for example, Brazil or Ireland — are categorized as belonging to Brazilian and Irish "ancestry groups." However, individuals from countries of birth or communities associated with a "race," i.e., Asian, black, Hispanic, or Native American, are categorized racially, rather than according to ethnicity. One cannot choose Pakistani "ancestry"; he or she can choose to be of the Asian "race": and then a subcategory by country. Thus, in this study, we have two ancestry groups and two race groups. To complicate matters further, beginning with the 2000 Decennial Census, individuals can choose more than one race, but only about 2 percent do so.

† Figures for Ireland on this variable not available for Massachusetts only; stated percentages are based on the U.S. foreign-born population from Ireland.

among those with management or professional occupations the men outnumbered the women two to one. Nearly 40 percent of the households owned their own homes. Finally, although many Gujaratis spoke a language other than English at home (80 percent), only 19 percent claimed to speak it less than "very well."

PAKISTANIS

Community leaders' estimates of 2,500 Pakistanis in Massachusetts
and 6,000 in New England are probably closer to official census figures
(2,356 for Massachusetts and 5,144 for New England) because the percentage of undocumented immigrants in this community is quite
small. Most people were foreign born (just under 80 percent), and most
came to Massachusetts during the 1990s (63 percent). The majority
came directly to the United States. About 15 percent of the newest arrivals were U.S. citizens. Naturalization increased dramatically with
time in the United States. Forty-four percent of the people who came in
the 1980s were now citizens, as were 82 percent of those who came before then. Twenty-three percent of Pakistani individuals in Massachusetts lived below the poverty line. Again, this reflects the better-off
status of my sample compared to the statewide community as a whole.

The median income for Pakistanis ($45,087) was nearly that of the
entire state population ($50,502). There were more male immigrants
(56 percent) than females (44 percent). Massachusetts' Pakistanis were
very well educated. Over 81 percent had at least a high school diploma.
Nearly 60 percent had a college degree or higher. Many had a college
degree when they arrived in the United States and had come to pursue
graduate education. While almost 31 percent of Pakistanis in the state
have a master's, professional, or doctorate degree, the number was
higher among men (35 percent) than women (25 percent). And as one
would expect in a male-majority population, a higher percentage of the
men were single. Only 40 percent of the men were married, in contrast
to more than half of the women (53 percent). Overall, the Pakistani
community was quite young, with a median age of twenty-seven, a full
decade younger than the median for the state.

About 60 percent of the Pakistanis in Massachusetts over the age of
sixteen participated in the labor force. While most of the people interviewed for this book were professionals and managers, the majority of
the Pakistanis in the state were employed in management, professional,
and related occupations (45 percent), or sales and office occupations (40
percent), with small numbers in service (8 percent) or production,
transportation, and construction (7 percent). The vast majority worked
for a wage or salary with private employers (90 percent) or the govern-

ment (6.3 percent), and a few were self-employed in their own businesses (3.5 percent). More men were employed than women. Nearly three-quarters of the men worked, while less than half (47.8 percent) of the women had jobs. Not only did fewer of the state's Pakistani women work, but as in the United States as a whole, fewer worked in higher-paying jobs—just 29 compared to 55 percent of the men. (Interestingly, in our sample more of the women had professional, high-paying jobs than men, but this was offset by all the men who owned their own businesses.) Virtually all Pakistanis in Massachusetts spoke a language other than English at home (94 percent), yet only 28 percent spoke English less than "very well." For those under eighteen years old, the figure dropped to just 5 percent.

THE IRISH

In 2000, there were nearly 1.5 million people of Irish ancestry in Massachusetts, one of the largest Irish enclaves in the country. A small proportion was foreign born (1.6 percent, or 22,387 individuals), reflecting their generations-long presence. Unfortunately, at the time of this writing, a demographic profile of the Irish at the state level was not available (although it is scheduled to be released by the U.S. Bureau of the Census shortly). The picture I offer therefore describes foreign-born Irish throughout the United States, a population of 156,475. Where state-level data are available, on nativity, citizenship, and poverty status, I include them.

Most of the Irish immigrated to Massachusetts before 1980 (55 percent), and nearly all came from Europe (85 percent) or Canada (12 percent). Among the newest arrivals, citizenship levels were quite low—about one-quarter of those coming in the 1990s (26 percent) were citizens. The rate was even lower for those arriving between 1980 and 1989 (19 percent), but rose to just over half (55 percent) among the people who came before 1980. Citizenship was not nearly as correlated with poverty status as for the other groups—about 6 percent of the foreign-born Irish in Massachusetts had incomes below the poverty line, and equally so for citizens or noncitizens.

There were more foreign-born Irish women (54 percent) than men (46 percent) in Massachusetts—the same as among foreign-born Irish overall in the United States. The majority of the Irish throughout the United States were married (58 percent). Three-quarters of the foreign-born Irish had a high school degree or higher, and one-quarter of these had a bachelor's degree or higher, which was more education than Brazilians but less than the Pakistanis and Indians.

The employment situation was also different. The Irish were the least likely to participate in the labor force, and had the highest numbers working in production, transportation, and construction (21 percent). Less than half (41 percent) had managerial or professional occupations, followed by sales and office (22 percent), and then the service sector (16 percent). Like Brazilians, however, a significant number were self-employed in a business that was not their own (9.3 percent). The proportion of government workers was also higher than for the other groups (10.1 percent). Yet the majority remained private wage and salary workers (80.2 percent). The median household income ($49,780) was a little higher than the national (just under $42,000) and about the same as the Massachusetts median. Nearly two-thirds of the foreign-born Irish in the United States owned the home they live in, however, which is much higher than the levels among the other groups.

Transnational Activism

Here, I outline several broad patterns of homeland-oriented activities exhibited by the four groups as well as highlight some of the differences between them.

Eighty percent of the people we interviewed had traveled back to their homelands at least occasionally. Even if they had not been able to return home yet, as was the case for many Brazilians (over 40 percent had not visited Brazil since they left), nearly all (97 percent) of the migrants said they definitely planned to visit their homelands in the future.[10] Although many indicated they wanted to stay longer, most visits lasted between one and three months. The exception was the Irish; they generally stayed one month or less. And although many people insisted they would stay in the United States only temporarily and return home as soon as they reached their financial goals, only 12 percent had actually lived back in their homelands. These were primarily people from Pakistan and Brazil—20 percent of each group had gone home to live. Among those who did, Pakistanis stayed between one and three years while Brazilians remained for more than three years. Most people were

Table 5. Transnational Practices

		Brazil	India	Ireland	Pakistan	Total
Has subject visited home?	Never	40.6%	5.6%	20%	3.3%	18.5%
	Occasionally	37.7%	25 9%	30%	13.3%	27%
	Periodically	0%	25.9%	24%	31.7%	19.3%
	Regularly	21.7%	42.6%	26%	51.7%	35.2%
Has subject voted?	U.S.	10.1%	47.9%	38.5%	50.8%	35.2%
	Homeland	14.5%	14.6%	7.7%	4.9%	10.4%
	Both	7.2%	4.2%	1.9%	6.6%	5.2%
	No place	68.1%	33.3%	51.9%	37.7%	49.1%
Has subject contributed to charity?	U.S.	37.1%	5.8%	39.1%	6.6%	22.3%
	Homeland	0%	21.2%	2.2%	6.6%	7%
	Both	27.1%	69.2%	41.3%	86.9%	55.5%
	None	35.7%	3.8%	17.4%	0%	15.3%
Subject or family sends remittances to homeland?	Occasionally	18.6%	44.2%	This group was asked "yes" or "no"	45.9%	27.2%
	Periodically	12.9%	23.1%		1.6%	9.4%
	Regularly	14.3%	7.7%		13.1%	9.4%
	Never	54.3%	25%	61.5%	39.3%	45.5%
	Yes			38.5%		8.5%

undecided about where they would ultimately retire (36 percent). But nearly 20 percent overall envisioned that as senior citizens, they would live transnational lifestyles. This was highest among the Pakistanis (30 percent) and lowest among the Irish (4 percent). Approximately one-quarter planned to retire in the United States (24 percent) while close to another quarter (23 percent) planned to retire in their homeland.

Migrants were very much on top of sending country affairs. The majority read ethnic newspapers (73 percent) and watched ethnic movies (72 percent) or television shows (60 percent), sometimes exclusively, but more often in combination with U.S. programming.

Most people sent money home at least occasionally (55 percent). Gujaratis sent the most money (three-quarters sent remittances and, among those, close to 40 percent did so at least periodically if not more).

Sixty percent of the Pakistanis reported sending money, although most did so only occasionally (76 percent). We also collected data on other kinds of economic activities: whether the subject owned land, home(s), or business(es) in the homeland, the United States, or both; whether they contributed to charitable causes in the United States, the homeland, or both; and how they planned to invest and give to charity in the future.

The immigrants we spoke with were overwhelmingly "givers," with 85 percent reporting some form of philanthropic activity. Of these, a majority gave to charities in both the United States and their homelands. Only 7 percent gave money only to homeland concerns and a quarter donated only to U.S. charities.[11] Long-term charitable giving projects were even bolder—96 percent intended to contribute in the future, with big increases anticipated in the Brazilian and Irish communities.

Things were less clear with respect to investment. Almost half the sample had a transnational outlook (48 percent), planning to invest in both the United States and the homeland—a view particularly common among Valadarenses and Pakistanis. Nevertheless, a sizable percentage answered "neither" (14 percent) or "undecided" (9 percent). And while many migrants owned either land (39 percent), a home or homes (76 percent), or businesses (42 percent), who owned what and where they held title varied considerably across the four groups.

More than 50 percent of the Pakistani and Gujarati respondents owned a home both in the United States and in their homelands, although property in the homeland was often jointly owned with extended family members. Valadarenses were more likely to own businesses in the United States (41 percent) and Gujaratis were equally likely to own a business in the United States and in India (12 percent versus 14 percent), while 30 percent of the Pakistani respondents had business interests in both places.

Twenty-six percent planned to work in both countries and 13 percent were undecided, but more than half (51 percent) planned to continue earning their livelihood in the United States. Clearly, no single economic present or future easily characterizes these immigrants' experiences. The range, dimension, and amount of economic transnationalism form a complex picture that is not easy to generalize across groups.

Another way of keeping one's feet in both worlds is through political activism. Unfortunately, like their native-born counterparts, as many migrants reported they don't vote at all (49 percent) as those who say they do, whether in the United States (35 percent), the homeland (10 percent), or both (5 percent). This was relatively consistent for three of the four countries. Among the Valadarenses, the scenario was a bit different. Only one-third voted, and 17 percent had voted in the United States. Almost one-quarter (22 percent) voted in Brazilian elections, compared to figures ranging from 10 percent among Inishoweners to 19 percent among Gujaratis. Participation in formal political groups, in either the homeland or the United States, also mirrored native-born patterns. The majority in all groups were not political party members either in this country or in their homeland, although they did participate in political events and rallies.

We did find differences between groups, however, among those who *do* participate. Valadarenses were more likely to participate in political organizations connected to the homeland (24 percent), followed by Gujaratis (20 percent), and Pakistanis (19 percent). When it came to participating in political activities oriented toward the United States, the Irish stepped up to the plate (39 percent), with Pakistanis (32 percent), Valadarenses (26 percent), and Gujaratis (22 percent) not far behind. One significant finding, and one emphasized throughout the book, is that migrants do not save their political loyalty and energy just for their homelands. In all four cases, more people participated in U.S. groups than in groups aimed at their homelands. In the Pakistani, Gujarati, and Valadarense cases, nearly half participated in both.[12]

Social exchanges also occur transnationally, across the gulf that separates families, friends, and business associates. Unlike prior periods of heavy migration, letter writing is rare. Across all four groups, only a small proportion wrote letters either occasionally (6 percent) or regularly (11 percent). About one-quarter sent video recordings of family or social events. Brazilians and Gujaratis did so more frequently, and the Irish did so the least. Most often, people kept in touch with their relatives via phone. Virtually everyone phoned home at least occasionally (97 percent), and just over 80 percent did so regularly. The numbers were consistent except for Ireland, where even though 100 percent made contact at least occasionally, less than two-thirds did so on a regular basis. Many immigrants had also moved into the electronic age—about 30 percent sustained regular e-mail communication with someone in the homeland.

Figure 1. Political Participation of Study Sample

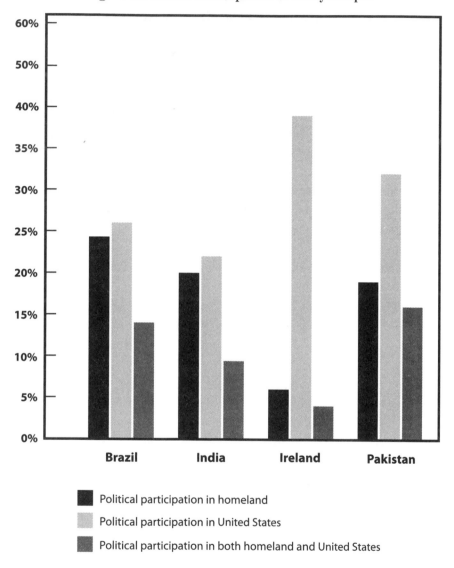

This was much more common among Pakistanis—80 percent did so regularly, compared to only 29 percent from India. Among Brazilians, more than 20 percent used e-mail, but only 10 percent did so regularly. Inishoweners had the lowest rate of electronic communication—just 15 percent.

Migrants from all groups were much more likely to participate in

Figure 2. Social Organizational Participation of Study Sample

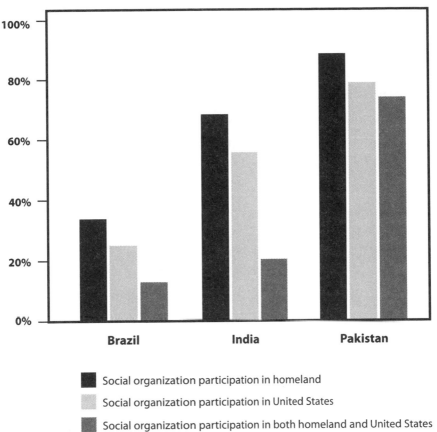

Data unavailable for the Irish sample.

transnational social and cultural groups than political ones. The vast majority from India (68 percent) and Pakistan (89 percent) belonged to and/or participated in social organizations related to the homeland; Brazilians did so to a much lesser degree (34 percent).[13] But, again, this did not preclude participation in the U.S. context. Nearly as many Pakistani and Indian migrants participated in U.S. social organizations as they did in homeland-oriented causes—79 and 56 percent, respectively.

Although the stereotype of immigrants is that they come to the United States because it is the land of opportunity, the picture we found was not that simple. Nor were the factors straightforward that determined where people move once they arrived. The Brazilians I spoke with came to the United States primarily for economic reasons (71 per-

Table 6. Transnational Plans

		Brazil	India	Ireland	Pakistan	Total
Plans to visit homeland	No	8.7%	0%	0%	1.7%	3%
	Yes	91.3%	100%	100%	98.3%	97%
Plans to work in	U.S.	59.4%	73.6%	42%	30%	51.3%
	Homeland	5.8%	5.7%	4%	1.7%	4.3%
	Both	14.5%	18.9%	8%	60%	25.9%
	Neither	1.4%	1.9%	10%	8.3%	5.2%
	Undecided	18.8%	0%	36%	0%	13.4%
Plans to retire in	U.S.	20.3%	27.6%	27.5%	20%	23.5%
	Homeland	37.7%	22.4%	23.5%	5%	22.7%
	Both	14.5%	20.7%	3.9%	30%	17.6%
	Neither	0%	0%	0%	1.7%	0.4%
	Undecided	27.5%	29.3%	45.1%	43.3%	35.7%
Plans to invest in	U.S.	16.7%	20.5%	52.6%	20.3%	27.9%
	Homeland	0%	2.6%	0%	1.7%	1.3%
	Both	61.1%	38.5%	15.8%	71.2%	48.1%
	Neither	16.7%	28.2%	13.2%	3.4%	13.6%
	Undecided	5.6%	10.3%	18.4%	3.4%	9.1%

cent) while Pakistanis came for education (57 percent). Inishoweners were divided between those who said they came for "fun/adventure" (53 percent) and those who came for economic reasons (43 percent). Gujaratis came primarily for economic reasons (57 percent), but a significant number came for more education (26 percent).

Brazilians came overwhelmingly (91 percent) to the Boston/Metro West area because they had family (two-thirds) or other contacts (one-quarter) who had already settled here, as did the Irish (96 percent). Fifty-five percent of the Gujaratis also had family or friends who lived in the area, but a significant number also came for occupational reasons (38 percent). The case of Pakistanis was completely different. The majority came for reasons related to a job (53 percent) or for an education (36 percent).

Table 7. Transnational Contacts

		Brazil	India	Ireland	Pakistan	Total
Reads newspapers	None	0%	9.6%	0%	0%	2.1%
	U.S.	14.3%	34.6%	25.5%	26.7%	24.5%
	Ethnic	35.7%	7.7%	3.9%	1.7%	13.7%
	Both	50%	48.1%	70.6%	71.7%	59.7%
Watches movies	None	0%	1.9%	0%	0%	0.4%
	U.S.	24.6%	3.8%	34.7%	47.5%	27.9%
	Ethnic	53.6%	0%	0%	1.7%	16.6%
	Both	21.7%	94.2%	65.3%	50.8%	55.0%
Watches television	None	0%	3.8%	2%	0%	1.3%
	U.S.	39.1%	21.2%	54%	41.7%	39%
	Ethnic	37.7%	0%	0%	1.7%	11.7%
	Both	23.2%	75%	44%	56.7%	48.1%
Listens to the radio	None	10.5%	5.8%	0%	0%	2.8%
	U.S.	63.2%	63.5%	25%	88.3%	61.5%
	Ethnic	5.3%	0%	0%	1.7%	1.1%
	Both	21.1%	30.8%	75%	10.0%	34.6%
Phones home	Never	7.1%	5.4%	0%	0%	3.3%
	Occasionally/periodically	7.1%	10.7%	38.5%	13.1%	16.3%
	Regularly	85.7%	83.9%	61.5%	86.9%	80.3%
Sends e-mails home	No	78.6%	65.5%	84.6%	11.5%	59.8%
	Occasionally/periodically	11.4%	5.2%	This group was asked "yes" or "no"	8.2%	6.6%
	Regularly	10%	29.3%		80.3%	30.3%
	Yes	0%	0%	15.4%	0%	3.3%
Sends videos home	Never	67.6%	63.5%	92.3%	82%	76%
	Occasionally/periodically	26.5%	32.7%	7.7%	14.8%	20.6%
	Regularly	5.9%	3.8%	0%	3.3%	3.4%

Table 8. Migratory Experiences of Study Sample

		Brazil	India	Ireland	Pakistan	Total
Number of years in U.S.	Less than one	7.1%	0%	1.9%	1.6%	3.1%
	1–5	27.1%	16.7%	21.2%	4.9%	17.8%
	6–10	8.6%	14.3%	13.5%	19.7%	13.8%
	11–20	50%	19%	34.6%	26.2%	34.2%
	21+	7.1%	50%	28.8%	47.5%	31.1%
Age of arrival in U.S.	0–9	1.4%	5.9%	0%	0%	1.7%
	10–19	10%	37.3%	34.6%	19.7%	23.9%
	20–29	67.1%	47.1%	59.6%	67.2%	61.1%
	30–39	14.3%	7.8%	5.8%	9.8%	9.8%
	40–49	0%	2%	0%	3.3%	1.3%
	50+	7.1%	0%	0%	0%	2.1%
Who came with subject to U.S.?	Came alone	15.7%	20.9%	57.7%	41.7%	33.3%
	Family/friends	84.3%	79.1%	42.3%	58.3%	66.7%
Who else is in U.S.?	No one	8.2%	2.3%	3.8%	16.4%	8.3%
	Nuclear family	22.4%	54.5%	36.5%	26.2%	34%
	Extended family	69.4%	43.2%	59.6%	57.4%	57.8%
Straight or step migration?	Straight	66.7%	91.1%	73.1%	91.8%	79.7%
	Step	33.3%	8.9%	26.9%	8.2%	20.3%
Why did subject migrate to U.S.?	Economic	71.4%	57.1%	43.1%	31.1%	51.3%
	Education	2.9%	26.2%	0%	57.4%	21.4%
	Family	14.3%	14.3%	3.9%	6.6%	9.8%
	Marriage	0%	2.4%	0%	4.9%	1.8%
	Fun/adventure	11.4%	0%	52.9%	0%	15.6%
Citizenship status	U.S. citizen	20%	63%	21.2%	70.5%	43.5%
	Resident alien	40%	27.8%	26.9%	16.4%	28%
	Undocumented	29.2%	0%	13.5%	0%	11.2%
	Dual	4.6%	1.9%	30.8%	0%	8.6%
	Work visa	0%	5.6%	7.7%	11.5%	6%
	Tourist visa	6.2%	0%	0%	0%	1.7%
	Student visa	0%	0%	0%	1.6%	0.4%
	Marriage visa	0%	1.9%	0%	0%	0.4%

Finally, as one might guess, there are considerable differences in religious demographics and participation. While nearly all of the groups exhibited extremely high levels of religious participation, their doctrine as well as where and with whom they worship differs. All groups had about a 90 percent participation rate, with Ireland somewhat lower at 73 percent. Of the Irish who did participate, 100 percent were Catholic. The vast majority (87 percent) of the Irish who said they were not currently active were still members of the church, however, and many (75 percent) responded that they "used to" worship regularly, again mirroring the homeland.

Migrants from India and Pakistan were also exclusively of a single faith, Hindu and Muslim, respectively. But the difference lay in the types of venues they attended and whose faces they saw next to them. A full 100 percent of Hindu and Muslim migrants described their houses of worship as ethnic or homeland establishments, and stated that they attended with "immigrants" 90 percent of the time.[14] In contrast, Inishoweners reported attending an "ethnic" church 71 percent of the time. The remainder considered their churches both "U.S." and ethnic. While 100 percent of those who participated in religious organizations from India were Hindu, they were divided by sect including Swadhyaya (49 percent), Swaminarayan (33 percent), and Bhagat (18 percent).

The Brazilians, on the other hand, were split when it came to the faith they follow. Almost everyone belonged to a religious organization (89 percent). Those who attended were divided 30 to 70 percent between Catholics and other Christians. The Christians further subdivided into sects. The majority belonged to Baptist groups (39 percent) or the ICFSG (23 percent). Another 13 percent identified simply as *"Protestante"* (Protestant). The remaining quarter belonged to Presbyterian, *Igreja Christa*, Assembly of God, Seventh Day Adventist, or interfaith groups. But even as the faith and sect varied considerably, the type of church did not. Three-quarters of the Brazilians attended what they considered "ethnic" churches, with the remainder described as U.S. churches.

Transnational Lifestyles: Why Here, Why Now?

What explains why increasing numbers live transnationally and why do they do so in different ways? Variations in the structured and cultural characteristics of the cross-border social fields migrants inhabit give rise to different patterns of transnational involvement.

For one thing, lifestyles are about constraints as well as choices. Immigration regimes, visa status, and sending and receiving country economies matter. The current visa system favors technical and financial wizards, and leaves low-skilled workers out. Undocumented immigrants need the safety net provided by strong homeland connections. That many migrants arrived during a period of economic decline in New England also made it difficult for them to establish a secure base in the United States and heightened the attractiveness of transnational strategies.

Second, the U.S. economy depends on surplus labor from poor countries to do jobs that native-born workers no longer want to do.[15] Sending countries simply do not have enough jobs to employ everyone. In some cases, they are alarmingly dependent on remittances to resolve their economic woes.[16] Even countries that enjoy fairly high levels of growth, such as India and Brazil, have regions such as Gujarat and Valadares, where the economy is partially supplemented by emigration. The Irish and Gujarati cases also illustrate how migration is self-perpetuating. Even when people enjoy good prospects at home, emigration is a hard habit to break.

A third factor is race. Valadarenses, Pakistanis, and Gujaratis are people of color according to most Americans' racial yardsticks. Particularly after September 11, many people felt real limits to how American the native born allowed them to become. Their loyalty was called into question, and their ability to become integrated into this country could go only so far. People turned to their homelands to counteract these barriers. The best response to a glass ceiling at work was to know how to do business in India or Pakistan. The best protection against things turning sour was to have a full bank account back home. Most felt, however, that class trumped race as the primary marker that native-born Americans used to define them. Professional status and economic success eased the sting of discrimination. They also allowed Pakistanis, and to a certain extent Gujaratis, to opt out of U.S. institutions and create their own.

A fourth key theme in this story is history and cultural memory. How people combine incorporation with their continuing involvement in their home countries depends, in part, on the context of departure, the context of arrival, and the history leading up to those events. With the exception of Valadarenses, each group has had lots of practice maintaining strong ties with people far away because they have been migrating, in their own way, for decades. Being separated did not compromise family closeness or liberate individuals from their responsibility to their kin.

A tragic history also motivates people to remain active in their ancestral homes. Like Jews or Armenians, whose experience of holocaust inspires a sense of responsibility to a real or imagined home, so Inishoweners also strongly identified with Ireland because of the poverty and hardships their relatives had endured. Doing things for Ireland was a way to honor their ancestors. Some undertook this duty more willingly than others. Either you could never stop being Irish even if you wanted to because it would be like walking out on your family, or you didn't want to forget you were Irish for a minute because that meant you would always remember how brave your ancestors had been and how much you owed them in return.

History strongly influences what it is you feel attached to as well. Since Pakistan is barely sixty years old, feeling Pakistani is not the same as belonging to a country that has been on the map, in one form or another, for centuries. Pakistan is a work in progress, while what it means to be Indian, Brazilian, or Irish has been defined and redefined many times over. Since many Karachiites are themselves Mohajirs, their feeling of rootlessness is even stronger. Because their ties to their villages were severed following Partition, they did not feel the same sense of attachment to the soil or a native place that motivates Gujaratis' and Inishoweners' sense of belonging.

Similarly, generational experiences strongly influence the strength of sending country ties.[17] What people's homelands mean to them and how much they care about their affairs are shaped by when they emigrate. Migrants from the Dominican Republic, for example, often say they are born with the Partido Revolucionario Dominicano or the Partido de la Liberación Dominicana in their genes. The next presidential campaign starts the day after the previous election is over. Because they come from a country with high levels of political participation, it is no surprise that Dominicans remain active in expatriate politics. In contrast, while emigrant Valadarenses have the right to vote, and Brazilian political parties are hard at work trying to mobilize people in the

United States, the political life of the Brazilian community pales by comparison.[18] Most Brazilians left their country during the Figueiredo dictatorship or soon after it. They are democratic novices who are only just beginning to form allegiances to particular candidates or groups.

The fifth factor explaining variations in transnational activism is cultural practices. Gujaratis and Pakistanis often live in extended family households whose members pool resources with one another. Each group also has a way to invent kinship ties that widen the family circle to include people not related by blood. When Valadarenses name someone their compadre or the godfather of their child, they are signaling a sense of mutual responsibility and obligation to that person. When second-generation Gujarati and Pakistani youngsters are taught to call their adult family friends "auntie" or "uncle," their parents are extending the family boundaries as well. When Gujaratis call their first cousins "cousin brothers," they express a similar tight bond and agreed-on set of mutual commitments. Sixty-eight-year-old Mary Doherty, describing her experience at the Doherty clan reunion, said, "All the Irish are related, you know. The older ones can tell you how. You might be the sixth cousin but it doesn't matter. You are still part of the same family. It was interesting to go to the reunion and after everybody got talking, we knew where we fit. We didn't really know the people, but we knew where we fit in this maze."

This cultural capacity to name and label someone as family, or to highlight the closeness between certain types of kin, influences a group's ability to engage transnationally. If family ties take precedence over other kinds of relationships, once everyone emigrates, transnational activism is likely to decline. On the other hand, being able to create family makes a group better able to act transnationally because there will always be people to partner with at home.

In addition, embedded within each national group are ethnic and religious identities that buttress transnational ties. In the Gujarati case, a person might be an Indian, a Gujarati, a Patel, a Leuva Patel, or a Bhagat. They may also be Swaminarayan or a Swadhyayee. These subnational religious and ethnic identities motivate Gujaratis to be transnational activists on several fronts. They can pick and choose within which ethnic or religious arena they want to act on these affinities. Pakistanis have their own version of overlapping identities that fit together like the parts of a Russian nesting doll. While Pakistani national identity is a work in progress, belonging to an occupationally based clan or a particular religious lineage is not.

People from Inishowen also construct their identities in ways that encourage transnational practices. Storytelling and a reverence for history act as built-in mechanisms for transmitting information across generations. Both private businesspeople and the Irish government have gotten into the "genealogy" business. Realizing the potential rewards of "roots tourism," county governments now create heritage centers where Irish emigrants from around the globe can research their family histories. Irish universities offer master's degrees in heritage studies. Clan associations operate headquarters where staff organize reunions, sell memorabilia, and conduct customized genealogical searches on request. The accoutrements of a transnational lifestyle are readily available for purchase.

Certain values also reinforce a transnational outlook. Each group strongly proclaimed its commitment to family. This makes them constitutionally unable to walk away from relatives left behind because it would violate deeply held beliefs about right and wrong. In many cases, migrants' social circles are still so firmly bounded that people who break the rules are ostracized.[19] Gujaratis and Pakistanis also place an extremely high value on hospitality. As a result, they host a steady stream of visitors and newcomers who reinforce homeland attachments. Inishoweners also placed a premium on keeping in touch. "How many times," asks Tricia McLaughlin, a second-generation Irish American, "have I been asked if I know so and so, even though the only thing we have in common is that we both live in the United States? People just expect that you know each other because your families are from Donegal."

Finally, each group has a different relationship to place that, in turn, affects the ways in which it stays connected to the homeland. In his book *Urban Exodus*, Gerald Gamm argues that the Irish remained in Boston while the Jews fled because the Irish built schools, hospitals, and parishes that kept them there.[20] A similar dynamic also reinforces Inishoweners' ties to Donegal. Births, baptisms, marriages, and deaths are noted in the records of the local parish. The second- and third-generation Irish Americans who want to learn more about their families find easy reference materials in the parish archives and on the cemetery headstones with which to construct a relationship with Ireland. This experience, described by the same Rosemary Wahlberg I mentioned at the beginning of the book, captures the importance of place.

Peggy said now we have to find out where your father is. So I had the name of the cemetery. So off we go to find it. And when we saw it, and just to see my name. My name is Mcgrory. And I don't often see that name. I said, "Oh Peggy, it's a waste of time, my family was so poor, they didn't put stones over them when they died, they threw stones at them." She said, "You don't know anything. You always think you know everything, but you don't know a damn thing." Peggy's down on her hands and knees looking around, and she says, "Are you going to look or are you just going to stand there?" It was interesting to see the way the cemetery was laid out and then there was the holy ground where the original church had been. And then they built the larger parish, so now I'm kind of getting with the program, and she says, "What did you say the names were?" And I said, "Michael and Frances were my grandparents." And she says, "Here they are, here they are."

NOTES

Prologue

1. "United States: A hot line to heaven; George Bush and God," *Economist*, December 16, 2004.

2. See Bagby 2004; Elliot 2006.

3. All the names of the people interviewed for this book are pseudonyms.

4. In his controversial book *The Clash of Civilizations and the Remaking of World Order*, Huntington (1996) suggested that the end of the Cold War would bring about a shift in the nature of world conflicts. It would not be political, economic, or ideological differences that produced global clashes but the incompatibility of cultures and traditions (especially religion). Although he "divides" the world's cultures into seven civilizations, many felt his message was really about the East versus the West, with particularly acute conflicts arising between the West and Islam.

5. This book includes the perspectives of labor migrants who speak little English and have limited job skills, and the experiences of PhDs in engineering and computer science who are founders of their own start-up companies. It is about Inishoweners, who have been coming to Boston for more than a century, and about Pakistanis, Valadarenses, and Gujaratis who have been in the United States for much less time. It is about a white group and people of color.

These pages could not have been written without help from a wonderful team of students and colleagues in each sending country. I interviewed between sixty and a hundred people from each community in the United States, and conducted at least fifty interviews with their family members and friends who stayed home. We began by getting to know a few key people who then introduced us to other immigrants. In the Pakistani case, I met Ali Khan, who invited me to a meeting of the Organization of Pakistani Entrepreneurs of North America (OPEN) and an *iftar* celebration. In the case of Inishowen, I met Father Tim, who invited me to a mother's group meeting. The women I met there then took us to church, Gaelic football games, and parties where we were introduced to other community members. In fact, my research team spent a lot of time between 1997 and 2004 at religious celebrations, political rallies, and social organization events in Massachusetts and in each sending country.

Many people generously contributed their time and energy to this project, and are anxiously awaiting the finished product. They want to know when my book about their group will come out because they want their stories to be told. But as I tried to explain many times, this is not a definitive account of the Brazilian or the Gujarati experience. Rather, I wanted to look comparatively, across experiences, to uncover common themes and emerging patterns. The strength of my effort is that it brings religion to the fore, that it offers a nuanced, complicated account of how people from different traditions actually live their faith across borders, and it illustrates how that informs their political and civic lives. It shows how the globalization of the sacred actually gets done. It is not, however, totally comparative across groups nor does it represent the experiences of the broader population.

This book is written with two different audiences in mind. I want to bring the discussions I have with my academic colleagues around the conference room table to a broader public. But I also want to contribute to ongoing debates in the social sciences about immigration and religion. This is a tall order, and both constituencies are likely to feel frustrated at some point along the way. My academic colleagues may find some of the arguments simplistic. I hope they will be satisfied by the "second book" that is included in the appendix and the notes. General readers will no doubt complain about the jargon (one friend has already warned me to "drop the transnational"). I have tried to do this wherever possible without compromising my analytic and conceptual goals. Despite the risks, I stand by my decision to reach out to several constituencies simultaneously. I believe strongly in sociology's public role, which my discipline has often backed away from, and the urgent need to have a more informed conversation about religion, immigration, and public life.

1   Redefining the Boundaries of Belonging

1. Eck 2001; Marty 1997; Wuthnow 1998, 2005; Wolfe 2003. They argue that America's sacred texts, like the Constitution, laid the groundwork for religious diversity to flourish. In the 1960s and 1970s, the civil rights and antiwar movements simply transformed this "culture of pluralism" into something mainstream.

2. Quoted from an interview with Bob Abernathy, *Religion and Ethics Newsweekly*, episode 535, May 3, 2002, produced by Thirteen/WNET New York. Available at http://www.pbs.org/wnet/religionandethics/transcripts/535.html.

3. My book is part of a growing body of work that looks at religion from a transnational perspective. Some of this research focuses on how migrants use religion during the migration journey and the process of settlement. Hagan and Ebaugh (2003), for example, draw out the connections that arise at various stages of the migration process—decision making, preparing for the trip, the journey, and the arrival—as well as the role of ethnic churches in settlement and the subsequent development of transnational linkages. Richman (2005) and McAlister (2002) examine transnational religious ties among Haitians.

Other researchers analyze institutional forms. Ebaugh and Chafetz (2002) studied the relationship between network ties among individuals, local-level corporate bodies, and international religious bodies, and found that ties frequently crossed between nodes. Yang (2002) discovered three-layered transpacific networks formed by contacts between individuals, single churches, and para–Chinese Christian churches that connected migrants in Taiwan, Hong Kong, and mainland China to their counterparts in the United States and Canada. Transnational institutional connections transformed immigrant community religious life along with the political and religious life of the home country (Kurien 2001), and enabled immigrant religious communities to exert power within their global religious systems (Yang 2002).

Other studies ask how religion encourages or impedes transnational membership. Wellmeier (1998) argued that because Guatemalan Mayans belonged to independent storefront ministries that were ethnically homogeneous, they had more energy and resources to make improvements in their hometowns. Similarly, because many members of the Protestant churches that Menjívar (1999) looked at came from the same regions of El Salvador, they also engaged in hometown-oriented activities with little conflict.

Some churches are better at generating transnational ties than others. Menjívar (1999) found that Catholic Church membership was far less conducive to transnational activism because the church wanted to emphasize pan-ethnic allegiances and feared that home-land-oriented activities might reignite schisms within the Salvadoran community. Be-longing to Charismatic, Neucatecumenal, or Cursillo movements produced similar mixed results. While Levitt (2001b) found that membership in Charismatic Catholic groups of-fered Dominican migrants a membership card that worked everywhere, Peterson, Vásquez, and Williams (2001) found that Charismatic Catholic activities encouraged indi-vidualized transnational religious practices but produced few collective transnational re-sponses. For others who also argue for the need to study religion across borders and pay attention to its multisited, multilayered production, see also Carnes and Yang 2004; Rudolph and Piscatori 1997; and the January 2005 Latin American Perspectives Special Volume on the American Hemisphere, edited by Manuel A. Vásquez and Philip J. Williams.

4. Religious historian William Hutchinson explains that pluralism as it is defined today only began to be understood as such very recently—beginning in the 1920s. Prior to that, he writes, there had been moments of acceptance (tolerance) or even occasionally the welcoming (inclusion) of religious diversity, but that this differed from actual engage-ment. This distinction is important to his argument: that diversity *happened* to American religion at the beginning of the nineteenth century, but pluralism was a *conscious* effort that did not take hold until the second half of the twentieth century (2003, 4). He empha-sizes that even as we realize religious pluralism means more than mere tolerance and in-clusion, it is still a work in progress. Diana Eck adds to this discussion: *"Pluralism* is not the sheer fact of *plurality* alone, but is active engagement with plurality. Pluralism and plural-ity are sometimes used as if they were synonymous. But plurality is just diversity, plain and simple—splendid, colorful, maybe even threatening. Such diversity does not, however, have to affect me. I can observe diversity. I can even celebrate diversity, as the cliché goes. But I have to participate in pluralism. . . . Pluralism requires the cultivation of public space where we all encounter one another" (1993, 14). See also *Taking Faith Seriously* (Bane, Coffin, and Higgins 2005), a collection of essays that looks at the constructive po-tential of religion in American public life—fostering pluralism and a healthy democracy through commitment and participation.

5. See, for example, Juergensmeyer 2000; Casanova 1994; Held 1999; Vásquez and Marquardt 2003. This book builds on this crucial literature by arguing for a move beyond a cross-cultural or comparative lens where the unit of analysis is generally the national society or a "world" religion. Demerath (2001), for instance, compares the relationship be-tween religion and politics in a variety of countries, but doesn't look at how those relation-ships interact with each other. Others report on different manifestations of the same religion around the globe but not the connections between them.

Since the worldwide and often parallel "resurgence" of religion and nationalism in the 1980s (the Islamic revolution in Iran, religious and counternationalist movements in the former Soviet bloc, and so on), there has been a revival of interest in religion and national-ism. Much of this work is based on an implicit surprise: "modern" nationalism should have been secular, thus presenting a theoretical dilemma for mainstream social sciences married to a modernization paradigm (Spohn 2003, 265–66). For example, a recent article seeking to "address the absence of religion in the literature on nationalism" discusses two of the countries in this study, India and Ireland, without mentioning the relationship of their diasporas to the national conflicts (Rieffer 2003). This book makes the case for the importance of taking emigrants' transnational political activities into account.

A growing body of work uses a broader optic, generating critical insights into the role of religion in today's world and how it differs from prior experiences. These theorists emphasize the need to use the global system as the primary unit of analysis to understand contemporary social life (Beyer 2001; cf. Robertson 1991; Queen 2002).

What are the cultural and religious consequences of "thick" contemporary globalization, with its increasing velocity? First, many religions have become multicentered, which differs from their multisitedness of the past (Beyer 2001). Buddhist ideas and practices, for instance, now move with unprecedented speed to non-Asian countries, but it's not simply a move from the religion's center to periphery—it's about the emergence of multiple new centers, with regionalized Buddhist interpretations and practices, that are socioculturally particularized (Prebish and Baumann 2002, 7). Because the centers are constantly in communication with each other, East and West as well as old and new infuse and transform one another. These changes in the Buddhist worldview, from mutual encounters between Asia and the West, represent an example of a "profound mutual assimilation," displaying "hybridity all the way down" (Queen 2002, 331).

Second, if globalization is the ever-changing state of "mutability" (Beyer 2001) and we no longer have the security of an ascribed or fixed sense of self (Robertson and Chirico 1985), then several problems arise to which religion offers solutions. Robertson and Chirico (1985, 238) define two of them: the "legitimacy of the world order of societies (nations)" and "the meaning of what mankind 'really is.' " These are essentially problems of definition, both at the universal level (what is happening to my society/nation in this globalizing world?) and the level of the self (who am I as a member of this society/nation and as a member of humanity at large?). These concerns engender a paradoxical response: we search not only for particularistic identities (the local) but also for the meaning of the universal whole (the global). Thus, globalization is about the universalization of particularisms and the particularization of universalisms (Robertson 1991; cf. Beyer 2001; Casanova 2001).

These largely theoretical accounts tell us little about how religion is actually lived. Further, as Spohn (2003) asserts, globalization theories are macroparadigms that are not unlike modernization paradigms in some respects. One essentializes the global system and the other the nation-state system. Both tend to "correlate the political, socioeconomic and cultural phenomena and dimensions, instead of considering the local, national and transnational macro-micro linkages, relations and interactions" (Spohn 2003, 266). Vásquez and Marquardt (2003, 3) warn similarly that there is a danger of "glossing over the contested, uneven, and situated impact of globalization. Abstract readings of globalization risk obscuring the conflict-laden relations among global, regional, national, local, and individual actors and processes. That is why we prefer to talk about 'anchored' or 'grounded' globalization" (cf. Fox and Starn 1997; Burawoy 2000). They use case studies, as I do, to stress the significance of local places and thick descriptions.

6. According to Vásquez and Marquardt (2003, 35), religion "is one of the main protagonists in [the process] of unbinding culture from its traditional referents and boundaries and in its reattachment in new space-time configurations." Individuals use religion to create new spatiotemporal arrangements and invent new mental maps with which to locate themselves within terrains that globalization is constantly changing. See also Tweed 2002.

7. Hervieu-Léger 2000.

8. Tweed 2002; Queen 2002.

9. Precise religious statistics are almost impossible to come by. Because the U.S. Census no longer asks religiously based questions, scholars must rely on private or sectarian figures, which are sometimes small studies of varying quality. I used figures from the World Christian Database (2002, 2004) and the General Social Survey (2004) to cross-check fig-

ures from private groups that do surveys more frequently, such as the Gallup Organization, the Pew Research Center for the People and the Press, and the Pew Forum on Religion and Public Life. The variation across different surveys was anywhere from 1 to 3 percent in each category of religious preference, and slightly higher when looking at the proportion of individuals who are nonreligious, as described in the following note.

Another problem arises because of the changing use of the identifier "Christian" or "Protestant." Religions that at one time would have been labeled as such, without question, are now identified in different ways. For example, Gallup polls from 1994 report 60 percent Protestant and "Other Specific" religions (4 percent) or "Undesignated" religions (2 percent). In 2006, only 49 percent were Protestant, while the percentage of "Other Specific" religions named jumped to 10 percent and only 1 percent remained "Undesignated."

10. Again, estimates vary considerably concerning people without a religious preference for the same reasons that make the categories "Christian" or "Protestant" increasingly problematic. Some surveys simply have the ambiguous category "None" or "No Preference," while others subdivide into "Atheist," "Agonistic," or "Don't Know." Regardless of the wording or the source, however, there are a remarkable number of individuals who say they have no religion as such, up from about 7 to 8 percent in the early 1990s to anywhere between 10 to 14 percent a decade later. Kosmin, Mayer, and Keysar (2001), who place this proportion at the higher end (13.6 percent), cite that the number of adults "who do not subscribe to any religious identification" doubled from 14.3 million in 1990 to 29.4 million in 2001. Data from the General Social Survey (GSS) also support this view. A GSS Social Change Report (Smith and Kim 2005) cites the percentage of respondents whose current religion is "none" at 7.7 percent in 1990 and 14.1 percent in 2000; the 2004 GSS is even higher—14.3 percent. But a PBS survey (2002) raises some nagging questions by breaking down the "nonpreferenced" responses. Given more choices, only 2 percent were "Atheists." Another 3 percent were "Agnostic," and the same number each specifically volunteered they had "No Preference" or had "another religion." And 2 percent "didn't know" or refused to answer. All this indicates that Americans may be even more religious than we think, but in complicated ways.

11. Kosmin, Mayer, and Keysar 2001, using their figures from the 1990 National Survey of Religious Identification and the 2001 American Religious Identification Survey.

12. All the major statistical sources for current and recent figures are within small fractional percentages of one another: the World Christian Database (2002), the GSS (2004), the Pew Research Center (2002, 2004), the Gallup poll (2004 through 2006 figures), and the American Religious Identification Survey (Kosmin, Mayer, and Keysar 2001).

13. Divali is the Hindu New Year, often celebrated with a festival of lights, and the Muslim Eid al-Fitr is a celebration marking the end of the fast during Ramadan.

14. Jasso et al. 2003, 221.

15. Although secular sources vary widely on their estimates, with surveys of the general population differing by double-digit percentage points from bilingual or Latino-sponsored ones, it is safe to assume about 70 percent of Hispanics identify as Catholics (Perl, Greely, and Gray 2004). And they account for the vast majority of the church's growth in the United States—86 percent from 1970 to 2000—prompting the National Conference of Catholic Bishops (2001) to estimate that within one generation, Latinos would make up half of all U.S. Catholics. They are almost there. As of 2005, the approximately 30 million Hispanics within the nation's 69.1 million Catholics represent just over 43 percent of the nation's Catholics (figures calculated with data from USCCB 2005 and "Nation's Population One-Third Minority," U.S. Census Release, May 10, 2006, available at http://www.census.gov/Press-Release/www/releases/archives/population/006808.html).

16. Kosmin, Mayer, and Keysar 2001.

17. The researchers carrying out this work differed as to how much. Gallup polls (2004) found about 5 percent professing "Other, non-Christian religions," while the Pew Research Center's (2005b) *Trends* report showed slightly more (6.4 percent). A survey by the Barna Research Group (2004) that looked at "Religious Beliefs and Practices by Race" uncovered 11 percent "aligned with a non-Christian faith," including 45 percent among Asians.

18. Except for the influence of German Lutheranism on the predominantly Calvinist pre–Civil War religion, Protestantism largely sidestepped the "problem" of religious accommodation throughout the nineteenth and early twentieth centuries. The first and most obvious reason was that a large number of "newcomers" were Catholic. By 1860, a nation that had been virtually 100 percent Protestant in 1790 was only three-quarters so, or even 60 percent if you looked at actual church membership instead of ethnic or religious identification (Hutchinson 2003, 26–27). On an ideological level, however, "integration" was only allowed from within; "if you were a 'cultural insider,' [meaning Euro-American] you could be about as different as you wished in actual religious views" (Hutchinson 2003, 57). Yet newcomers had to become *"like us"* first—American that is, and by default Protestant—before their sectarian differences would be acceptable.

19. The extensive missionary work, which was an outgrowth of American Protestantism from the start, has not been a one-way religious export. Flows from the missionized, even if a trickle, constantly change the Christianity of the missionizers at the same time, introducing ideological conflict. In the early twentieth century, many Protestant missionaries turned their focus toward social service provision rather than conversion and also began to question some of the culturally imperialist assumptions at the root of many of their activities. In fact, more evangelically minded preachers were shocked when, in 1925, E. Stanley Jones suggested that American Christians had as much to learn from Indian Hindus as the other way around, and noted that should Indians indeed adopt Christianity, it would be different—it "will be essentially Eastern and not Western" (Gaustad and Schmidt 2002, 270).

20. See Machacek 2003; Warner 1997, 2005.

21. Bowen 2004; Gaborieau 1999.

22. Levitt 2004.

23. In fact, Bowen (2004) and Kahani-Hopkins and Hopkins (2002) argue that a Muslim transnational public sphere has been in place since the beginning of the Islamic era. The Koran urges followers to turn away from localized deities and worship the transcendent God. The caliphate is not limited to one particular region or center. As Bowen (2004, 882) concludes, "This sense of Islam's transnational character is diffuse but powerful, and it derives its power from the ways in which rituals reproduce, and histories remind Muslims of, the shared duties and practices of Muslims across political boundaries. In its impulse to refuse particularistic loyalties to ethnic groups or to a nation-state, this consciousness first and foremost creates an imagination of an Islamic community transcending specific boundaries and borders."

24. According to Tweed (2002), scholars of religion still assume that identity is singular and fixed, and characterized by a core essence. They characterize people as either adherents or nonadherents, based on their adoption of a particular set of beliefs, norms, membership, and attendance. What gets left out are those who consider themselves followers without adopting the entire package, the ways in which traditions change through contact with each other, and the hybrid forms that result. Religious identity is much more complex because religions can be functionally compartmentalized, people will mix and

match when there are no negative consequences, and even when there are negative consequences people still mix and match. See also McGuire 2003.

25. "Religious Bodies of the World with at Least 1 Million Adherents." 2003. Adherents.com. Available at http://www.adherents.com/adh_rb.html (last modified June 21, 2006).

26. The Baptist World Alliance is officially the largest organization of Baptists around the globe, with 211 Baptist Conventions (the Southern Baptists left in 2004) and approximately 110 million members (http://bwanet.org/AboutUS/index.html).

27. For more on these developments, see Jenkins 2002.

28. Eck (2001) and Harvey and Goff (2005), in fact, claim the United States is *the* most religiously diverse and complex nation on earth. Statistics support their assertion. While it is not the most religious—90 percent of the populations of Pakistan, India, Indonesia, and several countries in Africa state that "religion plays a very important role in their lives"— the United States stands alone among "wealthy" countries for the number of residents who affirm that statement (59 percent—about or nearly double that of Canada, Great Britain, and both Eastern and Western Europe [Pew 2002b]). Citing the profound secularity of even traditionally Catholic Italy (at just 27 percent), results from the first wave of the Pew Global Attitudes Project (Pew 2002a) confirm that America's religiosity is closer to that of developing nations. While a high percentage of people in some industrialized nations believe in God (56 and 65 percent of those in the United Kingdom and Russia, respectively), the United States still surpasses them, with 86 percent of the population saying they believe in a higher power (BBC 2005). When it comes to religious participation, according to the World Values Survey (Swanbrow 1997), the United States again has a higher level of church attendance than any other country at a "comparable level of development." World Values Survey researchers, along with Presser and Stinson (2004) and Chaves and Stevens (2003), offer the same caveat, however, warning that people are inclined to say they go to church far more often than they actually do. But even so, if only 20 percent attend services weekly, instead of the self-professed 44 percent, the closest country in the Westernized cohort, Canada, has much lower church attendance figures— 10 percent (Inglehart 1997).

Church attendance dropped slightly from its peak of about 50 percent in the 1950s and 1960s to the 40 to 44 percent that is seemingly the norm today (Carroll 2004). Yet the number of Americans who consider themselves members of a religious group remained steady—at about 65 to 70 percent—during the same period (Carroll 2004; Gallup 2005). In his 1998 National Congregations Survey, Chaves (2004, 3, 18–19) reported that there were three hundred thousand religious congregations in the United States, but that their distribution was skewed. Most people were associated with a large congregation, but the majority of congregations were small (a median of seventy-five persons) and struggling financially (with a median budget of $56,000). Protestant groups were, in general, experiencing significant declines in membership. Catholic membership vacillated up and down, but on average ended up the same. The Jewish population was declining slightly. The most significant growth was among non-Christian groups and non-Protestant Christians (Lyons 2005; Kosmin, Mayer, and Keysar 2001).

How is it that so many Americans are seemingly so "unchurched" yet the nation remains so religious? Scholars propose both structural and cultural explanations. Once the much-heralded secularization thesis (Hammond 1985; D. Martin 1969; Weber 1958) proved wanting, one way religious scholars explained the persistence of religion was to argue that although it had disappeared from the "public square" and was no longer a holistic social institution, it was very much alive in the hearts and minds of Americans. It had been *privatized* (Berger 1967; Luckmann 1967; Wilson 1982). Many understand this as part of a large "de-traditionalizing" trend in modernity that sacralizes the "self." Individuals now live in a culture of choice (Bellah et al. 1985; Heelas 1996; Roof 1993; Wuthnow 1998) where the individual is preeminent. Others contend that what is happening is neither secularization renamed nor privatization but a "reenchantment" with religion, or *sacralization*. This happens, in large measure, in response to religious growth and intensification, and, claims Casanova (1994), because of religion's de-privatization. He asserts that religion remains public—the sphere that was evacuated by religion is now being reinfused with it.

Regardless of their theoretical perspective, one thing most scholars agree on is that the meaning of religion for Americans has become much more malleable—it's "spiritual," "experiential," or "expressive." Stark and his colleagues (2005) believe that although as many as one-third of Americans are "unchurched," they are far from irreligious. The majority pray (only 4 percent never pray), and believe in God or a higher power (2005, 12). Roof (1999) also found that among the 14 percent of Americans who were "not religious," two-thirds claimed to be "spiritual." It is the "failure to define religion with sufficient breadth and nuance" that blinds us to what Grace Davie has called "believing nonbelongers" (quoted in Stark et al. 2005, 20; Wuthnow 1998).

If it seems that there are more questions than answers, and more theories than solid facts, it is because no theory is totally mistaken. America's deep religiosity carries with it a deep ambivalence and often outright contradictions. Religious historian E. J. Dionne states, "It isn't simply that we Americans are divided into opposing camps . . . secular and religious . . . [It's] a great ambivalence within ourselves." He cites the Pew's (2004) survey on religion in public life, which asked Americans if they wanted a president with strong religious beliefs (70 percent), on the one hand, but if they disliked politicians who talked too much about how religious they are (50 percent), on the other. Dionne uses David Brooks's term from *Bobos in Paradise*, "flexidoxy," as an apt metaphor: "Many Americans want the moral and spiritual certainty of orthodoxy, but being Americans of their age, they also want their orthodoxy to be flexible" (see event transcript from E.J. Dionne Jr.'s discussion with the Pew Forum on Religion and Public Life, *Religion Returns to the Public Square: Faith and Policy in America*, February 28, 2003, available at http://pewforum.org/events/index.php?EventID=44.

Wolfe (2003) describes these seeming contradictions in his recent work about the transformation of American religion. Although some Americans continue to define themselves by their religion, they "shape and reshape" their traditions and identities to suit their own sense of egalitarianism and personal identity (246). They want fellowship and community, but are often suspicious of the religious institutions that provide it. Finally, they find their faith highly valuable and important to their lives, yet are "reluctant to shove anything down anyone else's throat" (246). His findings about what believers actually know about the details of their faith provide a fitting capstone for this portrait of religious America— "58 percent of Americans cannot name five of the ten commandments, just under half know that Genesis is the first book of the Bible . . . and 10 percent believe that Joan of Arc was Noah's wife" (247).

For more on Muslims in the United States, see Haddad and Lummis 1987, Haddad et al. 2003, and Haddad et al. 2006.

29. Herberg 1955.

30. A uniquely open and voluntaristic marketplace also characterizes the American religious experience. There is no official state religion. Religious affiliation is not ascribed on the basis of race, ethnicity, or class. Intense competition between religious groups means that Americans enjoy a range of religious choices. We are encouraged, sociologists like

Roger Finke and Rodney Stark say, to choose our faith based on the product giving us the most satisfaction (see, for example, Finke and Stark 1992; Iannoccone 1994; Stark 1994). This generally comes in the form of congregations, which look remarkably similar across the country (Ammerman 1997a, 1). No longer established from above, by a universal church or parish structure, American religious groups tend to embody de facto congregationalism. In other words, the local religious community is made up of people who come together voluntarily, and in large part, it remains under their control (Warner 1993, 1066–67).

31. According to Ahlstrom (2004, 67), "A traveler in 1700 making his way from Boston to the Carolinas would encounter Congregationalists of varying intensity, Baptists of several varieties, Presbyterians, Quakers, and several other forms of Puritan radicalism; Dutch German and French Reformed; Swedish, Finnish and German Lutherans; Mennonites and radical pietist Anglicans; Roman Catholics; here and there a Jewish congregation; a few Rosicrucians; and of course, a vast number of the unchurched—some of them powerfully alienated from any form of institutional religion." In fact, the bitter struggles, especially between colonizers France and England, were more than "competition for empire"; they were a conflict of cultures, beneath which lay two contrasting interpretations of the Christian faith. The cultural creation of a "popish menace" remained a symbol that continued to underwrite Protestant anti-Catholicism in the United States for the better part of two centuries.

32. Hall, introduction to Ahlstrom 2004, xiii–xiv. D'Agostino (2004) offers a second example of a transnational perspective on American religious history. In his discussion of American Catholics' involvement in the "Roman Question," he dismantles a "trope" of American Catholicism that depicts it as "a quirky Protestantism, divorced from its international matrix" (3–4). Catholics throughout the world, D'Agostino argues, took up the issue of a papal state, which was seen as a "prisoner" within the kingdom of "Liberal Italy," rather than a sovereign territory of its own; "Rome, not Jerusalem, Washington, Baltimore, or Dublin, was the center of the American Catholic world from 1848 to 1940" (3). "Even within the heyday of the nation-state system, modern Catholics within states forged an "imagined community" with myths, shared symbols, and a calendar of prescribed rituals . . . and the Holy See was at the center of this community" (6).

33. Their tolerance was not as ideologically based as it might be today. The directors' motivation was successful conduct of trade and commerce without the interference of cultural or religious conflict. See Gaustad and Schmidt 2002, 74–77.

34. Even when historians acknowledge the cross-fertilization that occurred in eighteenth-century revivalism, they generally limit their focus to George Whitefield, a minister who made numerous transatlantic journeys. But O'Brien (1986, 815) suggests putting the mid-eighteenth-century awakening, led by Jonathan Edwards and his compatriots, on a continuum of Protestant evangelical development that begins with Puritans' transatlantic networks of the seventeenth century and extends to contemporary global movements. Edwards, along with key players such as Whitefield, Isaac Watts, and John Guyse, were part of an established network of evangelists that encompassed the colonies, England, Scotland, Wales, and Holland. With just ten ministers at its center, thousands of letters containing ministerial narratives and advice, testimonial and thanks from lay people, and missives organizing prayer days were transnationally disseminated. Lay persons, including financial backers and printers, contributed not simply by copying and distributing but also by founding newspapers and journals as well as doing public readings. When Edwards wrote to Boston's core member Benjamin Colman of the Northampton, Massachusetts, awakening, the letter "took on a life of its own." It immediately traveled overseas, and was soon published in London (Marsden 2003, 171–73). Many have since followed in

this mission of Christianizing the world. By World War I, the Student Volunteer Movement, created in 1886, had sent out five thousand volunteers, and saw itself replicated in Britain, Holland, Germany, Norway, Sweden, Denmark, Finland, Switzerland, and South Africa. In the last two decades, the Campus Crusade for Christ has distributed its motion picture on the life of Christ in 638 separate languages, and boasts the film has been viewed by over four billion people. Both of these groups draw on tried-and-true transnational evangelism strategies that are centuries old (Gaustad and Schmidt 2002, 266; "Jesus Film Passes 4 Billion Mark," *Christian Week*, February 6, 2001, 12).

35. Noll 2002, 2–3.

36. Noll 2002.

37. Ahlstrom 2004, 518–22.

38. Nardi and Simpson 1916; Astori 1968.

39. Bodner 1985.

40. Quoted in Tseng 1999, 31.

41. Wyman 1993.

42. Dobkin Hall 1998, 101. Norris and Inglehart (2004, 17).

43. In 1900, there were 43 generally recognized nation-states; by 1998, there were 193, and today the number is over 200 (P. Martin 2003). The number doubled (from 90 to 180) from 1960 to the mid-1990s (Held et al 1999).

44. Quoted in Bennhold 2005.

45. Other scholars have grappled with the distinction between the global and the transnational. Kearney (1995, 48) differentiates them as follows: "Whereas global processes are largely decentered from specific national territories and take place in a global space, transnational processes are anchored in and transcend one or more nation-states." Glick Schiller (1999, 96) writes that " 'global' is best reserved for processes that are not located in a single state but happen throughout the entire globe. . . . I employ the word transnational to discuss processes that extend beyond the borders of a particular state, including actors that are not states, but are shaped by the policies and institutional practices of states." For a more in-depth discussion, see Khagram and Levitt 2007.

46. For example, Held and his colleagues (1999, 16) conceptualize globalization as "a process (or set of processes) which embodies a transformation in the spatial organization of social relations and transactions generating transcontinental or interregional flows and networks of activity, interaction, and the exercise of power."

47. Silver (2003, 25–26) points out that for world-systems and world-society perspectives, "local attributes and behavior are seen as the product of a unit's location in the system. The larger system has a steamroller-like quality, transforming social relations at the local level along a theoretically expected path."

48. For an introduction to transnational migration scholarship, see Abelman 1998, 2002; Al-Ali and Koser 2002; Basch, Glick Schiller, and Szanton Blanc 1994; Caglar 2002; Duany 2000; Ebaugh and Chafetz 2002; Eckstein and Barberia 2002; Espiritu 2003; Faist 2000a, 2000b; Fitzgerald 2004; Georges 1990; Glick Schiller, Basch, and Szanton Blanc 1992; Glick Schiller and Fouron 2001; Gold 2002; Goldring 2002; Grasmuck and Pessar 1991; Guarnizo, Portes, and Haller 2003; Itzigsohn 2000; Itzigsohn, Cabral, and Medina and Vasquez 1999; Itzigsohn and Saucedo 2002, 2005; Jackson, Crang, and Dwyer 2004; Karim 2002; Kastoryano 2000; Kennedy and Roudometof 2001; Kivisto 2001; Koopmans and Statham 2001; Kyle 2000; Laguerre 1998; Landolt 2001; Levitt 2001a, 2001b; Mahler 1998; Morawska 1989, 2003; Morgan 2001; Morkavasic 1996; Nyíri 1999; Østergaard-Nielsen 2003; Portes, Guarnizo, and Landolt 1999; Portes, Guarnizo, and Haller 2002; Pries 2001; Purkayastha 2005; Raj 2003; Riccio 2001; Rouse 1992; Salih 2001; Schiffauer 1999; Sklair 2000; Skrbiš 1999; R. C. Smith 2003, 2006; M. P. Smith and Guarnizo 1998;

Van der Veer 2002; Vertovec 1999, 2002; Yeoh and Willis 1998; Yeoh, Charney, and Tong 2003; Yeoh, Willis, and Fakhri 2003; Yeoh, Huang, and Lam 2005. A transnational perspective on migration is not without its critics. See Dahinden 2005; Waldinger and Fitzgerald 2004; Lucassen 2004. For a response, see Glick Schiller and Levitt 2006.

49. Levitt 1998, 2001b.

50. World Bank 2006, 88; cf. Hussain 2005.

51. Buch and Kuckulenz 2004; World Bank 2006, 88–89.

52. Glick Schiller and Levitt 2006.

53. See Menjívar 2003; Hamilton and Chinchilla 2001.

54. Caglar 2002.

55. Levitt and Glick Schiller 2004; Morawska 2003.

56. In his book *Who Are We?* Huntington (2004, xvii) calls for Americans to "recommit themselves to the Anglo-Protestant culture, traditions, and values that have been embraced by Americans of all races, ethnicities, and religions," and warns against the dangers of "Hispanization."

57. Among sociologists of religion, the parallel debate is about whether increased religious pluralism undermines religion's social solidarity function. If the classic role of religion was as a unifying force, that ritually reinforced solidarity (Durkheim 1915), then wouldn't the potential legitimacy of alternative moralities erode the authority of them all? (Gertrude Himmelfarb, cited in Machacek 2003, 150). In reformulating what he considers America's "new religious pluralism," Machacek (2003) argues that most scholars have seen the outcome as either "bubble or Babel" (151)—assimilation or social disorder. He explains that neither has taken place because secularization and civil religion are operating at the same time (151–58).

58. See work on religious violence by Appleby 2000; Bromley and Gordon 2002; Ellens 2004; Juergensmeyer 2000; D. Martin 1997; Stern 2003.

2 Transnational Lives

1. U.S. Department of Homeland Security 2004.

2. U.S. Bureau of the Census 2000.

3. U.S. Department of Homeland Security 2004.

4. Only 13.7 percent were from Europe (Larsen 2004).

5. Saenz 2004.

6. Gibson and Lennon 2001.

7. This figure includes "race alone" or "in combination" ("in combination" indicating that the respondent checked off two or more racial categories). There are 11.6 million Asians in the "race alone" category. Lott 2004.

8. Nine out of twelve of the most popular destinations are located in the Sun Belt or the West, bringing migration patterns of the foreign and native born more in sync with each other (Spain 1999).

9. The three states that experienced more than a 200 percent change in the foreign-born population from 1990 to 2000 were Georgia, Nevada, and North Carolina; many midwestern states saw at least a 100 percent change (all figures from Malone et al. 2003). Dalla and Christensen (2005) discuss the "browning" of Midwest meatpacking communities prompted by Hispanic and Asian migrants who respond to recruiting efforts and fill labor-intensive, difficult jobs in the industry.

10. Wyman 1993.

11. Foner 2000.

12. See Portes, Guarnizo, and Haller 2002; Guarnizo, Portes, and Haller 2003.

13. See http://www.ibge.gov.br/home/estatistica/populacão/estimativa2004.

14. International Religious Freedom 2003. Most members of these sects speak in tongues, subscribe to millennialist beliefs, and believe in spiritual healing. Many highly debated explanations have been offered for Pentecostalism's dramatic increase, including alienation caused by rapid social change, class differences that heighten social marginalization, modernization that left its promises unfulfilled, and globalization (Cox 1995; Droogers 2001; Freston 2001; Lalive d'Epinay 1968; D. Martin 1990).

15. Including an estimated 1.2 million between 1985 and 1988 alone (Sales 2003).

16. Researchers, Catholic Church officials, the Brazilian consulate of Boston, and community action groups all agree that between 800,000 and 1.2 million would approximate the U.S. Brazilian population much more closely. They estimate that 150,000 to 200,000 Brazilians live in Massachusetts. In my sample, about 30 percent lived without documents in the United States, and another 6 percent stated they were on a tourist visa, without specifying its expiration date.

17. U.S. Bureau of the Census 2000; Marcuss and Borgos 2004. In 2003, the Brazilian consulate reported that there were nearly 650 Brazilian immigrant firms in New England (Martes 2004).

18. *Istoé Independente*, March 12, 1997.

19. Ministério das Relações Exteriores n.d. In countries like the Dominican Republic, it is 10 percent. The current population of Mexico is approximately 106 million, and about 10 million live outside the country (CIA 2006b). Many count not only emigrants but also their offspring, however. For example, Juan Hernández, head of the now-defunct Office for Mexicans Living Abroad, reminded Americans, "Vicente Fox sees the nation of Mexico as being one of 123 million people—100 million people within the borders, and 23 million living outside of Mexico" (quoted in Sutherland 2003). Sutherland, Howard. 2003. Mexico's northern strategy: Vicente Fox takes active measures to keep Mexico's emigrants from assimilating. Available at http://www.amconmag.com/03_10_03/feature.html.

20. Until recently, these included Minas Gerais, followed by Rio de Janeiro, São Paulo, Santa Catarina, Goiás, and Espírito Santo, although the number of source communities is expanding.

21. Levitt and de la Dehesa 2003.

22. Kocian 2005; Mineo 2005.

23. Called Yagneopavit or Upanayana, the thread ceremony was once performed only by high Hindu castes. Current readings of the Vedas suggest that the ceremony can be done for lower castes as well as girls. The thread is placed around the child, and has three knots signifying the individual soul, the individual body, and the creator. The thread ceremony is a means of initiating the child into secular and religious learning.

The Bhagat experience reveals the malleability of the caste system, and the way in which some groups have slowly reinvented themselves by imitating the customs and traditions of those above them in the social hierarchy. Four hundred years ago, the Bhagats were Shoudras, the lowest of the four categories in the Varna system, who were not twice born but were above the "pollution line" marking untouchability. Over the next two centuries, they gradually transformed themselves into Kshatriyas or the warrior caste. At that time, India was divided into hundreds of small kingdoms frequently at war with each other. Each king appointed a local leader to maintain control over and defend his territories. Loyal, brave subjects received money and privileges as a reward. The more they acquired, the more these former Shoudras could act like warriors and adapt the customs and trappings of the warrior caste. Like Kshatriyas, they could also cultivate land, which also increased their wealth. The British built on this system, calling these leaders Jagirdars, and charging them with maintaining law and order as well as collecting taxes. In the twentieth century, as India moved from feudalism to capitalism, it became more advantageous to belong to the commercial, or Vaishya or Bania, caste in Gujarat. Gujaratis are known throughout India for their business acumen, and so the Bhagats, once again, gradually assumed the activities and customs of the business caste. Many have adopted the last name Patel to signal this higher status.

24. Bhagat Samaj Vasti Ganatsi (census) 2002.

25. See population statistics by Thomas Brinkhoff "City Population (Gujarat)," available at http://www.citypopulation.de/India-Gujarat.html.

26. Sixty-year-old Kirin Patel, who now lives in Baroda, represents one example of this experience. He worked as an engineer in a sugar factory in Uganda. His uncle went in the late 1920s, recruited by the British to build railroads. His father followed in 1935. The Patel community of his youth and early adulthood was incredibly tight-knit. In Kampala, he said, if someone dropped you from a helicopter, you would have thought you were in India. On Saturdays and Sundays, all you saw were Indians, most of them Patels. Everyone would get together for marriages and religious ceremonies. "We even had the *Cha Gham* and all that." During my interview with him, he pulled out a directory, as thick as a telephone book, from his days in Uganda with "The Patels of East Africa" printed in large black letters across the cover. It did not really matter, he explained, what country you were in, as long as you were connected to the Patel community. For more historical background, see Gregory 1993.

27. On middleman minorities, see also Sowell 1991, 1994; Bonacich 1973.

28. For more on the changing Indian economy, see Denoon 1998, Thakur 1991.

29. Tara Shankar and Onkar Singh, "States Woo NRIs/PIO in Contrasting Styles," Rediff.com News, January 11, 2004, available at http://us.rediff.com/news/2004/jan/11pbd3.htm; "Dual Citizenship for PIOS May Be Launched on Jan 9," Business Line India, December 24, 2003, available at http://www.thehindubusinessline.com/2003/12/24/stories/2003122402380500.htm.

30. The third annual Pravasi Bharatiya Divas, a three-day event from January 7–9, 2005, hosted over 1,700 members of the Indian diaspora from 63 countries. With over 3,061 participants (1,300 Indian delegates participated from different regions), it was the largest to date (see http://www.moia.gov.in/showinfo.asp?linkid=156).

31. The Navratri, or the Festival of Nine Nights, is a dance festival that is both religious and cultural, devoted to the Divine Mother, who is worshipped in different forms on different days. Modi spearheaded a major, multilocation summit, Global Investor's Summit 2003: Vibrant Gujarat (September 30–October 2), to coincide with the festival. His goal was to attract not only tourists and members of the diaspora but also foreign and domestic investors: "The idea was to combine commerce and culture, trade and tradition, entrepreneurship and entertainment, and development and disaster management" (Shri Narendra Modi, "Speech Delivered on the 30th Sept 2003," available at http://www.gujaratindia.com/Media/Speeches/Ghandhidham.pdf).

32. Which in 2003 included 275 groups in the United States, 50 in Africa, and 25 in the United Kingdom (interview with Nikil Shah, Gujarati State government, July 2003).

33. These types of programs are on the increase, especially in countries that receive large sums of overseas remittances. Nearly 10 percent of those who send remittances to Latin and Central America belong to hometown association, where members of the diaspora pool their resources and work with NGOs in the homeland that promote infrastructure and social service programs in local communities (Orozco 2006). Mexico's hometown associations are a classic example, with an estimated two thousand groups throughout the United States (Leiken 2000). The U.S. group might work with a counterpart that already exists in the community or they may be the impetus for such a group's formation. Manuel

Orozco (2003) estimates that hometown associations contribute up to $60 million a year for public works projects in Mexico, above and beyond what they are already sending to their families. In response, the Mexican government instituted a "3 x 1" program whereby migrant-generated funds are matched by funds contributed at the local, state, and federal government levels. El Salvador and Guatemala have followed suit with similar matching funds programs (Goldring 2002; Orozco 2006; Popkin 2003).

34. Interestingly, the Gujarati government has received just as many requests for help with property management, land ownership, and problems with customs as it has about potential business ventures. The law stipulates that when a tenant has rented a dwelling for seven years, he cannot be evicted. Nonresidents, who live abroad for years at a time, often have trouble reclaiming their property. Because of these concerns, some are reluctant to rent their farmland, causing problems with neighbors who want access to this increasingly scarce resource. Nonresident Gujaratis look to the state to help sort things out.

35. For more on OPEN's New England chapter, see http://opennewengland.org.

36. Many of the Pakistanis in New York come from rural Punjab as well as urban centers throughout Pakistan. They tend to be less educated and less skilled than their counterparts in Massachusetts (see Tahir Mirza, "Beyond the Window," available at http://www.pakistanlink.com/letters/2003/Feb/21/01.html).

37. Jalal (1995) explains that although the religious establishment initially opposed the creation of Pakistan, once secular groups within the country began to promote their concept of nationalism, Islamic groups increasingly sought to recast Pakistan in their own religious image. The "religious divines that had so strenuously fought the creation of Pakistan were reincarnated in the official discourse of the 1980s as true heroes of the Muslim saga of suffering and sacrifice" (82). The ulema (religious scholars) abandoned their historical opposition to Pakistan as the benefits of equating national identity with the Islamic movement became increasingly evident. Most members of this first cohort came of age before this occurred.

Ziring (2003) argues that the Islamization of Pakistan came as a direct result of the civil war in 1971 that prompted many questions about national identity. The war was frequently depicted as a struggle between righteous Muslim Pakistan and evil Hindu India. "Not only was the war seen as part of a larger Indian and therefore Hindu conspiracy, but after India's invasion of the country, its defeat of the Pakistani garrison, and the humiliation suffered as a consequence of army surrender, Pakistanis found new resolve in their Islamic faith" (166). Although defeated, the Pakistani army was seen as having fought the good fight "against forces that would undo the Islamic tradition in India. The civil war and India's intervention therefore provided the Pakistani army with its true baptism, that is, a liberation war to free Pakistan from the grip of the nonbeliever" (166).

The divisive electoral politics of Bangla versus Urdu as well as the ethnocentrism advanced by Zulfikar Ali Bhutto and Sheikh Mujib that characterized the 1970s gave way to military rule of an openly devout Muslim, Zia ul Haq. Zia had been influenced by Islamic parties such as Jamaat-i-Islami, and advanced the cause of the Islamization of Pakistan through new ordinances, courts, and increased funding for madrassas (religious schools). He also supported Islamist armies fighting communists along Pakistan's western Afghan border.

During his entire military rule, Zia supported religious groups, which doubled as political parties, while banning secular political parties. The effect on Pakistan was the creation of a seemingly more religiously devoted country, but also one that was divided politically. The Islamists were less interested in heightening spirituality and more concerned about narrowing the definition of what it meant to be Pakistani.

38. Hasan and Mohib 2003.

39. Pakistani last names reveal a great deal about where their bearers come from and what their legacies might be. For one thing, Pakistan as a national identity is fairly fragile. The country is only fifty-nine years old. Eight percent are Mohajirs or immigrants whose families only arrived in this corner of the former India after partition (Library of Congress n.d.). They are Urdu-speaking and tend to be more educated than the average Pakistani. For many in that first generation, said one of their children I interviewed, "nothing about their experience says this is my people, this is my culture, this is the land where my ancestors are buried." Instead, when forced out of India, Mohajirs lost their centuries-old claim to place on which strong national identities are built. They are, though, justifiably proud of the contributions they have made to Pakistan. Several claimed that Mohajirs built Pakistan from the ground up through the businesses they created and their government service.

Being Pakistani competes with strong clan, ethnic, and religious identities that in some cases bolster national belonging, but in others take precedence over it. One is either a Sunni Muslim (77 percent), a member of the Shia Muslim community (approximately 20 percent), or an Ismaeli or a member of another sect (CIA 2006c). The Sunni community is itself divided according to a family's lineage to the Prophet. Those with the last name Syed or Sayeed, or who use these as titles preceding their surnames, for example, are said to be the Prophet's direct descendants. Usmanis are descended from one of the four khalifs: Abu Bakr, Umar, Usman, and Ali. Many Pakistanis also identify strongly with a particular ethnicity. Each province has a distinct language and culture. Within these provincial groups are also embedded clan, brotherhood, or tribal ties that until a generation or so ago, functioned as endogamous marriage communities. Punjabis, for instance, might also be Gujjars or Arains.

In 1981, the Mohajirs made up 24 percent of the population in Sindh Province, where Karachi is located. They generally identify as a unique cultural and linguistic group (Malik 1997), which is itself internally divided according to where a family came from in India. Mohajirs from Bihar, Utter Pradesh, or Delhi prefer to marry one another because they are said to share distinct cultural and personality traits. From the outset, ethnic and professional lineages were reinforced in Karachi because the various housing authorities, to which the government gave land to build homes, were organized by ethnicity. For example, one of the oldest, the Pakistani Expatriate Community Housing Society, was built for people who came from India following Partition.

The Mohajirs grew to outnumber the native Sindh population in government and professional positions. In response, the provincial government instituted a form of affirmative action, allocating jobs according to ethnicity. Intergroup relations, that until then had been fairly peaceful, soured. Following the example of their fellow Pakistanis, the Mohajirs created their own ethnic rights movement, the Muttiheda Qaumi Movement. This movement grew out of a student organization called the All Pakistan Mohajirs Students' Organization, which renamed itself in 1977 (Chitkara 1996).

40. This might be several generations actually living in the same house, two separate apartments in the same building, or separate houses in the same compound.

41. In 2004, Pakistan received $3.9 billion in worker remittances (World Bank 2006), representing about 4 percent of the country's GDP (Bouhga-Hagbel 2006). This represents a comeback, after remittances had approached $3 billion annually in the mid-1980s, and then plummeted to about $1 billion in 1999. Much money comes into the country via the hawala system. Hawala is a form of remittance where no money is actually moved between countries. The hawala system is particularly popular among South Asian Muslims, and is considered Islamic because it charges a fee rather than an interest rate on the money being transferred. Recently, however, the Pakistani government has begun to encourage

migrants to remit through the state banking system. In October 2001, remittances to Pakistan through the banking system totaled $185.5 million (Orozco 2002); currently, they average over $380 million monthly (latest data available from the State Bank of Pakistan Statistics Department, available at http://www.sbp.org.pk/ecodata/Homeremit.pdf). For more work on the impact of migrant remittances, see Adams 1998; Orozco 2002, 2006; Siddiqui and Kemal 2002.

42. Muzaffar Rizvi, "Trends since September 11," *Nation* (Pakistan), September 9, 2002, available through Lexis-Nexis Academic.

43. Adil Najam, personal communication, August 2004. Also property prices have increased an average of 25 percent all over Pakistan between 1999 and 2004 (Noshad Ali, "How Long Can Meteoric Rise of Property Prices Last?" *Daily Times* [Pakistan], October 4, 2004, available at http://www.dailytimes.com.pk/default.asp?page=story_4-10-2004_pg7_23).

44. See http://www.opf.org.pk/html/Deptt/ferc/benefit.htm.

45. Abdul Sattar Edhi, its founder, said during an interview that 30 percent of the monies he raises each year comes from the United States and the United Kingdom. People give *tzakat* or charity to him because they believe he runs an honest organization. The majority of the donors and beneficiaries are Pakistani (interview by author, September 10, 2004).

46. The latest findings (Najam 2006) are summarized in a report drafted for a workshop on diaspora philanthropy and equitable development held by the Global Equity Initiative at Harvard University in May 2006.

47. Based on giving patterns in the United States, which indicate that Americans who contribute to fulfill religious obligations give about twice as much as other households, Najam finds the Pakistani "half and half" giving comparable (see, for example, Toppe et al's 2001 report, "Giving and Volunteering in the United States 2001"). The issues that Pakistanis in America consider most important are split almost equally between poverty and helping the needy (29 percent), civil and human rights (25 percent), religion (25 percent), and education/literacy (21 percent). There is a profound distrust of formalized organizations, regardless of whether they are NGOs or educational or religious institutions. Thus, many funds go directly to family and friends, or to needy individuals, identified by kinship networks that "research" appropriate, accountable, and trustworthy causes. In fact, the vast majority of respondents felt that giving would increase significantly if people could be reassured they were giving to honest causes. The single most important consideration, not surprisingly given the post–9/11 climate in the United States, was "more clarity on U.S. laws about giving to organizations in Pakistan," followed by the desire for easier transfer mechanisms, communication, accountability, and the legitimacy of receiving organizations.

48. Carroll 1999.

49. In towns like Roxbury and Dedham, and Boston neighborhoods such as South Boston, Charlestown, Dorchester, and Jamaica Plain, the Irish traditionally predominated.

50. Ireland, in fact, has become "Exhibit A" for those who believe that entering the EU can make you richer. When Ireland "joined Europe" in 1973, its per capita income was just 62 percent of the EU average; by 2002 it was 121 percent (Ruhs 2004). Pat Cox, the Irish president of the European Parliament, said membership "turned us from a stagnant, backward, failed part of the British regional economy into a modern and prosperous European country" ("Dancing an Irish Jig," *Economist*, April 15, 2004, available at http://www.economist.com/displayStory.cfm?story_id=2597266).

51. The Irish government even allows children of Irish citizen-parents to apply for citizenship, whether the parents were born in Ireland or not ("citizenship by descent").

Many Irish Americans are doing this not just because of heritage or even to speed through customs lines but because it gives them the right to live and work in Ireland and the other EU countries, according to Joe Hackett of the Irish Embassy in Washington, DC (Sarah Max, "When One Passport Won't Do: An Estimated 40 Million Americans Are Eligible for Citizenship in Another Country. Any Takers?" CNNMoney.com, October 11, 2004, available at http://money.cnn.com/2004/10/08/real_estate/mil_life/twopassports).

52. The Fianna Fáil, literally translated as Soldiers of Destiny, is currently the largest political party in Ireland. Its association and fund-raising efforts within the United States date back prior to its founding, with peak periods in the 1960s and 1980s.

Fine Gael, approximately translated as Family of the Irish, is the second-largest political party in both the Republic of Ireland and Northern Ireland (see http://www.fine gael.com/index.cfm). Like Fianna Fáil, it also actively engages in U.S. fund-raising efforts.

Besides the mainstream parties, there is a substantial drive to raise funds for Sinn Fein, the political wing of the Irish Republican Army, primarily by its American-based support group, Friends of Sinn Fein. Donations from America have made Sinn Fein Ireland's wealthiest political party. A ban on the party fund-raising in the United States was lifted by President Bill Clinton in 1995, and since then Sinn Fein has raised more than $11 million dollars (Baldwin 2006). In addition, there is the Irish Northern Aid, a nonprofit organization that supports by "peaceful means a free and independent 32 county Republic of Ireland offering justice and equality for all of its citizens in accordance with the Proclamation of the Irish Republic issued on Easter 1916." This group "fully supports Gerry Adams and Sinn Fein in their efforts to get the peace process back on track" (see http://www.inac.org).

53. Pollack 1994.

54. Twomey (2003) argues that prior to the Second Vatican Council, the loss of political autonomy among the Irish prompted them to identify primarily as Catholics. Unlike other predominantly Catholic countries such as Poland and Italy, Catholicism was a fundamental part of the national identity.

55. Although church affiliations remain high, active participation has plummeted. Consistent with these trends, a 2002 referendum on a constitutional amendment banning abortion failed by less than 1 percent. Despite the Vatican's clear antiabortion stance, more than half the population rejected its position. The vote was 618,485 in favor of the government motion, with 629,041 against. The referendum was the fifth in twenty years, and was an effort on the part of Prime Minister Bertie Ahern to reconcile the 1983 constitutional ban on abortion and the 1992 Supreme Court decision entitling a fourteen-year-old rape victim to an abortion. See "Irish Reject Abortion Change," CNN.com, March 7, 2002, available at http://archives.cnn.com/2002/WORLD/europe/03/07/ireland.result/index.html.

56. Their activities vary along four dimensions. The first is scope. Some migrants are involved in a full gamut of economic, political, social, and religious activities. Others participate in a single arena. The former participates comprehensively while the latter is selectively engaged. Another dimension is the target. Some activities are directed at homeland goals while others are aimed at the United States. Other activities benefit members of social and political communities regardless of their address. A third dimension is frequency. Some migrants keep in touch with their homelands on a regular basis. These regular transnational activists stand in contrast to people who participate periodically when there are elections, economic crises, hurricanes and earthquakes, or important family events. The fourth dimension is class. Some migrant communities are pushed into transnational lifestyles because economic security eludes them at home and in the United States. They lack the educational, job, and language skills to be able to make it in either

place. Other groups choose to live across borders. They reap the rewards of transnational living, and avoid the costs, because of their education, language, and cultural cachet. For further discussion of different ways to conceptualize the dimensions of transnational migration, see Levitt 2001b; Guarnizo 2003; Itzigsohn 2000; Vertovec 2001.

57. To capture this, Vásquez and Marquardt (2003) call religion a "multi-scalar" phenomenon.

3 Between the Nation, the World, and God

1. Gujarati cultural organization that organizes holiday celebrations, dance recitals, and musical presentations.

2. Luiz Inácio Lula da Silva, or Lula, is Brazil's current president.

3. Many theorists emphasize a distinction between "rooted" or "rootless" cosmopolitanism (Ackerman 1994; Appiah 1998; Cohen 1993; Tarrow 2001, 2005). The primary distinction is not necessarily physical location or movement in space throughout the globe but the cognitive, affective, or ideological orientation to "home" context(s). For example, in his work on transnational activists, Tarrow asserts that cosmopolitans are not deterritorialized members of a global civil society; instead, they are "people rooted in their specific national contexts, but who engage in regular activities that require their involvement in transnational networks of contacts and conflicts" (2001, 6).

4. What Rubina describes is similar to the idea of "glocalization" as elaborated by Swyngedouw (1992, 1997) and Robertson (1991). The term originates from *dochakuka*, the Japanese practice of adapting a global institution's practices to local conditions. When in response to the call for flexible specialization Japanese corporations tailor products to local markets around the world, they are not simply selling a global, homogenized product. Rather, glocalization "sets-up power-laden tensions between heterogeneity and homogeneity, between tradition and modernity, which both global institutions and dispersed consumers must negotiate" (Vásquez and Marquardt 2003, 57). The term carries over into the religious arena perfectly. As Vásquez and Marquardt (2003) point out, Christian organizations have long practiced this—crafting symbolic goods that maintain orthodoxy but meet local needs. See also Beyer 1994, 2001.

5. Burdick (1998, 123) goes on to suggest, however, that this view is at odds with the ethnic project, "for the universalizing insistence that before Christ every human being is the same is in tension with a focus on group-centered discourse."

6. The call to prayer that is recited from mosque minarets five times a day affirms monotheism and the prophethood of Muhammad (Pickthall 1938).

7. The Pickthall (1938) version of the Koran translates chapter 3, verse 103 as, "And hold fast, all of you together, to the cable of Allah, and do not separate. And remember Allah's favor unto you: how Ye were enemies and He made friendship between your hearts so that Ye became as brothers by His grace; and [how] Ye were upon the brink of an abyss of fire, and He did save you from it. Thus Allah maketh clear His revelations unto you, that haply Ye may be guided."

8. Calhoun 2002.

9. Appiah 1998.

10. Nussbaum (1996, 5). Most references to a Stoic cosmopolitanism refer back to the famous quote by Diogenes the Cynic, who when asked from where he came replied, "I am not an Athenian or a Greek, but a citizen of the world." A cosmopolitan outlook was a cornerstone of Stoic philosophers who embraced Diogenes' idea of the *kosmou politês* (world citizen) and took it a step further into the pragmatic realm. They argued that while each of us essentially lives in two communities—the one of our birth as well as the one of human-

ity at large—our greatest ethical responsibility lies in the burden of enriching and improving the fellowship of humanity.

11. Nussbaum 1996, 9.

12. Sen 1996.

13. There are, of course, certain exceptions. Durkheim (1915, 1984) defended a secularized religion of humanity (meaning a kind of implicit, taken-for-granted public morality that would bind together all members of the society, in this case the nation, in the face of increasing social differentiation and complexity). This religion elevated the self-legislating individual—both in the concrete sense, as the law-abiding citizen of the nation-state, and in the abstract sense of representing the species being of civilized humanity—as the apex of human progress. Implicit in Saint Augustine's idea of the *City of God*, where the legacy of Roman global society would be perfected, was the idea of belonging to several communities at the same time. Martin Luther spoke of "two kingdoms"—the kingdom of Christ, inhabited by true believers who were "subject to Christ," and the kingdom of the world, where non-Christians lived under the rule of the law. He believed people could belong to the kingdom of God and contribute to the kingdom of the world at the same time, although one was clearly more important than the other (Ahern 1999). Saint Thomas Aquinas saw individuals as members of families, nation-states, and the human community, and grappled with how life could be organized across all three. The classic phrase "Every fatherland is a foreign land, and every foreign land is a fatherland" captures this notion of being at home and a stranger simultaneously.

14. See Betancourth 2004; Ghils 1992.

15. On the Jesuits, see O'Byrne 2003, 58.

16. Peter van der Veer (2002) has argued convincingly that associating religion with cosmopolitanism is not an automatic non sequitur. The cosmopolitan ideology grew out of the European Enlightenment. There was both a Christian and a liberal, progressive variety. British missionary movements taught the public about the world beyond Britain and about British Christians' imperial duty toward it. Liberal and evangelical cosmopolitanism emerged hand and hand in the colonial era. What they shared was captured by phrases like "the white man's burden," which still underlies some global charitable and developmental activism. If openness and a willingness to engage are characteristics of cosmopolitanism, one has to recognize that there are many ways to engage with the world. Appiah (1998, 92) also acknowledges, "Some cosmopolitan patriots are conservative and religious. . . . Christian cosmopolitanism is as old as the merger with the Roman Empire."

17. In contrast to the paucity of scholarship linking religious belonging to global citizenship, there is an increasing focus on religion as the source from which the *standards* for global/world citizenship can emerge. One proponent, Roman Catholic theologian and religious scholar Hans Küng (1997, 2002), describes a "global ethic," underwritten by the moral principles common to all religions, as an ethical minimum for the "universal civilization" of a "world century." It is not a clash of civilizations on a grand scale that we need worry about but rather the clashes that occur in local or particular contexts, "all sorts of cultural and religious conflicts between specific countries or in a specific country often even in the same city, the same street, the same school"; thus, there will be "no peace among nations until there is peace among religions" (2002, 134). Even secular conceptions of universal human rights often acknowledge the religious basis in their moral construction. For example, O'Byrne (2003, 71) states that the ideas contained "within this Western discourse [of human rights], such as equality, liberty, and even property, are found in many of the world's major religions, and not just in the West." See also Küng and Hassan 1997; Küng and Moltmann 1990; Ven, Dreyer, and Pieterse 2004; van der Veer 2002.

18. See, for example, Bauböck 1994, 2003; Fox 2005; Turner 1993, 2001a; October 2005

special issue of *Political Science and Politics* on "Changing Citizenship Theory and Practice," with essays by Seyla Benhabib, Rainer Bauböck, Riva Kastoryano, Ahiwa Ong, and others.

19. See Kymlicka and Norman 1994; Sassen 1999; Basok 2004; Turner 2001b.

20. Bauböck 1994; Habermas 1998.

21. Chidester 2003; Isin and Wood 1999; Werbner 2000; Yuval-Davis 1999.

22. Habermas 1998; Jones and Gaventa 2002.

23. Mouffe 1992. See also Sewell (1992) and his notion of transposibility—that social actors are agents because they occupy multiple structures and can import resources and schemas from one to another. Minow (1997) calls identities "intersectional" because we are always many things at the same time—female, white, Catholic, disabled, daughter, and so on.

24. Each individual experiences and expresses different forms as well as combinations of citizenship (Isin and Wood 1999). They participate and make claims at various sites and levels of social interaction. They decide what spaces and scales of citizenship matter most (Cornwall and Gaventa 2001, 54). For example, when a woman demands changes in the health care system, she expresses a form of social-gendered citizenship. When she fights for changes in World Trade Organization policies, she acts as a global economic citizen. She has different expectations about what she should give and receive from the many institutions that shape her life. She is included on the basis of one status and excluded on the basis of another (Jones and Gaventa 2002).

4   Values and Practices

1. In fact, some scholars call into question the very category religion, and ask us to critically explore the power and history behind the use of this term. Asad (1993, 29), for example, argues that religion as a conceptual category was superimposed on to colonial subjects, writing, "There cannot be a universal definition of religion, not only because its constituent elements and relationships are historically specific, but because the definition is itself the historical product of discursive processes." He states that "anthropologists who seek to describe rather than to moralize will consider each tradition on its own terms—even as it has come to be reconstructed by modern forces—in order to compare and contrast it with others" (200). Hinduism, in particular, was never a unified canon. This becomes evident when we compare how the members of the three Hindu communities in this study talk about the key components of their faith. See also J. Smith 1982; Bhabha 1990.

2. The types of religiosity I encountered differed along three broad dimensions—people's orientations toward truth, identity, and action—and the boundaries they constructed between themselves and others as a result. The first was how much they believed in one enduring religious truth that their faith encapsulated. Some people described religious traditions incorporating a fixed set of values and practices that could not be tampered with, while others felt that individuals and communities should not be afraid to question, pick and choose, and transform what they believe in. The second was how people constructed their individual and group identities in response to that truth. Some felt that faith was there to provide a moral compass and behavioral guidelines, while others felt it was about achieving greater self-satisfaction. And finally, given how people construct their religious truths, and the normative individual and group identities that follow, the third axis of variation concerns how groups relate to the broader society. Some interpreted their faith as a call to look inwardly and create a mini moral world that reflects its own values and

only cares for its own. Others heard it as a call to reach out to the larger society. See also McRoberts 2003.

3. Wolfe 2003, 2.

4. Halal meat is known by the Arabic term *zhabiha*, and has been slaughtered in the proper Islamic manner involving slitting the throat and removing all blood from the animal.

5. What people say when they convert to Islam.

6. This, again, is similar to what Wolfe (2003) argues about native-born Americans. Although many of the people he interviewed did not know what was in the Bible, their beliefs and commitments remained strong. As in politics, people who participate (believers) may not know the "fine print. Both commitments come . . . 'tax-free'; citizenship and salvation go to those pure in spirit, not necessarily to those who can cite either the constitution or the Bible chapter and verse" (247).

7. The mainstream view in the sociology and economics of religion that has dominated from the late 1980s until recently sees the American religious panorama as an open and unregulated "marketplace" where consumers choose the "product" that will provide the highest satisfaction based on the associated costs and benefits. In this paradigm, rival churches and denominations compete for congregants in the religiously pluralistic environment of the United States. Ironically, it is not always what a particular group offers religious consumers but sometimes what it requires of its clientele. For example, Iannaccone (1994, 1998) argues that Dean Kelly's 1972 book *Why Conservative Churches Are Strong* still holds true today. Utilizing economic models, Iannaccone shows how organizational strictness increases commitment, raises levels of participation, and enables a group to provide more benefits to current and potential members, thus offering a competitive advantage over other churches (1998, 269–71).

It is also the highly individualistic environment in the United States, which appears to support the basic assumption of *homo economicus*—that people make rational choices in order to maximize their utility (in other words, their happiness and satisfaction). This perspective emerged to explain America's persistent religiosity compared to the declining religiosity of Europe and other industrial countries. Religion has not disappeared—it has simply been reworked to meet the needs of a nation of individually minded consumers living in a culture of choice. For example, Roof (1993, 1999) studied baby boomers and found that nearly half "drop out" of organized religion at some point. But while some return to the fold, many others "privatize" their experience, becoming a "generation of seekers" in a spiritual marketplace, searching for what will best suit their own particular needs (on privatization, cf. Bellah et al. 1985; Berger 1967; Wuthnow 1998). For an introduction to rational choice theory in religion, see, among others, Finke and Stark 1992; Iannoccone 1992, 1994; Stark 1994; Stark and Bainbridge 1987; Stark and Glock 1968. For some of the rejoinders, critiques, and clarifications, see Bruce 1999; Spickard 1998; Vásquez and Marquardt 2003; Warner 1993, 2004.

8. The Koran encourages Muslims not to delay their prayer and pray at appointed times (7:29). The tradition of the Prophet Muhammad, however, includes some leniency to permit worshippers to perform their prayers at different times in cases of hardship.

9. In their book *Vanishing Boundaries*, Hoge, Johnson, and Luidens (1994) examine the religious lives of a cohort of Presbyterian baby boomers to see how they have changed since they were confirmed in the 1950s and 1960s. The authors called the majority of those who still attend church "lay liberals." These lay liberals scored low on "orthodox" Christian beliefs, such as traditional views about the Bible, believing that Jesus is the only way to salvation, and emphasizing the next world over this one. In fact, they saw themselves as part of this world, rejecting the idea that the Bible should be taken literally or that Chris-

tianity had a monopoly on the truth. The authors of the study seem to disapprove. They implicitly measured strength of belief and commitment against a norm defined by evangelicalism. They placed less-involved, less-exclusivist practitioners in a "lapsed-practice" category that was lower on their validity scale.

Sociologist Ammerman (1997b, 2005) disagrees. Lay liberals, from her perspective, are not just watered-down evangelicals but practice a type of faith that should be taken seriously in its own right. Rather than categorizing religiosity according to what people believe, we should categorize it based on their practice. In her study of nearly two thousand individuals, in twenty-three congregations, Ammerman has identified three types of religious individuals. Twenty-nine percent of her respondents gave evangelically oriented responses. They emphasized prayer, Bible study, and witnessing as key practices. They wanted their churches to spread the word and help them resist temptation in this world while they got ready for the world to come. Nineteen percent of her respondents qualified as "activists" who stressed social action and working for justice. But more than half qualified as what she called "golden rule Christians"—individuals who said that the most important thing about being a Christian was "caring for the needy and living one's Christian values every day" (1997b, 198). They also believed that the church's primary function was to serve people in need. Golden rule Christians filled the pews of mainline, Catholic, and evangelical denominations in middle-class, suburban neighborhoods across America. As Ammerman writes, "What I am describing may in fact be the dominant form of religiosity among middle-class suburban Americans" (199). Fifty years ago, Herberg (1955) alluded to a similar phenomenon when he described a somewhat homogeneous, 1950s' blend of values he called "the American way of life" that supported the three prongs of his religious melting pot: Protestant, Catholic, and Jew. Here, I take up Ammerman's challenge to take different forms of religiosity seriously in their own right and build on her golden rule category.

10. Gans 1979.

11. Gans 1994.

12. Bellah et al. 1985.

5   A New Religious Architecture

1. National and local churches enjoy varying degrees of autonomy. Vatican II, for example, reversed a century-long trend toward centralization by acknowledging the plurality of national Catholicisms at the same time that it instituted a set of liturgical changes that homogenized Catholicism around the world (Hervieu-Léger 2000). Catholic authorities' open acceptance of local popular religious forms or *inculturation* was also taken as an indicator of a heightened tolerance for more diverse practices.

2. See Menjívar 1999; Cook 2002; Peterson, Vásquez, and Williams 2001.

3. That same year, a task force composed of religious and organizational leaders and academics recommended an increase of up to €1 million ($1.2 million) for the Irish Episcopal Commission's work with emigrants in the United States (Task Force 2002). Although they did not receive the entire amount, Foreign Minister Brian Cowen did establish the "Irish Abroad Unit" within the Ministry of Foreign Affairs in 2004, and as of July 2006 the amount earmarked for U.S. groups topped $1 million (Department of Foreign Affairs, press release, July 26, 2006, available at http://www.foreignaffairs.gov.ie/Press_Releases/20060726/2122.htm).

4. Southern and Brazilian Baptists used to meet each other at the annual congresses of the Baptist World Alliance. The Southern Baptist Convention withdrew from the alliance in June 2004.

5. Groups of devotees (Satsangees) have been getting together informally to hold Satsang Sabhas in each other's homes throughout England since the 1960s (see http://www.swaminarayan.info/events/leicesterutsav/history.asp). According to its Web site, in 1976, the ISSO, headquartered in Leicester, was created "to further the Maharajashri's divine vision of creating a global Satsang network of young and old Satsangees across the continents." Presently, ISSO Europe has temples in Mariestad, Sweden, and in Leicester, Streatham (London), and Portslade (Brighton), all in the United Kingdom. Additionally, there are Swaminarayan temples in Bolton, London (Willesden, Harrow, Forest Gate, and Woolwich), Cardiff, and Oldham. The Maharajashri's dream was carried to the United States in 1978 to "meet the religious needs of the present generations, rather than the future ones," with the help of a single devotee who offered to travel all over the United States with him. The result was the creation of numerous chapters (branches) across the North American continent, including Swaminarayan temples in Weehawken (New Jersey), Boston, Chicago, Houston, and Los Angeles (http://www.swaminarayan.info/isso/isso.asp). This follows a pattern in many immigrant religions that assume a congregational form when they are transplanted to the United States. This "de facto congregationalism" (see Warner 1993, 1066–67) follows and re-creates the Protestant model of voluntary church organization with lay leadership, rather than a universal or parish structure dictated from above (Yang and Ebaugh 2001; Bankston and Zhou 2000).

6. They divided India into four regions. Ahmedabad alone has forty-two temples, organized into three areas. Leaders attend a yearly religious retreat, where they choose projects to work on together. People who want to become leaders must pass a test demonstrating their mastery of the material. The most important leaders have passed nine levels of exams. For more on BAPS, see Williams 1988, 2001. See also Barot 2002 on the Swaminarayans, and Srivastava 1998 on Swadhyaya.

7. Swadhyaya also has the Bal Sanskar Kendra for young children, the Yuva Kendra and Divine Brain Trust for older children and young adults, and the Mehila Kendra for women.

8. Transnational political parties employ a similar strategy. Young people first participate in youth groups and then in groups for young adults. Ultimately, they graduate into groups of male and female supporters, often after a political education similar to the ISSO's nine exam levels.

9. The term "flexible specialization" was first introduced by Piore and Sabel (1984).

10. Castells's depiction of the current "information age" and his multivolume work about the emergence of a network society (1996, 1997, 1998) transformed the way many scholars conceptualized identity and social relationships in a global world. Network societies do not arise in response to globalization but the other way around—globalization is the consequence of a global network society (Rantanen 2005). A network society is one where decentralized, flexible, yet connected networks provide customized services and goods. Its "social structure is made of networks powered by microelectronics-based information and communication technologies" (Castells 2004, 1). In Castells's formulation, a network has no center, just interconnected multiple "nodes" that play multiple roles. Some nodes may be more important than others, based on what they contribute to the network's goals, but all are necessary for its performance. Networks continuously evolve and adapt, adding and deleting nodes as necessary and/or useful. Exchanges of flows or streams of information circulate through and between the nodes; there is no line in the sand between receivers and senders as traditionally conceived in communication research. Nor can there be any one model for network societies, Castells adamantly asserts (cited in Rantanen 2005)—they are inherently flexible, and may exhibit more or less connectivity according to the other social structures in a given society.

11. Peterson, Vásquez, and Williams (2001) make this same argument in their study of the Charismatic Catholic Renewal Movement. While parish life is characterized by a Fordist mode of production that results in a one-size-fits-all product, the renewal movement is post-Fordist, flexibly creating a customized product that is successful because it does not challenge established hierarchies.

12. Satsang means "the company of the truth." It is a gathering of seekers who chant, meditate, and listen to scriptural teachings or readings together.

13. Although they accept the rightful inheritance of the family of the Prophet Muhammad as leader of the Muslims, Shia groups are divided over who that leader is. Disputes over time have led to the establishment of distinct branches or denominations such as Dawoodi Ismaeli or Khoja. The Masumeen Center, or the Islamic Center of Hopkinton, is a Jaafari mosque, or one that follows the Ithna Ashari tradition within Shia Islam. The Jaafari community is the largest Shia community globally, and is predominant in southern Lebanon, southern Iraq, Bahrain, and Iran. The imam of a Shia mosque is someone who is learned in that tradition but does not necessarily come from the family of the Prophet Muhammad himself.

14. Karabala is believed to be the site where Imam Ali, the nephew and son-in-law of Prophet Muhammad, was martyred.

15. Hannerz 2004.

16. This is similar to Sklair's (2000) "transnational capitalist class" that promotes the globalization of capitalism and an associated consumer culture. This emerging class includes four main factions: the corporate (business executives and local affiliates), the state (globalizing bureaucrats and politicians), the technical (globalizing professionals), and the consumerist (merchants and media). Their (primarily economic) interests are globally linked and outwardly reaching, rather than locally situated, and they share similar tastes, lifestyles, educational levels, and consumption styles. Projecting themselves as citizens of the world as well as their nations, they include individuals such as Akio Morita (the founder of Sony) and Australian-born media mogul Rupert Murdoch.

17. According to Sheth (1994), the video baghan, or the act of receiving discourse through a video, has become a ritual in itself.

6   Getting to the Other Side of the Rainbow with Faith as the Car

1. Hunter's (1991) book *The Culture Wars* described an America deeply polarized by social and political cleavages. Since then, academics and pundits have hotly debated our national differences. Some, like Wolfe (1998; cf. Baker 2004), argue that the so-called culture wars are exaggerated and that most Americans fall in the "unopinionated middle." Others, like Wuthnow (2005), find evidence of "a continuing and significant divide in American religion" that might be even bigger than what Hunter first described.

2. I am interested in religion and politics broadly defined. This chapter is more about how religion influences civic engagement than about how it influences how immigrants vote.

3. Building on Fleck's (1979) idea of "thought collectives," Zerubavel (1997, 54) calls these "thought communities," social groups that foster the development of categories and mindscapes that people share with others: "Perhaps the most striking evidence of the social nature of classification is the fact that different cultures often carve out of the same reality somewhat different islands of meaning. Not everybody who is considered 'black' in Utah or New Hampshire, for example, would necessarily be regarded as such in Puerto Rico or Brazil. Nor for that matter, are 'cancer,' 'depression' or 'viral infection' universal diagnostic categories."

4. Favell 2001. See also Davie 2007.

5. Although, in 1991, an overwhelming 92 percent of the Irish population was Roman Catholic, Inishoweners' "troubles" with their Protestant neighbors were clearly on their minds, and came up frequently in our interviews, particularly because so many families had been directly affected by them. Gujarat, where Muslims represent only 10 to 12 percent of the population, has also been a site of major communal violence in the last four decades. While sectarian violence between Sunni and Shia Muslims is what ails Pakistan of late, the specter of Hindu India still looms large.

6. Exact numbers of Muslims living in India are hard to ascertain. The India Census (2001), with which the U.S. Department of State concurs (2005), states the figure as 13.4 percent (approximately 138 million). Others, however, especially those concerned with political underrepresentation, put the estimate much higher, anywhere between 150 and 200 million, or 20 to 30 percent of the country's population (see, for example, Kamal 1997; Rahmani 2000).

7. While the Pakistani Constitution guarantees freedom for all religions, Islam is the state religion and Muslims receive preferential treatment. The 1979 implementation of Islamic criminal law, also known as the Hudood Ordinances, for example, treats the testimony of Muslims and non-Muslims differently, and requires different evidence from individuals based on their religious persuasion (U.S. Department of State 2004). Further, the Ministry of Religious Affairs spends more money per Muslim than it does on other religious minorities because it coordinates the annual hajj pilgrimage for Pakistani travelers and manages their *zakat* (charitable giving), which can be automatically deducted from a paycheck and channeled to a government account. See the Ministry of Religious Affairs Web sites for the hajj, zakat, and ushr divisions at http://www.pakistan.gov.pk/divisions/index.jsp?DivID=31&cPath=3 80).

Article forty-four of the Irish Constitution guarantees religious freedom to minorities and those without religion. It also forbids the state from supporting any religion, including the Catholic Church. The government is required to distribute aid equally among schools of all faiths. Religious instruction in schools is permitted but not required. Most primary and secondary schools are denominational, and sectarian instruction is common, although parents can have their children excused.

The Indian Constitution created a secular nation and guaranteed religious freedom to all faiths. No government office regulates religious life. Muslim personal law is recognized as a separate legal framework. While religious education is not required in state-run schools, private schools can teach religion as long as they refrain from missionary activities. Many Hindu groups, particularly Hindu nationalists, have their own schools, as do Muslim communities. Christian private schools, remnants from the colonial era, also serve a primarily Hindu student population.

Brazil established the separation of religion from politics in the late nineteenth century (Novaes 2005). Religious freedom is a guaranteed right, and the government's concordat with the Vatican is largely symbolic. There is no ministry of religious affairs nor are religious groups required to register with the state. The government allows religious instruction in state-run schools but does not require it. Nearly all religious groups are eligible for tax-exempt status, although not all are officially classified as philanthropic organizations. Groups receive public funds for providing services to the general community without a religious bias, including religious schools working in areas the state does not reach. As a result, both Catholic and Protestant churches receive state funds for their educational activities.

8. The Chamber of Deputies is one of two bodies in the Bicameral National Congress.

9. The evangelical bench is divided ideologically, and observers disagree over the

strength of its political influence. For a summary of the ebbs and flows of evangelical ascendancy in Brazil, see Novaes 2005.

10. Quoted in "Murder in the Temple," *Economist*, U.S. ed., December 18, 2004, Asia section. In his book *The Saffron Wave,* Blom Hansen (1999) chronicled the rise of Hindutva, or India's "cultural" nationalism, claiming that while in theory it is religiously inclusive, in practice it is far less so. India's democratic transformation, he argued, allowed lower castes to become politically mobilized and granted civil protections to religious minorities. Hindu nationalism successfully addressed the anxieties and desires these raised among India's large and amorphous middle class. Privileged groups, which feared losing their dominance, as well as "plebian" and impoverished groups that sought recognition through a majoritarian rhetoric of cultural pride, order, and national strength, were attracted to its message.

In Gujarat, the Sangh Parivar, the socioreligious wing of the Rashtriya Swayamsevak Sangh (RSS), supported initiatives requiring Hindus and Muslims to wear different kinds of clothing, and to have Hindu prayers be recited in state-run orphanages. The state's public school system has also been criticized for its increasingly Hindu nationalist bias. Many see the RSS as actively spreading Hindu nationalist ideologies, working through a network of organizations ranging from the parliamentary (that is, the BJP party) to the cultural, religious, and social service realms. Their activities are also allegedly supported through the long-distance nationalism of the middle- and upper-class Hindu diaspora in various countries. As Kapur (2003) points out, however, there is little evidence on which to base such claims. Even in the well-documented cases of the India Development and Relief Fund in the United States and Hindu Sewa Sangh and Sewa International in the United Kingdom, of the $18 billion that flowed into India in 2003 as remittances, the combined flows from these organizations represent less than 0.05 percent. (See "The Foreign Exchange of Hate: IDRF and the American Funding of Hindutva," available at http://stopfundinghate .org/sacw/; Awaaz: South Asia Watch, "In Bad Faith? British Charity and Hindu Extremism," 2004, available at http://www.awaazsaw.org/ibf/ibflores.pdf; report of the International Initiative for Gujarat [IIJ], available at http://www.onlinevolunteers.org/gujarat/ reports/iijg/.) But, Kapur warns, this does not mean that the Indian diaspora is not a significant supporter of the Sangh Parivar—it could be a lack of detail in the data kept about foreign contributions in India, or the obvious conclusion that those who give to extremist organizations are not likely to admit it (Kapur 2003; cf. Geithner et al. 2004).

Not everyone sees Swadhyaya and Swaminarayan as positive forces. Both communities are known throughout the United States and India for their good works. Both build hospitals and schools, and mount de-addiction campaigns. In 1997, Dadaji was awarded the Sir John Templeton Prize for Progress in Religion for his humanitarian contributions. But each group has also received its share of negative attention. The ISSO has recently been plagued by accusations of sex abuse and financial mismanagement (recent tabloid-type news headlines include: "Reserve Bank Cancels Licence of Gujarat-Based Shri Swaminarayan Co-operative Bank," *Hindustan Times*, June 8, 2005; "Fight for Control Reflects Poorly on Religious Bodies," *Hindu*, May 20, 2005; "Sex CDs: Priest Sent to Police Custody," *Hindustan Times*, February 16, 2005; "Swaminarayan Temple Priest, 3 Others Held in Sleaze Case," *Statesman* [India], February 16, 2005).

Critics accuse the Swadhyaya Parivar of similar wrongdoings, even when Dadaji was still alive. They centered around the misappropriation of organizational funds for personal use and lavish gifts as well as discrepancies in the substantial amount of money collected for victims of the Gujarat earthquake (about $4.2 million from the United States through the Devotional Associates of Yogeshwar). The latest news, though, has essentially put the Swadhyaya Parivar on trial for murder as far as the Indian and nonresident Indian media are concerned. Pankaj Trivedi, forty-three and a U.S.-based Swadhyayee who had been very active in the organization, was murdered outside a club on June 15, 2006. Many (including some local police) believe that Trivedi was killed for his criticisms of the group ("Five Held in NRI Murder Case," *Hindu,* online ed., (July 5, 2006, available at http://www.hindu.com/2006/07/05/stories/2006070518181100.htm). In early July, police arrested five members of the Swadhyaya Parivar who allegedly confessed to the murder, but it was unclear whether it had been officially sanctioned.

Further, critics from inside and outside these organizations, in the United States and India, consider them to be neo-Hindu organizations promoting the creation of an India where only Hindus are welcome. They say they are using Hinduism to keep women in their place. Evaluating this claim is beyond my scope. Human rights groups and advocacy organizations have clearly documented the fundamentalist agendas and violence perpetrated against non-Hindu minorities in India by the RSS, and facilitated by the Gujarati government (see, for example, reports by Human Rights Watch 2002; South Asian Citizens Web 2002; Dharkar 2002). But as Kapur (2003) reminds us, the connection between U.S. groups and the RSS has not been empirically established. And it would be yet another step removed to connect the giving practices of the ISSO, BAPS, and Swadhyaya with these other U.S. groups.

Setting aside the issue of financial support and focusing on ideology reveals an important aspect of transnationalism in a globalized world. What Hindutva *means* for believers in India may be substantially different for believers in the diaspora. Kamat and Mathew (2003) point out that U.S. Hindus adopt the cultural ideology of Hindutva even within (and paradoxically because of) U.S. liberal discourse since it is the perfect ethnoreligious identity to further their integration into U.S. racial politics. A multiculturalist discourse, which reifies "neglected" minorities, encourages a Hindu Americanness of this kind. Because it is also a relativist ideology, a certain amount of fundamentalism might be tolerated (Kamat and Mathew 2003, 12–13). Raj (2000) documents a similar process for young Hindus in Great Britain, but also writes that these youth use their Hindu identities to differentiate themselves from Muslims or other "Asians." Even though they don't officially endorse Hindutva, Kurien (2004b, 281) contends that there is an overlap of ideology and rhetoric within the various Hindu umbrella groups in the United States. The Hindutva category of "Hindu" becomes translated into "Indic" by Westerners (academics, in particular), and accommodates a wide variety of different and even contradictory traditions, allowing for what Williams (1992, 239) calls an "ecumenical Hinduism" that is truly "made in America."

Finally, the official line of any religious organization is often quite different than what ordinary followers believe. A classic example of this is Catholicism in the United States. An increasing number are viewed as "Cafeteria Catholics," picking and choosing among the religious doctrines they embrace. According to a recent Gallup study, there are hard-core older Catholics who attend church frequently and express beliefs that are more or less in line with official Vatican doctrine, but they are far from the majority. A considerably younger, larger group "seldom or never attend church," and take "positions on moral issues that tend to be quite at odds with official church dogma" (Newport 2005).

For a more general discussion of these debates, extending beyond the groups discussed here, see Blom Hansen 1991; Cossman and Kapur 1999; Kurien 2004a, 2004b, 2005; Poros 2001; and a special issue of *Ethnic and Racial Studies* 23, no. 3 (2000), devoted to the debates surrounding Hindu nationalism, titled "Hindutva Movements in the West: Resurgent Hinduism and the Politics of Diaspora," in particular, articles by Mukta and Bhatt (401–41), Matthew and Prashad (516–44), Raj (535–58), and Rajagopal (467–96).

11. Not only was Modi denied a diplomatic visa, the tourist/business visa he had al-

ready been granted before was revoked. According to U.S. embassy spokesperson David Kennedy, the chief minister was denied a diplomatic visa because he was not traveling for diplomatic purposes. His tourist/business visa was revoked under Section 212 (a)(2)(g) of the Immigration and Nationality Act. This section makes any foreign government official who was "responsible for or directly carried out, at any time, particularly severe violations of religious freedom" ineligible for the visa ("No entry for Modi into US: Visa denied," *India Times News Network*, March 18, 2005, available at http://timesofindia.indiatimes .com/articleshow/1055543.cms).

12. The former has randomly sampled populations covering 85 percent of the world since 1981 (Inglehart 2006), and the Pew project, which started with a benchmark study in 1991, includes face-to-face survey interviews with more than ninety thousand people in fifty nations (see http://pewglobal.org/about).

13. Esmer 2003; Inglehart and Baker 2000; Norris and Inglehart 2004; Pew Research Center 2002a.

14. Pew Research Center 2002a; Inglehart 2006.

15. Esmer 2003. In fact, the cultural changes we see in some countries as well as the persistence of a particular values package in others around sexuality, gender, and "life and death" issues (abortion, euthanasia, and suicide) is largely a product of economic conditions, not variation across "civilizations" or religion. Increasing economic development is associated with a shift away from absolute norms and values toward an increasingly rational, tolerant, and participatory outlook. As a society develops economically, levels of religiosity and sexual attitudes may change (meaning they become more liberal like the United States and Western Europe), but core political values and democratic ideals stay the same (meaning that unlike the stereotypes of developing countries, they were never "backward" or "fundamentalist" to begin with).

How do American values stack up against the rest of the world? Many believe what Swedish Nobel Prize winner Gunnar Myrdal called the "American Creed" still captures the nation's core values, "the essential dignity of the individual human being, of the equality of all men, and of certain inalienable rights to freedom, justice, and a fair opportunity" (see Myrdal et al. 1944). Answers to questions on the 2004 General Social Survey confirm these sentiments. When asked how important it was that government authorities treat everybody equally regardless of their position in society, on a scale of one (not at all) to seven (very), more than 80 percent chose the highest value. Less than 1 percent replied "not at all." But only about 70 percent felt it was realized in practice, and were "proud" of the "U.S. fair and equal treatment of all groups in society." Similarly, when asked about whether government authorities should "respect and protect the rights of minorities," over three-quarters of the sample rated this highly—a six (16 percent) or a seven (61 percent) in importance. People, both immigrants and native born, were overwhelmingly proud of America overall, however, with 95 percent answering either "very" (77 percent) or "somewhat" (17 percent). The majority are in the middle as far as their political views (38 percent), followed closely by a conservative orientation (37.7 percent), and about one-quarter are liberal (24.4 percent).

And although people in general weren't terribly interested in politics, with only 21 percent "very interested," and over 30 percent "not very" or "not at all," it is nevertheless crucial that individuals have their say. What "it takes to be a good citizen" would be "to help people in America who are worse off than yourself"—about 90 percent gave this a five, six, or seven in importance. And it extended beyond the boundaries of the United States. "To help people in the rest of the world who are worse off than yourself" was a five, six, or seven in importance to 60 percent of those surveyed, with less than 5 percent saying it was "not at all" important. Beyond equality and other political rights for people living in a democracy, "all citizens should have an adequate standard of living"—over 90 percent gave this a five, six, or seven. The single highest thing that was "very important" for a "good citizen" to do was "never to try to evade taxes"—72 percent rated this a seven.

Obeying the law, paying taxes, voting, and being active in a social or political association were also part of one's civic responsibilities, with 95, 91, 87, and 55 percent, respectively, ranking these qualities a five, six, or seven. And true to the Protestant ethic, hard work and honesty were important for getting ahead in life. In response to, "Some people say that people get ahead by their own hard work; others say that lucky breaks or help from other people are more important. Which do you think is most important?" two-thirds replied "hard work." Only 9 percent thought it was getting a break or help from others, but one-quarter realized that social capital was also important and said it was equal parts of both. Regardless of their individual efforts, however, God plays an important role—about half ask for God's help in the midst of daily activities, at least once a day, and 25 percent many times a day. Only 13.4 percent never ask for divine assistance.

16. In the United States this was more than three out of five individuals. In African countries, overwhelming majorities felt their religious leaders were a good influence on society. Japan and several European countries (Germany, Turkey, and the Czech Republic) had the most unfavorable opinions, and among Muslim publics, the results varied considerably (Pew 2002).

17. Even in the most secular realm, when people don't believe in God, religion still has an influence, "We are all atheists; but I am a Lutheran atheist and they are Orthodox atheists" (Norris and Inglehart 2004, 17, citing an Estonian colleague describing the differences between Estonians and Russians).

18. Barna Research Group, "How 'Christianized' Do Americans Want Their Country to Be?" July 26, 2004, available at http://www.barna.orgFlexPage.aspx?Page=Barna Update&BarnaUpdateID=168.

19. See note 10 earlier in this chapter.

20. See Malkin 2004; Kasinitz, Mollenkopf, and Waters 2004; Kasinitz et al. forthcoming.

21. While this is not a new idea—Durkheim (1915) long ago pointed to the benefits of group association—contemporary formulations have quickly caught on because they offer policymakers a noneconomic alternative for addressing social problems (Portes 1998). Articulated in recent years by Bourdieu (1984), Coleman (1988), Loury (1977), and others, theorizing about social capital exploded in the mid-1990s in response to Putnam's (1995) declaration that Americans were "bowling alone," and that associational life was steadily plummeting. Putnam and his collegues (Putnam 2000; Putnam, Feldstein and Cohen 2003) see the renewal of voluntary associations as critical to addressing social inequality and the lack of trust associated with ethnic diversity. Although many scholars are equally optimistic about the democratizing potential of social capital, some think that Putnam's original claims may be overstated (Skocpol 1997). Most debates about social capital scholarship center on one of two broad issues, ambiguity in its definition and/or its "cure-all" normative implications. For various critiques and debates, see, among others, Navarro 2002, Portes and Landolt 1996, Baron and Hannan 1994, Woolock 1998, and McLean, Schultz, and Steger's 2002 edited volume titled *Social Capital: Critical Perspectives on Community and "Bowling Alone"*.

22. Putnam (2000, 66). These differences have prompted some scholars to coin the term "spiritual capital," which they are working to distinguish from its "social" counterpart. Smidt (2003) argues that the social capital generated by religion is unique for several reasons. It is more durable, because religions evaluate success differently. It may also be stronger and broader in its scope of influence. Religious social relationships may be less instrumental, not following the logic of self-interest but based on the calling to help others

and advocate for people who cannot advocate for themselves. Its rewards may be transcendent rather than material, rooted in such ideas as getting to heaven through good works on earth. Finally, the religious institutional realm is one where opportunities are distributed in a relatively democratic fashion. Regardless of their socioeconomic status or educational attainment, active members learn leadership, administrative, and other skills important for civic engagement and political participation. Smidt concludes, echoing Putnam, that "religion rivals education as the most important variable related to most forms of civic engagement." See Smidt 2003, 216–18; Putnam 2000, 67. On the potential for religious social capital to operate beyond the boundaries of the church, see also the chapters by Warren, Wood, and Nemeth and Luiden in Smidt 2003.

23. Putnam and others distinguish between social capital that is "bonding" or reinforces homogeneous identities and positions, and that which is "bridging," coming from networks encompassing people from a wide spectrum of social strata and political ideologies. With regard to immigrants, some further distinguish between the effects of social capital as leverage (help in solving problems, or getting ahead in terms of employment, housing, and so on) and social capital as social support (help coping with new surroundings, small loans or child care, and emotional confidants). Hardwick 2003; cf. Hannerz 1996; Portes 1995.

24. Putnam 2000; see also Berger and Hefner 2003; Cheong 2006; Portes and Landolt 1996.

25. And whether enough bonding social capital is present depended on shared religious worldviews. Curry (2003) found that in the small communities she studied in Iowa, intimate, face-to-face interactions did not generate the trust that is normally associated with social capital. It was only in communities that combined bridging social capital with enough bonding social capital where sustainable institutions emerged. See also Halpern 2005.

26. There are major debates about how this actually works. For example, attaining civic skills may not always translate into civic engagement (Verba, Schlozman, and Brady 1995). See also Jones-Correa and Leal 2001; Lee, Pachon, and Barreto 2002; DeSipio 2002; Ebaugh and Pipes 2001; Sherman 2003.

27. Hudood means "limitations or boundaries" in Urdu, and the Hudood Ordinance deals with the realm of theft and robbery, sexual relations, and alcohol or narcotic consumption. Zina are the specific ordinances dealing with rape, fornication, and adultery, which is punishable by death. The well-known cases of Zafran Bibi, a rape victim who was sentenced to die by stoning, and Mukhtar Mai, sentenced by a tribal council to be gang raped as punishment for the alleged misconduct of her twelve-year-old brother, serve as extreme examples of its implementation. Bibi was acquitted in June 2002 on a technicality and paid a small compensation (US$8,300) by the government, and Mai was given a similar compensation after Pakistan's chief justice publicly denounced the behavior of local authorities. Mai's perpetrators swiftly received a sentence of hanging from the anti-terrorist court, but were acquitted in March 2005, only to have the highest Islamic court suspend the acquittal. They remain in custody, and Mai speaks internationally in staunch opposition to the Hudood Laws (Asian American Network against Abuse of Human Rights Web site, available at http://4anaa.org/index.htm; "Mukhtar Mai: History of a Rape Case," *BBC News*, June 28, 2005, available at http://news.bbc.co.uk/2/hi/south_asia/4620065.stm). Although as many as 95 percent of the women accused under this ordinance are ultimately acquitted, they are subject to sexual and other police abuse during the average five years they spend in jail, and more important, their reputation is sullied, leaving them open to "honor killings" by male relatives (see http://www.pakistan-facts.com/

article.php?story=20030916000445575). Of the seven thousand women currently in jail, 88 percent are accused of crimes under the Hudood Ordinance and 90 percent have no lawyer (Baldauf 2005).

28. Based on selected variables chosen from questions asked in the General Social Survey (1972–2000, 2004) over the past thirty-two years. See also Etzioni (2004), who recounts numerous surveys highlighting the agreement among different racial and ethnic groups. When some surveys do show substantial differences, the media play them up while "areas of agreement are ignored." Differences do exist, Etzioni acknowledges, but they must be seen against the background of important shared understandings on basic values, attitudes, and policies (215–16).

29. Pew Research Center 2005b. A recent Gallup poll (Jones 2005) found that on life-and-death issues such as abortion, the death penalty, and euthanasia; medical research using stem cells; or views on sex and marriage, there was virtually no difference between Protestants and Catholics who attend church weekly. In a similar poll, Catholics as a whole shared similar views to non-Catholics—there was a much larger difference *among* Catholics, depending on how often they attended church (Newport 2005).

Conclusion

1. Casanova (2006) also makes this argument with respect to Europe, noting that secular and Christian cultural identities are intertwined in complex and rarely verbalized modes among most Europeans. Davie (2007) characterizes the European situation as "believing without belonging," while Hervieu-Léger (2000) calls it "belonging without believing."

2. Ammerman 2005, 259.

3. See the Presidency of Religious Affairs (Diyanet) Web site, available at http://www .diyanet.gov.tr/english/default.asp. See also Lemmen 2000; Laurence and Vaïsse 2006.

4. Laurence and Vaïsse 2006, 264.

5. Dilek Zaptcioglu, "Turkey's Religion Council: Setting Guidelines for Islam and Politics," *Qantara.de Dialogue with the Islamic World* (online journal), October 5, 2004 http:// www.quantara.org/webcom/show_article.php/_c=476/_nr=241/i.html.

6. Laurence and Vaïsse 2006, 260–61.

7. Laurence and Vaïsse 2006, 269. See also Bouzar 2004; Geisser and Finan 2002.

8. Warner (1997) also makes this point in arguing for cultural and religious *bridges* that build a "both/and" society, rather than rigid *boundaries* that solidify one that is "either/or."

9. I borrow the term "cultural wholism" from Vásquez and Marquardt 2003.

10. Taylor and Guttman et al. 1992, 61–73.

11. In fact, recent research suggests that transnational entrepreneurs are more likely to be U.S. citizens (Portes, Guarnizo, and Haller 2002). The same organizations that promote political participation in the United States double as vehicles for political involvement back in Central and South America (Escobar 2004).

12. Saxenian 1999; Saxenian, Motoyama, and Quan 2002.

13. Niebuhr 1944, 134–35.

14. Buruma (2005) warns that the war in the Islamic world can be won only by involving moderate Muslims who are committed to liberal democracy and willing to engage with other institutions of the modern world. To see this as a war between Christendom and Islam, or the West and the Middle East, can only make things worse.

Appendix

1. I also collected data from some second-generation respondents, including 28 Irish, 13 Brazilians, 38 Gujaratis, and 3 Pakistanis. There were not enough cases, however, to warrant their "statistical" inclusion in the book. Nevertheless, in several places, I use the data from these conversations to illustrate a particular point.

2. These numbers are skewed because of the large numbers of Pakistanis who came to the United States expressly to further their education—59 compared to 24 percent from India, and 13 to 14 percent among the Irish and Brazilians.

3. Some of this work debates the social solidarity or lack thereof among Brazilian immigrants (Goza 1994; Margolis 1998; Sales 2003; Martes (2000, 2004). A second body of work looks at how Brazilian immigrants identify racially (Fleischer 2002; Marrow 2003; Martes 2004; Sales 2003). A third focuses on Brazilian American families and the status of women (DeBiaggi and Dantas 2002; Fleischer 2002; Messias 2001).

Much of this work looks at the experiences of Brazilians in Boston and corroborates the need to look transnationally to understand this experience. Galvão (2005), who has examined the economic profile of New England's Brazilian community since the mid-1990s, found that there are more than 350 Brazilian-owned businesses spread over forty Massachusetts cities, generating an estimated $180 million in tax revenue. As entrepreneurship increased, Galvão also discovered increased mobility between the United States and Brazil. Assis (1995) examined the emergence of a "culture of migration" in Valadares by studying letters that migrants in the United States sent back to their relatives and friends. Along with Goza (2004), Millman (1997), and Martes, Reis and Sales 1999, she found that the factors drawing Brazilians to Massachusetts were tales of its mid-1980s' economic boom; the existing Portuguese-speaking immigrant population (from Portugal, the Azores, and Cape Verde); and the importance of social networks. Still, when people say they came for "economic reasons," as Beserra (2003, 13) notes, it is not simply about "making money" or pursuing a "better life." Migrants, she argues, also amass cultural, social, informational, symbolic, and economic capital: "Brazilians migrate to the United States to acquire skills to survive better in a transnational English-speaking world dominated by the United States." Because they cannot achieve these standards at home, they migrate, and in turn serve as ambassadors of capitalistic development, carrying this message to those who stay behind and teaching them to become transnational capitalists too.

With a few exceptions, far less attention has been paid to the religious aspects of the Brazilian community. Sales (2003), who also studied Brazilians in Framingham, Massachusetts, interviewed Catholics and Protestants and examined the emergence of an ethnic enclave and ethnic identity. Martes (2004) looked at the role of churches, particularly evangelical ones, in business expansion. Ribeiro (1999) explored the role of religious ceremonies and festivals in affirming Brazilian identity among migrants primarily from Goiás. The "Latino Immigrants in Florida: Lived Religion, Space, and Power" project, coordinated by Manuel Vásquez and Philip Williams, studied the transnational religious lives of Brazilians, Mexicans, and Guatemalans from Florida. In their theoretical reflections, Vásquez and Marquardt (2003) emphasized the need to look "beyond congregations," and concentrate instead on religious networks, overlapping sets of relations, and exchanges of religious discourses and practices that crisscross multiple levels of geography and history, and move from the self and the local to the national, the regional, the transnational, and the global.

4. Sales 2003.

5. Margolis 1994, 88.

6. Martes 2000 and 2004. The U.S. Bureau of the Census does not include questions about religion, but according to Brazilian scholar Martes, about 60 percent of the Brazilians in Massachusetts are Catholic. Evangelical Protestants, especially among business owners, are well represented. Martes (2004) estimated that at least 58 percent belonged to a religious organization of some type, and stressed that Brazilian churches are one of the principal means of support for Brazilians in Massachusetts.

7. Jennifer Moraz, "Flight to the U.S. Brings Brazilians Pain and Promise," *Philadelphia Inquirer,* October 10, 2005, available at http://www.philly.com/mld/inquirer/news/special_packages/riverside/12862117.htm.

8. Mineo 2005; Kocian 2005; Ordonez, 2005.

9. Unlike the Brazilians and the Irish, which are "ancestry" groups, both Pakistani and Asian Indian are "race" groups for the purposes of the census. Individuals can choose to be a single race (that is, "Asian Indian alone") or more than one race ("Asian Indian alone or in any combination"). Here, I use the numbers for the state's population who answered "Asian Indian alone," since they have a higher percentage of foreign born than those who report this race in combination with some other. The logical conclusion is that a good many of the additional five thousand or so people who are Asian Indian in some combination of multiple races are second generation, and would distort any comparisons with my sample.

10. A number of the Brazilians I interviewed were undocumented U.S. residents, and thus unable to freely travel out of the country. Over one-third were in the United States illegally (29 percent) or still on a tourist visa (6 percent), going through the lengthy and difficult process of obtaining U.S. citizenship. The situation with the Irish was similar, but to a lesser degree, with 14 percent of interviewees reporting they were here illegally. Consequently, among those from India and Pakistan, where no respondents reported an illegal or tourist status, the incidence of trips home was 94 and 97 percent, respectively.

11. A slightly higher proportion of the Gujaratis gave only to the homeland (20 percent). In contrast, Valadarenses were more likely to give to U.S. causes (37 percent compared to 26 percent overall).

12. In the case of the Brazilians, it is nearly equal.

13. I cannot comment on the case of the Irish because their interview guide initially contained this question in a different form and it was inadvertently never updated to match the others. Thus, while we know that 85 percent were members (52 percent) or substantive supporters (33 percent) of social organizations, we do not know the breakdown between homeland or U.S. concerns.

14. The discrepancy between the type of church and the type of attendee comes from the fact that the remaining 10 percent said they worshipped alongside someone who was "white." There are several ways to explain this—it might reflect the respondent's racial self-identification or there may be "white" converts who belong to these congregations.

15. Guarnizo 2003; Itzigsohn and Saucedo 2002; Portes 1995; Portes and Guarnizo 1990; Portes and Rumbaut 2001.

16. Buch and Kuckulenz 2004; Eckstein and Barberia 2002; Guarnizo, Portes, and Haller 2003; Portes 2003.

17. See Mannheim 1951; Eckstein 2004; Eckstein and Barberia 2002.

18. Since democracy came to the country in 1989, Brazilians residing outside the country have been obligated to vote. Yet only a small percentage registers to vote, and the number of those eligible who actually vote is about 5 percent (IDEA 2006). Of Brazilians residing in the homeland, about 80 percent have voted in each presidential or parliamen-

tary election, with the exception of the 1989 presidential election, which had an 88.1 percent turnout (see figures by year at IDEA's country Web site for Brazil, available at http://www.idea.int/vt/country_view.cfm?CountryCode=BR).

19. This is Portes's (1998; cf. Portes and Sensenbrenner 1993) notion of "enforceable trust." Because migrants are embedded in social networks, they develop expectations about reciprocity and trust. The broader community is capable of sanctioning members who do not observe these expectations.

20. Gamm 1999.

REFERENCES

Abelman, Nancy. 1998. Towards a transnational perspective on migration: Race, class, ethnicity, and nationalism reconsidered. *American Ethnologist* 25:24–25.

———. 2002. Mobilizing Korean family ties: Cultural conversations across the border. Working Paper No. WPTC-02-11, Transnational Communities Programme, Institute of Social and Cultural Anthropology, University of Oxford. Available at www.transcomm.ox.ac.uk/working_papers.htm.

Ackerman, Bruce A. 1994. Rooted cosmopolitanism. *Ethics* 104:516–35.

Adams, Richard H., Jr. 1998. Remittances, investment, and rural asset accumulation in Pakistan. *Economic Development and Cultural Change* 47:155–73.

Ahern, Annette Jean 1999. *Berger's dual-citizenship approach to religion.* New York: Peter Lang.

Ahlstrom, Sydney E. 2004. *A religious history of the American people.* New Haven, CT: Yale University Press.

Akam, Everett Helmut. 2002. *Transnational America: Cultural pluralist thought in the twentieth century.* Lanham, MD: Rowman & Littlefield.

Al-Ali, Nadje Sadig, and Khalid Koser. 2002. *New approaches to migration? Transnational communities and the transformation of home.* London: Routledge.

Ammerman, Nancy Tatom. 1997a. *Congregation and community.* New Brunswick, NJ: Rutgers University Press.

———. 1997b. Golden rule Christianity: Lived religion in the American mainstream. In *Lived religion in America: Toward a history of practice,* ed. David D. Hall, 196–216. Princeton, NJ: Princeton University Press.

———. 2005. *Pillars of faith: American congregations and their partners.* Berkeley: University of California Press.

Appiah, Kwame Anthony. 1998. Cosmopolitan patriots. In *Cosmopolitics: Thinking and feeling beyond the nation,* ed. Pheng Cheah and Bruce Robbins, 91–117. Minneapolis: University of Minnesota Press.

Appleby, R. Scott. 2000. *The ambivalence of the sacred: Religion, violence, and reconciliation.* Lanham, MD: Rowman & Littlefield Publishers.

Asad, Talal. 1993. *Genealogies of religions: Discipline and reasons of power in Christianity and Islam.* Baltimore, MD: Johns Hopkins University Press.

Assis, Gláucia de Oliveira. 1995. Estar aqui, estar lá Estar aqui, estar lá . . . O retorno dos emigrantes valadarenses ou a construção de uma identidade transnacional? *Travessia—Revista do Migrante* 22:8–14.

Astori, Guido. 1968. Scalabrini e Bonomelli Fraternalmente uniti nell' assistenza agli emigranti italiani. *Studi Emigrazione* 5:579–86.

Bagby, Ihsan. 2004. A portrait of Detroit mosques: Muslim views on policy, politics, and religion. Clinton Township, MI: Institute for Social Policy and Understanding.

Baker, Wayne E. 2005. *America's crisis of values: Reality and perception.* Princeton, NJ: Princeton University Press.

Baldauf, Scott. 2005. Pakistani religious law challenged: Rights groups condemn ordinances that call for harsh penalties for adultery, drinking, and premarital sex. *Christian Science Monitor,* March 2. Available at http://www.csmonitor.com/2005/0302/p06s01-wosc.html.

Baldwin, Tom. 2006. US at odds with allies over bar on Sinn Fein fundraising. *The Times* (London), June 6. Available at http://www.timesonline.co.uk/article/0,,11069-2212310,00.html.

Bane, Mary Jo, Brent Coffin, and Richard Higgins, eds. 2005. *Taking faith seriously.* Cambridge, MA: Harvard University Press.

Bankston, Carl L.I., and Min Zhou. 2000. De facto congregationalism and socioeconomic mobility in Laotian and Vietnamese immigrant communities: A study of religious institutions and economic change. *Review of Religious Research* 41:453–70.

Barna Research Group. 2004. Ethnic groups differ substantially on matters of faith. Available at http://www.barna.org/FlexPage.aspx?Page=BarnaUpdate&BarnaUpdateID=169.

Baron, James N., and Michael T. Hannan. 1994. The impact of economics on contemporary sociology. *Journal of Economic Literature* 32:1111–46.

Barot, Rohit. 2002. Religion, migration and wealth creation in the Swaminarayan movement. In *The transnational family: New European frontiers and global networks, cross-cultural perspectives on women,* ed. Deborah Fahy Bryceson and Ulla Vuorela, 197–216. Oxford: Berg.

Basch, Linda, Nina Glick Schiller, and Christina Szanton Blanc, eds. 1994. *Nations unbound: Transnational projects, postcolonial predicaments, and deterritorialized nation-states.* London: Gordon and Breach.

Basok, Tanya. 2004. Human rights and citizenship: The case of Mexican citizenship in Canada. *Citizenship Studies* 8:47–64.

Bauböck, Rainer. 1994. *Transnational citizenship: Membership and rights in international migration.* Brookfield, VT: Edward Elgar Publishing Company.

———. 2003. Towards a political economy of migrant transnationalism. *International Migration Review* 37:700–23.

———. 2005. Expansive citizenship: Voting beyond territory and membership. *Political Science & Politics* 38:683–87.

BBC (British Broadcasting System). 2005. What the world thinks of god: A survey. ICM Research Limited. Available at http://news.bbc.co.uk/2/hi/programmes/wtwtgod/3518375.stm.

Bellah, Robert, Richard Madsen, William M. Sullivan, Ann Swidler, and Steven M. Tipton. 1985. *Habits of the heart: Individualism and commitment in American life.* Berkeley: University of California Press.

Bennhold, Katrin. 2005. Taking networking to the next level. *International Herald Tribune,* January 26, 1.

Berger, Peter L. 1967. *The sacred canopy: Elements of a sociological theory of religion.* Garden City, NY: Doubleday.

Berger, Peter L., and Robert W. Hefner. 2003. Spiritual capital in comparative perspective. Working paper, Metanexus Institute, Philadelphia.

Beserra, Bernadete. 2003. *Brazilian immigrants in the United States: Cultural imperialism and social class.* New York: LFB Scholarly Publishing.

Betancourth, Carlos. 2004. Cosmopolitanism and Islam. *Archis* 5. Available at http://www.archis.org/.

Beyer, Peter. 1994. *Religion and globalization.* London: Sage Publications.

———, ed. 2001. *Religion im prozess der globalisierung.* Würzburg: Ergon Verlag.

Bhabha, Homi K. 1990. Introduction: Narrating the nation. In *Nation and narration,* ed. Homi K. Bhabha, 1–7. New York: Routledge.

Bhagat Samaj Vasti Ganatsi (Census 2002), Bhagat Samaj telephone directory.

Biju, Mathew, and Vijay Prashad. 2000. The protean forms of Yankee Hindutva. *Ethnic and Racial Studies* 23:516–34.

Blom Hansen, Thomas. 1991. *The saffron wave: Democracy and Hindu nationalism in modern India.* Delhi: Oxford University Press.

Bodner, John. 1985. *The transplanted.* Bloomington: Indiana University Press.

Bonacich, Edna. 1973. A theory of middleman minorities. *American Sociological Review* 38:583–94.

Bouhga-Hagbel, Jacques. 2006. "Altruism and workers" remittances: Evidence from selected countries in the Middle East and Central Asia. International Monetary Fund Working Papers #06/130, Washington, DC.

Bourdieu, Pierre. 1984. *Distinction: A social critique of the judgment of taste.* Cambridge, MA: Harvard University Press.

Bouzar, Dounia. 2004. *"Monsieur Islam" n'existe pas: Pour une désislamisation des débats.* Paris: Hachette.

Bowen, John. 2004. Beyond migration: Islam as a transnational public space. *Journal of Ethnic and Migration Studies* 30:879–94.

Bromley, David G., and J. Gordon Melton. 2002. *Cults, religion, and violence.* Cambridge: Cambridge University Press.

Bruce, Steve. 1999. *Choice and religion: A critique of rational choice theory.* Oxford: Oxford University Press.

Buch, Claudia M., and Anja Kuckulenz. 2004. Worker remittances and capital flows to developing countries. ZEW Discussion Paper 04–31, Zentrum Fuer Europaeische Wirtschaftsforschung (ZEW)/Centre for European Economic Research, Mannheim, Germany, April. Available at http://opus.zbw-kiel.de/volltexte/2004/1857/pdf/dp0431.pdf.

Burawoy, Michael. 2000. *Global ethnography: Forces, connections, and imaginations in a postmodern world.* Berkeley: University of California Press.

Burdick, John. 1998. *Blessed Anastacia: Women, race, and popular Christianity in Brazil.* New York: Routledge.

Buruma, Ian. 2005. On tolerance in the age of terrorism. *The Bardian,* summer, 24–28.

Caglar, Ayse. 2002a. The discrete charm of dual citizenship: Citizenship ties, trust and the "pink card." In *Unraveling ties: From social cohesion to new practices of connectedness,* ed. Yehuda Elkana et al., 248–62. Frankfurt: Campus.

———. 2002b. Encountering the state in migration-driven social fields: Turkish immigrants in Europe. Habilitationsschrift (postdoctoral thesis), The Free University, Berlin.

Calhoun, Craig. 2002. The class consciousness of frequent travelers: Towards a critique of actually existing cosmopolitanism. In *Conceiving cosmopolitanism: Theory, context, and practice,* ed. Steve Vertovec and Robin Cohen, 86–110. Oxford: Oxford University Press.

Carnes, Tony, and Fenggang Yang. 2004. *Asian American religions: The making and remaking of borders and boundaries.* New York: New York University Press.

Carroll, Joseph. 2004. Religion is 'very important' to 6 in 10 Americans. Gallup News Service, June 24. Available at http://www.gallup.com/.

Carroll, Michael P. 1999. *Irish pilgrimage: Holy wells and popular Catholic devotion*. Baltimore, MD: Johns Hopkins University Press.

Casanova, José. 1994. *Public religions in the modern world*. Chicago: University of Chicago Press.

———. 2001. Religion, the new millennium, and globalization. *Sociology of Religion* 62:415–41.

———. 2006. Religion, European secular identities, and European integration. In *Religion in an expanding Europe*, ed. Timothy A. Byrnes and Peter J. Katzenstein, 65–92. Cambridge: Cambridge University Press.

Castells, Manuel. 1996. *The rise of the network society*. Cambridge, MA: Blackwell.

———. 1997. *The power of identity*. Cambridge, MA: Blackwell.

———. 2004. *The network society: A cross-cultural perspective*. Cheltenham, UK: Edward Elgar.

Cesari, Jocelyn. 2002. Islam in France: The shaping of a religious minority. In *Muslims in the West: From sojourners to citizens*, ed. Yvonne Yazbeck, 36–51. Oxford: Oxford University Press.

———. 2004. *When Islam and democracy meet: Muslims in Europe and in the United States*. New York: Palgrave Macmillan.

———. 2005. Religion and politics: Interaction, confrontation and tensions. *History and Anthropology* 16:85–96.

Chaves, Mark. 2004. *Congregations in America*. Cambridge, MA: Harvard University Press.

Chaves, Mark, and Laura Stevens. 2003. Church attendance in the United States. In *A handbook of the sociology of religion*, ed. Michele Dillon, 85–95. Cambridge: Cambridge University Press.

Cheong, Pauline Hope. 2006. Communication context, social cohesion and social capital building among Hispanic immigrant families. *Community, Work & Family* 9:367–87.

Chidester, David S. 2003. Global citizenship, cultural citizenship and world religions in religion education. In *International perspectives on citizenship, education and religious diversity*, ed. Robert Jackson, 31–50. New York: Routledge Falmer.

Chitkara, M.G. 1996. *Mohajir's Pakistan*. New Delhi: P.H. Publishing Corporation.

CIA (Central Intelligence Agency). 2006a. *The world factbook: India*. Available at https://www.cia.gov/cia/publications/factbook/geos/in.html (last updated September 7, 2006).

———. 2006b. *The world factbook: Mexico*. Available at https://www.cia.gov/cia/publications/factbook/geos/mx.html (last updated September 7, 2006).

———. 2006c. *The world factbook: Pakistan*. Available at https://www.cia.gov/cia/publications/factbook/geos/pk.html (last updated September 7, 2006).

Cohen, Mitchell. 1993. Rooted cosmopolitanism. *Dissent* 39:478–83.

Coleman, James S. 1988. Social capital in the creation of human capital. *American Journal of Sociology* 94:S95–S120.

Cook, David A. 2002. Forty years of religion across borders: Twilight of a transnational field? In Ebaugh and Chafetz 2002.

Cook Martín, David. 2000. Iglesia Cristiana Evangélica: Arriving in the pipeline. In Ebaugh and Chafetz 2000.

Cornwall, Andrea, and John Gaventa. 2001. From users and choosers to makers and shapers: Repositioning participation in social policy. *IDS Bulletin* 31:50–62.

Cossman, Brenda, and Ratna Kapur. 1999. *Secularism's last sigh? Hindutva and the (mis)rule of law*. New Delhi: Oxford University Press.

Cox, Harvey Gallagher. 1995. *Fire from heaven: The rise of Pentecostal spirituality and the reshaping of religion in the twenty-first century.* Reading, MA: Addison-Wesley.

Curry, Janel. 2003. Social capital and societal vision: A study of six communities in Iowa. In Smidt 2003, 139–52.

D'Agostino, Peter R. 2004. *Rome in America: Transnational Catholic ideology from the Risorgimento to fascism.* Chapel Hill: University of North Carolina Press.

Dahinden, J. 2005. Contesting transnationalism? Lessons from the study of Albanian migration networks from former Yugoslavia. *Global Networks* 5:191–208.

Dalla, Rochelle L., and April Christensen. 2005. Latino immigrants describe residence in rural Midwestern meatpacking communities: A longitudinal assessment of social and economic change. *Hispanic Journal of Behavioral Sciences* 27:23–42.

Davie, Grace. 2007. Pluralism, tolerance, and democracy: Theory and practice in Europe. In *Democracy and the new religious pluralism,* ed. Thomas Banchoff, 364–94. New York: Oxford University Press.

DeBiaggi, Sylvia, and Duarte Dantas. 2002. *Changing gender roles: Brazilian immigrant families in the U.S.* New York: LFB Scholarly Publishing.

Demerath, N.J. 2001. *Crossing the gods: World religions and worldly politics.* New Brunswick, NJ: Rutgers University Press.

Denoon, David B.H. 1998. Cycles in Indian economic liberalization, 1966–1996. *Comparative Politics* 31:43–60.

DeSipio, Louis. 2002. Immigrant organizing, civic outcomes: Civic engagement, political activity, national attachment, and identity in Latino immigrant communities. Working Paper 02-08, Center for the Study of Democracy, University of California, Irvine.

Dharkar, Anil. 2002. *Crimes against humanity, volume II: An inquiry into the carnage in Gujarat, findings and recommendations.* Mumbai: Citizens for Justice and Peace.

Droogers, André. 2001. Globalisation and Pentecostal success. In *Between Babel and Pentecost: Transnational Pentecostalism in Latin America and Africa,* ed. André Corten and Ruth Marshall-Fratani, 41–61. Bloomington: Indiana University Press.

Duany, Jorge. 2000. Nation on the move: The construction of cultural identities in Puerto Rico and the diaspora. *American Ethnologist* 27:5–30.

Durkheim, Emile. 1915. *The elementary forms of the religious life: A study in religious sociology.* London: George Allen & Unwin.

———. 1984. *The division of labour in society.* Basingstoke, UK: Macmillan.

Ebaugh, Helen Rose, and Janet Saltzman Chafetz, eds. 2000. *Religion and the new immigrants: Continuities and adaptations in immigrant congregations.* New York: AltaMira Press.

———, eds. 2002. *Religion across borders: Transnational immigrant networks.* Walnut Creek, CA: AltaMira Press.

Ebaugh, Helen Rose, and Paula Pipes. 2001. Immigrant congregations as social service providers: Are they safety nets for welfare reform? In *Religion and social policy for the 21st century,* ed. Paula Nesbitt, 95–110. Walnut Creek, CA: AltaMira Press.

Eck, Diana L. 1993. Challenge to pluralism (God in the newsroom). *Nieman Reports* 47:9–15.

———. 2001. *A new religious America: How a "Christian country" has now become the world's most religiously diverse nation.* New York: HarperSanFrancisco.

Eckstein, Susan. 2004. On deconstructing immigrant generations: Cohorts and the Cuban émigré experience. Working Paper, Center for Comparative Immigration Studies, University of California at San Diego. Available at www.ccis-ucsd.org/PUBLICATIONS/working_papers.htm.

Eckstein, Susan, and Lorena Barberia. 2002. Grounding immigrant generations in history: Cuban Americans and their transnational ties. *International Migration Review* 36:799–837.

Ellens, J. Harold. 2004. *The destructive power of religion: Violence in Judaism, Christianity, and Islam.* Westport, CT: Praeger.

Elliot, Andrea. 2006. After 9/11, Arab-Americans fear police acts, study finds. *New York Times,* June 12, 15.

Ellis, Marc H. 1997. *Unholy alliance: Religion and atrocity in our time.* Minneapolis, MN: Fortress Press.

Escobar, Cristina. 2004. Dual citizenship and political participation: Migrants in the interplay of United States and Colombian politics. *Latino Studies* 2:45–69.

Esmer, Yilmaz. 2003. Is there an Islamic civilization? In Inglehart 2003, 35–68.

Espiritu, Yen Le. 1992. *Asian American panethnicity: Bridging institutions and identities.* Philadelphia: Temple University Press.

———. 2003. *Home bound: Filipino lives across cultures, communities, and countries.* Berkeley: University of California Press.

Etzioni, Amitai. 2004. Assimilation to the American creed. In *Reinventing the melting pot: The new immigrants and what it means to be American,* ed. Tamar Jacoby, 211–20. New York: Basic Books.

Faist, Thomas. 2000a. Transnationalization in international migration: Implications for the study of citizenship and culture. *Ethnic and Racial Studies* 23:189–222.

———. 2000b. *The volume and dynamics of international migration and transnational social spaces.* Oxford: Clarendon Press.

Favell, Adrian. 2001. *Philosophies of integration: Immigration and the idea of citizenship in France and Britain.* New York: Palgrave.

Finke, Roger, and Rodney Stark. 1992. *The churching of America, 1776–1990: Winners and losers in our religious economy.* New Brunswick, NJ: Rutgers University Press.

Fitzgerald, David. 2004. Beyond "transnationalism": Mexican hometown politics at an American labour union. *Ethnic and Racial Studies* 27:228–47.

Fleck, Ludwik. 1979. *Genesis and development of a scientific fact.* Chicago: University of Chicago Press.

Fleischer, Soraya Resendes. 2002. *Passando a América a limpo: O trabalho de housecleaners brasileiras em Boston, Massachussets.* São Paulo: Annablume.

Foner, Nancy. 2000. *From Ellis Island to JFK: New York's two great waves of immigration.* New Haven, CT: Yale University Press.

Fox, Jonathan. 2005. Unpacking transnational citizenship. *Annual Review of Political Science* 8:171–201.

Fox, Richard Gabriel, and Orin Starn. 1997. *Between resistance and revolution: Cultural politics and social protest.* New Brunswick, NJ: Rutgers University Press.

Freston, Paul. 2001. *Evangelicals and politics in Asia, Africa, and Latin America.* Cambridge: Cambridge University Press.

Gaborieau, Marc. 1999. Transnational Islamic movements: Tablighi Jamaat in politics? *ISIM* (International Institute for the Study of Islam in the Modern World) *Newsletter* 3, July 1999, 21. Available at http://www.isim.nl/files/newsl_3.pdf.

Gallup Organization. 1976–2006. KEYWORD=Religion. In *The Gallup Brain* database. Available at http://www.galluppoll.com/.

Galvão, Heloisa Maria. 2005. Brazilian immigrants in the greater Boston area. Paper presented at the Latino Immigrants in Florida: Lived Religion, Space, and Power conference, University of Florida, Antigua, Guatemala.

Gamm, Gerald H. 1999. *Urban exodus: Why the Jews left Boston and the Catholics stayed.* Cambridge, MA: Harvard University Press.

Gans, Herbert J. 1979. Symbolic ethnicity: The future of ethnic groups and cultures in America. *Ethnic and Racial Studies* 2:1–20.

———. 1994. Symbolic ethnicity and symbolic religiosity: Towards a comparison of ethnic and religious acculturation. *Ethnic and Racial Studies* 17:577–92.

Gaustad, Edwin S., and Leigh Eric Schmidt. 2002. *The religious history of America.* San Francisco: HarperSanFrancisco.

Geisser, Vincent, and Khadija Finan. 2002. *L'islam à l'école.* Paris: Institut National des Hautes Études de Sécurité.

Geithner, Peter F., Paula D. Johnson, Lincoln C. Chen, and Harvard University Global Equity Initiative. 2004. *Diaspora philanthropy and equitable development in China and India.* Cambridge, MA: Global Equity Initiative, Asia Center.

Georges, Eugenia. 1990. *The making of a transnational community: Migration, development, and cultural change in the Dominican Republic.* New York: Columbia University Press.

Ghils, Paul. 1992. International civil society: International non-governmental organizations in the international system. *International Social Science Journal* 133:417–29.

Glick Schiller, Nina. 1999. Transmigrants and nation-states: Something old and something new in the U.S. immigrant experience. In *The handbook of international migration: The American experience,* ed. Philip Kasinitz, Charles Hirshman, and Josh DeWind, 94–119. New York: Russell Sage Foundation.

Glick Schiller, Nina, and Georges Eugene Fouron. 2001. *Georges woke up laughing: Long-distance nationalism and the search for home.* Durham, NC: Duke University Press.

Glick Schiller, Nina, and Peggy Levitt. 2006. Haven't we heard this somewhere before? A substantive review of transnational migration studies by way of a reply to Waldinger and Fitzgerald. Working Paper #06-01, Center for Migration and Development, Princeton University, Princeton, NJ.

Glick Schiller, Nina, Linda G. Basch, and Cristina Szanton Blanc. 1992. *Towards a transnational perspective on migration: Race, class, ethnicity, and nationalism reconsidered.* New York: New York Academy of Sciences.

Gold, Steven J. 2002. *The Israeli diaspora.* Seattle: University of Washington Press.

Goldring, Luin. 2002. The Mexican state and transmigrant organizations: Negotiating the boundaries of membership and participation. *Latin American Research Review* 37:55–99.

Gómez, Ileana and Manuel Vásquez. 2001. Youth gangs and religion among Salvadorans in Washington and El Salvador. In Peterson, Vásquez, and Williams 2001, 165–86.

Goza, Franklin. 1994. Brazilian immigration to North America. *International Migration Review* 28:136–52.

———. 2004. Immigrant social networks: The Brazilian case. Working Paper Series 2004–2, Center for Family and Demographic Research, Bowling Green State University, Bowling Green, OH. Available at http://www.bgsu.edu/organizations/cfdr/research/pdf/2004/2004–02.pdf.

Grasmuck, Sherri, and Patricia R. Pessar. 1991. *Between two islands: Dominican international migration.* Berkeley: University of California Press.

GSS (General Social Survey). 1972–2000. Cumulative data file. Principal investigator, James A. Davis; director and co-principal investigator, Tom W. Smith; and co-principal investigator, Peter V. Marsden. Chicago: National Opinion Research Center, producer, 2002; Storrs, CT: Roper Center for Public Opinion Research, University of Connecticut, distributor. Microcomputer format and codebook prepared and distributed by

MicroCase Corporation. Accessed through the Inter-university Consortium for Political and Social Research at http://webapp.icpsr.umich.edu/GSS/.

———. 2004. Machine-readable data file. Principal investigator, James A. Davis; director and co-principal investigator, Tom W. Smith; co-principal investigator, Peter V. Marsden. Chicago: National Opinion Research Center, producer, 2002; Storrs, CT: Roper Center for Public Opinion Research, University of Connecticut, distributor. Microcomputer format and codebook prepared and distributed by MicroCase Corporation. Accessed through the American Religious Data Archive, available at http://www.thearda.com/Archive/Files/Descriptions/GSS2004.asp.

Guarnizo, Luis Eduardo. 2003. The economics of transnational living. *International Migration Review* 37:666–99.

Guarnizo, Luis Eduardo, Alejandro Portes, and William Haller. 2003. Assimilation and transnationalism: Determinants of transnational political action among contemporary migrants. *American Journal of Sociology* 108:1211–48.

Habermas, Jürgen. 1998. *The inclusion of the other: Studies in political theory,* ed. Ciaran Cronin and Pablo De Greif. Cambridge, MA: MIT Press.

Haddad, Yvonne Yazbeck, and Adair T. Lummis. 1987. *Islamic values in the United States: A comparative study.* New York: Oxford University Press.

Haddad, Yvonne Yazbeck, Jane I. Smith, and John L. Esposito, eds. 2003. *Religion and immigration.* Walnut Creek, CA: AltaMira Press.

Haddad, Yvonne Yazbeck, Jane I. Smith, and Kathleen M. Moore. 2006. *Muslim women in America: The challenge of Islamic identity today.* New York: Oxford University Press.

Hagan, Jacqueline, and Helen Rose Ebaugh. 2003. Calling upon the sacred: Migrants' use of religion in the migration process. *International Migration Review* 37:1145–62.

Hall, Peter Dobkin. 1998. Religion and the organizational revolution in the United States. In *Sacred companies: Organizational aspects of religion and religious aspects of organizations,* ed. N.J. Demerath III, Peter Dobkin Hall, Terry Schmitt, and Rhys H. Williams, 99–115. New York: Oxford University Press.

———. 2000. Moving targets: Evangelism and the transformation of American economic life, 1870–1920. In *More money, more ministry: Evangelicals and finance in modern America,* ed. Larry Eskridge and Mark A. Noll, 141–79. Grand Rapids, MI: Eerdmans Publishing Company.

Halpern, David. 2005. *Social capital.* Cambridge: Polity.

Hamilton, Nora, and Norma Stoltz Chinchilla. 2001. *Seeking community in a global city: Guatemalans and Salvadorans in Los Angeles.* Philadelphia: Temple University Press.

Hammond, Phillip E. 1985. *The sacred in a secular age: Toward revision in the scientific study of religion.* Berkeley: University of California Press.

Hannerz, Ulf. 1996. *Transnational connections: Culture, people, places.* London: Routledge.

———. 2004. *Foreign news: Exploring the world of foreign correspondents.* Chicago: University of Chicago Press.

Hardwick, Susan W. 2003. Migration, embedded networks, and social capital: Towards theorising North American ethnic geography. *International Journal of Population Geography* 9:163–79.

Harvey, Paul, and Philip Goff, eds. 2005. *Documentary history of religion in America 1945–2000: A Columbia documentary history.* New York: Columbia University Press.

Hasan, Arif, and Masooma Mohib. 2003. Understanding slums: Case studies for the global report on human settlements—the case of Karachi, Pakistan. Karachi: Mohd. Ali Society.

Heelas, Paul. 1996. *New age movement: The celebration of the self and the sacralization of modernity.* Oxford: Blackwell.

Held, David. 1999. *Global transformations: Politics, economics, and culture.* Stanford, CA: Stanford University Press.

Held, David, Anthony McGrew, David Goldblatt, and Jonathan Perraton. 1999. *Global transformations: Politics, economics, and culture.* Stanford, CA: Stanford University Press.

Herberg, Will. 1955. *Protestant, Catholic, Jew.* Garden City, NY: Doubleday and Company.

Hervieu-Léger, Danièle. 2000. *Religion as a chain of memory.* Cambridge, UK: Polity Press.

Hoge, Dean R., Benton Johnson, and Donald A. Luidens. 1994. *Vanishing boundaries: The religion of mainline Protestant baby boomers.* Louisville, KY: Westminster/John Knox Press.

Human Rights Watch. 2002. "We have no orders to save you": State participation and complicity in communal violence in Gujarat. New York: Human Rights Watch.

Hunter, James Davison. 1991. *The culture wars: The struggle to define America.* New York: Basic Books.

Huntington, Samuel P. 1996. *The clash of civilizations and the remaking of world order.* New York: Simon & Schuster.

———. 2004. *Who are we? The challenges to America's national identity.* New York: Simon & Schuster.

Hussain, Mushtaq. 2005. Measuring migrant remittances: From the perspective of the European commission. International Technical Meeting on Measuring Migrant Remittances, World Bank, Washington, DC, January 24–25. Available at http://siteresources.worldbank.org/DATASTATISTICS/Resources/2eHussain.pdf

Hutchison, William R. 2003. *Religious pluralism in America: The contentious history of a founding ideal.* New Haven, CT: Yale University Press.

Iannaccone, Laurence R. 1992. Sacrifice and stigma: Reducing free-riding in cults, communes, and other collectives. *Journal of Political Economy* 100:271–91.

———. 1994. Why strict churches are strong. *American Journal of Sociology* 99:1180–211.

Iannaccone, Laurence R. 1998. Introduction to the economics of religion. *Journal of Economic Literature* 36:1465–96.

IDEA (International Institute for Democracy and Electoral Assistance). 2006. A preview of the forthcoming International IDEA handbook on external voting. Stockholm: International IDEA.

India Census. 2001. *The first report on religion: Census of India 2001.* Available at http://www.censusindia.net/religiondata/Summary%20Muslims.pdf, http://www.censusindia.net/religiondata/Brief_analysis.pdf

Inglehart, Ronald. 1997. *Modernization and postmodernization: Cultural, economic, and political change in 43 societies.* Princeton, NJ: Princeton University Press.

———, ed. 2003. *Human values and social change: Findings from the values surveys.* Leiden, Netherlands: Brill.

———. 2006. The worldviews of Islamic publics in global perspective. World Values Survey Research Papers 06-02, Center for the Study of Democracy, University of California, Irvine.

Inglehart, Ronald, and Wayne E. Baker. 2000. Modernization, cultural change, and the persistence of traditional values. *American Sociological Review* 65:19–51.

Isin, Engin F., and Patricia K. Wood. 1999. *Citizenship and identity.* London: Sage.

Itzigsohn, Jose. 2000. Immigration and the boundaries of citizenship: The institutions of immigrants' political transnationalism. *International Migration Review* 34:1126–54.

Itzigsohn, Jose, Carlos Dore Cabral, Esther Hernandez Medina, and Obed Vazquez. 1999.

Mapping Dominican transnationalism: Narrow and broad transnational practices. *Ethnic and Racial Studies* 22:316–39.

Itzigsohn, Jose, and Silvia Giorguli Saucedo. 2002. Immigrant incorporation and sociocultural transnationalism. *International Migration Review* 36:766–98.

———. 2005. Incorporation, transnationalism, and gender: Immigrant incorporation and transnational participation as gendered processes. *International Migration Review* 39:895–920.

Jackson, Peter, Phil Crang, and Claire Dwyer. 2004. *Transnational spaces*. London: Routledge.

Jalal, Ayesha. 1995. Conjuring Pakistan: History as official imagining. *International Journal of Middle East Studies* 27:73–89.

Jasso, Guillermina, Douglas S. Massey, Mark R. Rosenzweig, and James P. Smith. 2003. Exploring the religious preferences of recent immigrants to the United States: Evidence from the new immigrant survey pilot. In Haddad, Smith, and Esposito 2003, 217–53.

Jenkins, Philip. 2002. *The next Christendom: The rise of global Christianity*. Oxford: Oxford University Press.

Jones, Emma, and John Gaventa. 2002. Concepts of citizenship: A review. In *IDS Bibliography 19*. Brighton, UK: Institute for Development Studies.

Jones, Jeffrey M. 2005. Preaching to another church's choir? Practicing Protestants' moral views more consistent with Catholic Church. Gallup News Service, April 26. Available at http://www.gallup.com.

Jones-Correa, Michael A., and David L. Leal. 2001. Political participation: Does religion matter? *Political Research Quarterly* 54:751–70.

Juergensmeyer, Mark. 2000. *Terror in the mind of God: The global rise of religious violence*. Berkeley: University of California Press.

Kahani-Hopkins, Vered, and Nick Hopkins. 2002. "Representing" British Muslims: The strategic dimension to identity construction. *Ethnic and Racial Studies* 25:288–309.

Kamal, Feroz Mahbub Kamal. 1997. Face to face with the Indian Muslims. *Daily Inqilab*, July 3. Available at http://www.paklinks.com/gs/archive/index.php/t-19876.html, trans. Abdullah Al Amin.

Kamat, Sangeeta, and Biju Mathew. 2003. Mapping political violence in a globalized world: The case of Hindu nationalism. *Social Justice* 30:4–17.

Kapur, Devesh. 2003. Indian diasporic philanthropy: Some observations. In *Workshop on Diaspora philanthropy to China and India*. Cambridge, MA: Harvard University, Global Equity Initiative.

Karim, Karim H. 2002. *The media of diaspora: Mapping the globe*. London: Routledge.

Kasinitz, Philip, John H. Mollenkopf, and Mary C. Waters, eds. 2004. *Becoming New Yorkers: Ethnographies of the new second generation*. New York: Russell Sage Foundation.

Kasinitz, Philip, John H. Mollenkopf, Mary C. Waters, and Jennifer Holdaway. Forthcoming. *The second-generation advantage: The children of immigrants inherit the city*. Cambridge, MA: Harvard University Press.

Kastoryano, Riva. 2000. Settlement, transnational communities and citizenship. *International Social Science Journal* 52:307–12.

Kearney, Michael. 1995. The local and the global: The anthropology of globalization and transnationalism. *Annual Review of Anthropology* 24:547–65.

Kennedy, Paul T., and Victor Roudometof. 2001. Communities across borders under globalising conditions: New immigrants and transnational cultures. Working Paper No. WPTC-01-17, Transnational Communities Programme, Institute of Social and Cultural Anthropology, University of Oxford. Available at www.transcomm.ox.ac.uk/working_papers.htm.

Khagram, Sanjeev, and Peggy Levitt. 2007. *The transnational studies reader.* New York: Routledge, forthcoming.

Kivisto, Peter. 2001. Theorizing transnational immigration: A critical review of current efforts. *Ethnic and Racial Studies* 24:549–77.

Kocian, Lisa. 2005. Tempest over illegal immigrants roils town. *Boston Globe.* May 26, Globe West sec., 1.

Koopmans, Ruud, and Paul Statham. 2001. How national citizenship shapes transnationalism. *Revue Europeenne des Migrations Internationales* 17:63–100.

Kosmin, Barry A., Egon Mayer, and Ariela Keysar. 2001. American religious identification survey. Graduate Center of the City University of New York.

Küng, Hans. 1997. A global ethic in an age of globalization. *Business Ethics Quarterly* 7:17–31.

———. 2002. A global ethic for a new global order. In *Global citizenship: A critical introduction,* ed. Nigel Dower and John Williams, 133–45. New York: Routledge.

Küng, Hans, and Mohammad Kamal Hassan. 1997. *Towards a common civilization: Public lectures.* Kuala Lumpur: Institute of Islamic Understanding Malaysia (IKIM).

Küng, Hans, and Jürgen Moltmann. 1990. *The ethics of world religions and human rights.* London: SCM Press.

Kurien, Prema. 2001. Religion, ethnicity, and politics: Hindu and Muslim Indian immigrants in the United States. *Ethnic and Racial Studies* 24:263–93.

———. 2004a. Multiculturalism, immigrant religion, and diasporic nationalism: The development of an American Hinduism. *Social Problems* 51:362–85.

———. 2004b. To be or not to be South Asian: Contemporary Indian American politics. *Journal of Asian American Studies* 6:261–88.

———. 2005. Being young, brown, and Hindu: The identity struggles of second-generation Indian Americans. *Journal of Contemporary Ethnography* 34:434–69.

Kyle, David. 2000. *Transnational peasants: Migrations, networks, and ethnicity in Andean Ecuador.* Baltimore: Johns Hopkins University Press.

Kymlicka, Will, and Wayne Norman. 1994. Return of the citizen: A survey of recent work on citizenship theory. *Ethics* 104:352–81.

Laguerre, Michel S. 1998. *Diasporic citizenship: Haitian Americans in transnational America.* New York: St. Martin's Press.

Lalive d'Epinay, Christian. 1968. *El refugio de las masas: Estudio sociológico del Protestantismo Chileno.* Santiago de Chile: Editorial del Pacifico.

Landolt, Patricia. 2001. Salvadoran economic transnationalism: Embedded strategies for household maintenance, immigrant incorporation, and entrepreneurial expansion. *Global Networks* 1:217–42.

Larsen, Luke J. 2004. The foreign-born population in the United States: 2003 (current population reports, P20–551). Washington, DC: U.S. Census Bureau.

Laurence, Jonathan, and Justin Vaïsse. 2006. *Integrating Islam: Political and religious challenges in contemporary France.* Washington, DC: Brookings Institution Press.

Lee, Jongho, Harry P. Pachon, and Matt A. Barreto. 2002. Guiding the flock: Church as vehicle of Latino political participation. Annual meeting of the American Political Science Association. Boston, MA, August 28.

Leiken, Robert S. 2000. *The melting border: Mexico and Mexican communities in the United States.* Washington, DC: Center for Equal Opportunity.

Lemmen, Thomas, 2000. *Islamische organisationen in Deutschland.* Bonn, Germany: Friedrich-Ebert-Stiftung.

Levitt, Peggy. 1998. Social remittances: Migration driven local-level forms of cultural diffusion. *International Migration Review* 32:926–48.

————. 2001a. Transnational migration: Taking stock and future directions. *Global Networks* 1:195.

————. 2001b. *The transnational villagers.* Berkeley: University of California Press.

————. 2004. Redefining the boundaries of belonging: The institutional character of transnational religious life. *Sociology of Religion* 65:1–18.

Levitt, Peggy, and Rafael de la Dehesa. 2003. Transnational migration and the redefinition of the state: Variations and explanations. *Ethnic and Racial Studies* 26:587–611.

Levitt, Peggy, Josh DeWind, and Steven Vertovec. 2003. International perspectives on transnational migration: An introduction. *International Migration Review* 37:565–75.

Levitt, Peggy, and Nina Glick Schiller. 2004. Conceptualizing simultaneity: A transnational social field perspective on society. *International Migration Review* 38:1002–39.

Library of Congress, Federal Research Division. n.d. *Pakistan* (as part of the Country Studies/Area Handbook Series sponsored by the U.S. Department of the Army between 1986 and 1998).

Lott, Juanita Tamayo. 2004. Asian-American children are members of a diverse and urban population. Washington, DC: Russell Sage Foundation and Population Reference Bureau.

Loury, Glenn. 1977. A dynamic theory of racial income differences. In *Women, minorities, and employment discrimination,* ed. Phyllis A. Wallace and Annette M. LaMond, chapter 8. Lexington, MA: Lexington Books.

Lucassen, Leo. 2004. Is transnationalism compatible with assimilation? Examples from Western Europe since 1850. Paper prepared for Migration, Nations, Citizenship conference, Centre for Research in the Arts, Social Sciences, and Humanities (CRASSH), University of Cambridge.

Luckmann, Thomas. 1967. *The invisible religion: The problem of religion in modern society.* New York: Macmillan.

Lyons, Linda. 2005. Tracking religious preferences over the decades. Gallup News Service, May 24. Available at http://www.gallup.com.

Machacek, David W. 2003. The problem of pluralism. *Sociology of Religion* 64:145.

Mahler, Sarah J. 1998. Theoretical and empirical contributions toward a research agenda for transnationalism. *Transnationalism from Below* 6:64–100.

Malik, Iftikhar H. 1997. *State and civil society in Pakistan: Politics of authority, ideology, and ethnicity.* New York: St. Martin's Press.

Malkin, Victoria. 2004. Who's behind the counter? Retail workers in New York City. In Kasinitz, Mollenkopf, and Waters 2004, 114–53.

Malone, Nolan, Kaari F. Baluja, Joseph M. Costanzo, and Cynthia J. Davis. 2003. *The foreign-born population: 2000.* Washington, DC: U.S. Census Bureau.

Mannheim, Karl. 1951. Das problem der generationen. Kölner vierteljahreshefte für soziologie. In *Essays on the sociology of knowledge,* ed. Paul Kecskemeti, 309–30. New York: Oxford University Press.

Marcuss, Mamie, and Ricardo Borgos. 2004. Who are New England's immigrants? *Communities and Banking,* fall, 10–21.

Margolis, Maxine L. 1994. *Little Brazil: An ethnography of Brazilian immigrants in New York City.* Princeton, NJ: Princeton University Press.

————. 1995. Transnationalism and popular culture: The case of Brazilian immigrants in the United States. *Journal of Popular Culture* 29:29–41.

————. 1998. *An invisible minority: Brazilians in New York City.* Boston: Allyn and Bacon.

Marrow, Helen. 2003. To be or not to be (Hispanic or Latino). *Ethnicities* 3:427–64.

Marsden, George M. 2003. *Jonathan Edwards: A life.* New Haven, CT: Yale University Press.

Martes, Ana Cristina Braga. 2000. *Brasileiros nos Estados Unidos: Um estudo sobre imigrantes em Massachusetts.* São Paulo: Paz e Terra.

———. 2004. Transnational institutions and ethnic entrepreneurship. Paper presented at the conference of the Business Association of Latin American Studies, Babson College, Wellesley, MA.

Martin, David. 1969. *The religious and the secular: Studies in secularization.* New York: Schocken Books.

———. 1990. *Tongues of fire: The explosion of Protestantism in Latin America.* Oxford: Blackwell.

———. 1997. *Does Christianity cause war?* Oxford: Clarendon Press.

Martin, Philip. 2003. Economic integration and migration: The U.S.-Mexico case. World Institute for Development Economics Research, United Nations University, Helsinki.

Marty, Martin E. 1997. *The one and the many: America's struggle for the common good.* Cambridge, MA: Harvard University Press.

McAlister, Elizabeth A. 2002. *Rara! Vodou, power, and performance in Haiti and its diaspora.* Berkeley: University of California Press.

McGuire, Meredith B. 2003. Contested meanings and definitional boundaries: Historicizing the sociology of religion. In *Defining religion: Investigating the boundaries between the sacred and secular,* ed. Arthur L. Greil and David G. Bromley, 127–38. Amsterdam: JAI.

McLean, Scott L., David A. Schultz, and Manfred B. Steger. 2002. *Social capital: Critical perspectives on community and "bowling alone."* New York: New York University Press.

McRoberts, Omar M. 2003. *Streets of glory: Church and community in a black urban neighborhood.* Chicago: University of Chicago Press.

Menjívar, Cecilia. 1999. Religious institutions and transnationalism: A case study of Catholic and evangelical Salvadoran immigrants. *International Journal of Politics, Culture, and Society* 12:589–612.

———. 2003. Religion and immigration in comparative perspective: Catholic and evangelical Salvadorans in San Francisco, Washington, DC, and Phoenix. *Sociology of Religion* 64:21–45.

Messias, DeAnne K. Hilfinger. 2001. Transnational perspectives on women's domestic work: Experiences of Brazilian immigrants in the United States. *Women & Health* 33:1–29.

Millman, Joel. 1997. *The other Americans: How immigrants renew our country, our economy, and our values.* New York: Viking.

Mineo, Liz. 2005. Out of the shadows: Immigration issues made a comeback in 2004. *Framingham Metrowest Daily News.* January 2. Available at http://www.metrowestdailynews.com/localRegional/view.bg?articleid=86563

Ministério das Relações Exteriores (Ministry of External Relations). n.d. Services: Consular assistance. Available at http://www.mre.gov.br/ingles/structure/foreing_relations/services/consular.asp.

Minow, Martha. 1997. *Not only for myself: Identity, politics, and the law.* New York: The New Press.

Morawska, Ewa. 1989. Labor migrations of Poles in the Atlantic world economy, 1880–1914. *Comparative Studies in Society and History* 31:237–72.

———. 2003. Immigrant transnationalism and assimilation: A variety of combinations and the analytic strategy it suggests. In *Toward assimilation and citizenship: Immigrants in liberal nation-states,* ed. Christian Joppke and Ewa Morawska, 133–76. Basingstoke, UK: Palgrave Macmillan.

Morgan, Glenn. 2001. Transnational communities and business Systems. *Global Networks* 1:113–30.

Morokvasic, Mirjana. 1996. Entre l'est et l'ouest: Des migrations pendulaires. In *Migrants: Les nouvelles mobilités en Europe*, ed. Mirjana Morokvasic and Hedwig Rudolph, 119–58. Paris: Editions L'Hartmann.

Mouffe, Chantal. 1992. Democratic citizenship and the political community. In *Dimensions of radical democracy: Pluralism, citizenship, community*, ed. Chantal Mouffe. London: Verso.

Mugridge, Donald Henry, and Blanche Prichard McCrum. 1960. *A guide to the study of the United States of America: Representative books reflecting the development of American life and thought.* Washington, DC: Library of Congress, General Reference and Bibliography Division.

Mukta, Parita, and Chetan Bhatt. 2000. Hindutva in the West: Mapping the antinomies of diaspora nationalism. *Ethnic and Racial Studies* 23:407–41.

Myrdal, Gunnar, Richard Mauritz, Edvard Sterner, and Arnold Marshall Rose. 1944. *An American dilemma: The Negro problem and modern democracy.* New York: Harper.

Najam, Adil. 2006. Portrait of a giving community: Philanthropy as a tool for managing diaspora identity. Paper presented at the Diaspora Philanthropy and Global Equity conference, Harvard University.

Nardi, Blanche P., and A.B. Simpson. 1916. Michele Nardi, the Italian evangelist, his life and work. New York: Blanche P. Nardi.

National Conference of Catholic Bishops/United States Catholic Conference (NCCB/USCC). 2001. Hispanic growth changing the face of U.S. Catholicism. *En Marcha*, summer. Available at http://www.nccbuscc.org/hispanicaffairs/enmarcha/summer01.htm.

Nemeth, Roger J., and Donald A. Luidens. 2003. The religious beliefs of charitable giving in America: A social capital perspective. In Smidt 2003, 107–20.

Newport, Frank. 2005. U.S. Catholics vary widely on moral issues: Active Catholics much more conservative. Gallup News Service, April 8. Available at http://www.gallup.com.

Niebuhr, Reinhold. 1944. *The children of light and the children of darkness: A vindication of democracy and a critique of its traditional defence.* New York: C. Scribner's Sons.

Noll, Mark A. 2002. *The old religion in a new world: The history of North American Christianity.* Grand Rapids, MI: Eerdmans.

Norris, Pippa, and Ronald Inglehart. 2004. *Sacred and secular: Religion and politics worldwide.* Cambridge: Cambridge University Press.

Novaes, Regina. 2005. The rise of the evangelicals in Latin America. Brazil: Religion of the poor. *Le Monde Diplomatique*, April. Available at http://mondediplo.com/2005/04/15evangelists.

Nussbaum, Martha C. 1996. *For love of country: Debating the limits of patriotism*, ed. Joshua Cohen. Boston: Beacon Press.

Nyíri, Pál. 1999. *New Chinese migrants in Europe: The case of the Chinese community in Hungary.* Aldershot, UK: Ashgate.

O'Brien, Susan. 1986. A transatlantic community of saints: The great awakening and the first evangelical network, 1735–1755. *American Historical Review* 91:811–32.

O'Byrne, Darren J. 2003. *The dimensions of global citizenship: Political identity beyond the nation-state.* London: Frank Cass.

Ordonez, Franco. Volunteers sought to guard border: US officials voice concerns on effort. *Boston Globe*, July 7. Available at http://www.boston.com/news/local/articles/2005/07/07/volunteers_sought_to_guard_border/.

Orozco, Manuel. 2002. Globalization and migration: The impact of family remittances in Latin America. *Latin American Politics and Society* 44:41–66.

———. 2003. Hometown associations and their present and future partnerships: New development opportunities. Report commissioned by the U.S. Agency for International Development. Inter-American Dialogue, Washington, DC, September.

———. 2006. Diasporas, philanthropy, and hometown associations: The Central American experience. Paper presented at the Diaspora Philanthropy and Global Equity conference, Harvard University.

Østergaard-Nielsen, Eva. 2003. The politics of migrants' transnational political practices. *International Migration Review* 37:760–86.

PBS (Public Broadcasting System). 2002. Exploring religious America: A poll conducted for *Religion & Ethics NewsWeekly* and *U.S. News & World Report*. Available at http://www.pbs.org/wnet/religionandethics/week534/specialreport.html.

Perl, Paul, Jennifer Z. Greely, and Mark M. Gray. 2005. How many Hispanics are Catholic? A review of survey data and methodology. Center for Applied Research in the Apostolate, Georgetown University, Washington, DC. Available at http://cara.georgetown.edu/Hispanic%20Catholics.pdf.

Peterson, Anna Lisa, Manuel A. Vásquez, and Philip J. Williams, eds. 2001. *Christianity, social change, and globalization in the Americas*. New Brunswick, NJ: Rutgers University Press.

PEW Research Center. 2002a. *What the world thinks in 2002: First major report of the PEW Global Attitudes Project*. Washington, DC: Pew Research Center for the People and the Press.

———. 2002b. Among wealthy nations . . . U.S. stands alone in its embrace of religion. News release, Pew Global Attitudes Project, Washington, DC, December 19.

———. 2004. Views of Islam remain sharply divided: Plurality see Islam as more likely to encourage violence. News release, Pew Forum on Religion and Public Life, Washington, DC, September 9.

———. 2005a. *Trends 2005*. Washington, DC: Pew Research Center.

———. 2005b. Support for terror wanes among Muslim publics: Islamic extremism, common concern for Western and Islamic publics. Report from the 17-Nation PEW Global Attitudes Project, Washington, DC.

Pickthall, Marmaduke William. 1938. *The meaning of the glorious Quran: Text and explanatory translation*. Hyderabad, India: Govern.

Piore, Michael J., and Charles F. Sabel. 1984. *The second industrial divide: Possibilities for prosperity*. New York: Basic Books.

Pollack, Andy. 1994. Losing faith in Ireland—decline of the Catholic Church. *Irish Times*, November 28–30, 13.

Popkin, Eric. 2003. Transnational migration and development in postwar peripheral states: An examination of Guatemalan and Salvadoran state linkages with their migrant populations in Los Angeles. *Current Sociology* 51:347–74.

Poros, Maritsa V. 2001. The role of migrant networks in linking local labour markets: The case of Asian Indian migration to New York and London. *Global Networks* 1:243.

Portes, Alejandro. 1995. Economic sociology and the sociology of immigration: A conceptual overview. In *Economic sociology of immigration: Essays on networks, ethnicity, and entrepreneurship*, ed. Alejandro Portes, 1–41. New York: Russell Sage Foundation.

———. 1998. Social capital: Its origins and applications in modern sociology. *Annual Review of Sociology* 24:1–24.

Portes, Alejandro. 2003. Conclusion: Theoretical convergences and empirical evidence in the study of immigrant transnationalism. *International Migration Review* 37:874–92.

Portes, Alejandro, and Luis E. Guarnizo. 1990. Tropical capitalists: US-bound migration and small enterprise development in the Dominican Republic. In *Migration, remittances and business development: Mexico and Caribbean basin countries,* ed. Sergio Diaz-Briquets and Sydney Weintraub, 101–31. Boulder, CO: Westview Press.

Portes, Alejandro, Luis E. Guarnizo, and William J. Haller. 2002. Transnational entrepreneurs: An alternative form of immigrant economic adaptation. *American Sociological Review* 67:278–98.

Portes, Alejandro, Luis E. Guarnizo, and Patricia Landolt. 1999. The study of transnationalism: Pitfalls and promise of an emergent research field. *Ethnic and Racial Studies* 22:217–37.

Portes, Alejandro, and Patricia Landolt. 1996. The downside of social capital. *American Prospect* 26:18–21.

Portes, Alejandro, and Rubén Rumbaut. 2001. *Legacies: The story of the immigrant second generation.* Berkeley: University of California Press.

Portes, Alejandro, and Julia Sensenbrenner. 1993. Embeddedness and immigration: Notes on the social determinants of economic action. *American Journal of Sociology* 98:1320–50.

Portes, Alejandro, and John Walton. 1981. *Labor, class, and the international system.* New York: Academic Press.

Prebish, Charles S., and Martin Baumann, eds. 2002. *Westward dharma: Buddhism beyond Asia.* Berkeley: University of California Press.

Presser, Stanley, and Linda Stinson. 1998. Data collection mode and social desirability bias in self-reported religious attendance: Church attendance in the United States. *American Sociological Review* 63:137–45.

Pries, Ludger. 2001. *New transnational social spaces: International migration and transnational companies in the early twenty-first century.* London: Routledge.

Purkayastha, Bandana. 2005. *Negotiating ethnicity: Second-generation South Asian Americans traverse a transnational world.* New Brunswick, NJ: Rutgers University Press.

Putnam, Robert D. 1995. Bowling alone: America's declining social capital. *Journal of Democracy* 6:65–78.

———. 2000. *Bowling alone: The collapse and revival of American community.* New York: Simon & Schuster.

Putnam, Robert D., Lewis M. Feldstein, and Don Cohen. 2003. *Better together: Restoring the American community.* New York: Simon & Schuster.

Queen, Christopher. 2002. Engaged Buddhism: Agnosticism, interdependence, globalization. In Prebish and Baumann 2002, 324–47.

Rahmani, Ahmad. 2000. Status of zakat in India today. *Milli Gazette: Indian Muslims' Leading English Newspaper,* January 15. Available at http://www.milligazette.com/Archives/15-1-2000/Art18.htm.

Raj, Dhooleka Sarhadi. 2000. "Who the hell do you think you are?" Promoting religious identity among young Hindus in Britain. *Ethnic and Racial Studies* 23:535–58.

———. 2003. *Where are you from? Middle-class migrants in the modern world.* Berkeley: University of California Press.

Rajagopal, Arvind. 2000. Hindu nationalism in the U.S.: Changing configurations of political practice. *Ethnic and Racial Studies* 23:467–96.

Rantanen, Terhi. 2005. The message is the medium: An interview with Manuel Castells. *Global Media and Communication* 1:135–47.

Ribeiro, Gustavo Lins. 1999. O que faz o Brasil, Brazil: Jogos identitários em São Francisco.

In *Cenas do Brasil migrante*, ed. Ana Cristina Braga Martes, Rosanna Rocha Reis, and Teresa Sales, 45–85. São Paulo: Boitempo.

Riccio, Bruno. 2001. Disaggregating the transnational community: Senegalese migrants on the coast of Emilia-Romagna. Working Paper No. WPTC-01-11, Transnational Communities Programme Institute of Social and Cultural Anthropology, University of Oxford. Available at www.transcomm.ox.ac.uk/working_papers.htm.

Richman, Karen E. 2005. *Migration and vodou.* Gainesville: University Press of Florida.

Rieffer, Barbara-Ann J. 2003. Religion and nationalism: Understanding the consequences of a complex relationship. *Ethnicities* 3, no. 2:215–42.

Robertson, Roland. 1991. The globalization paradigm: Thinking globally. In *New developments in theory and research: Religion and the social order,* ed. David. G. Bromley, 1:204–24. Greenwich, CT: JAI Press.

Robertson, Roland, and Joann Chirico. 1985. Humanity, globalization, and worldwide religious resurgence: A theoretical exploration. *Sociological Analysis* 46:219–42.

Roof, Wade Clark. 1993. *A generation of seekers: The spiritual journeys of the baby boom generation.* San Francisco: HarperSanFrancisco.

———. 1999. *Spiritual marketplace: Baby boomers and the remaking of American religion.* Princeton, NJ: Princeton University Press.

Rouse, Roger. 1992. Making sense of settlement: Class transformation, cultural struggle, and transnationalism among Mexican migrants in the United States. In Glick Schiller, Basch, and Szanton Blanc 1992, xv, 259.

Rudolph, Susann Hoeber, and James P. Piscatori. 1997. *Transnational religion and fading states.* Boulder, CO: Westview Press.

Ruhs, M. 2004. Ireland: A crash course in immigration policy. Migration Policy Institute, Washington, DC. Available at http://www.migrationinformation.org/Profiles/display .cfm?id=260.

Saenz, Rogelio. 2004. Latinos and the changing face of America. Washington, DC: Russell Sage Foundation and Population Reference Bureau.

Sales, Teresa. 2003. *Brazilians away from home.* New York: Center for Migration Studies.

Salih, Ruba. 2001. Moroccan migrant women: Transnationalism, nation-states, and gender. *Journal of Ethnic and Migration Studies* 27:655–71.

Sassen, Saskia. 1999. *Guests and aliens.* New York: The New Press.

Saxenian, AnnaLee. 1999. *Silicon valley's new immigrant entrepreneurs.* San Francisco: Public Policy Institute of California.

Saxenian, AnnaLee, Yasuyuki Motoyama, and Xiaohong Quan. 2002. *Local and global networks of immigrant professionals in Silicon Valley.* San Francisco: Public Policy Institute of California.

Schiffauer, Werner. 1999. *Islamism in the diaspora: The fascination of political Islam among second generation German Turks.* Working Paper No. WPTC-99-06, Transnational Communities Programme, Institute of Social and Cultural Anthropology, University of Oxford. Available at www.transcomm.ox.ac.uk/working_papers.htm.

Sen, Amartya. 1996. Humanity and citizenship. In Nussbaum 1996, 111–18.

Sewell, William H., Jr. 1992. A theory of structure: Duality, agency, and transformation. *American Journal of Sociology* 98:1.

Sherman, Amy L. 2003. The community serving activities of Hispanic Protestant congregations. Faith in Communities Initiative, Hudson Institute/Center for the Study of Latino Religion, Notre Dame University, December.

Sheth, N.R. 1994. Children of the same god: A spiritual approach to social transformation. Working Paper No. 59, Gujarati Institute of Development Research, Ahmedabad.

Siddiqui, Rizwana, and Abdul Razzaq Kemal. 2002. Remittances, trade liberalization, and poverty in Pakistan: The role of excluded variables in poverty change analysis. Study No. 1, Exploring the Links Between Globalisation and Poverty in South Asia project, Globalisation and Poverty Programme, Department for International Development (DFID), Warwick, UK, 1595–614.

Silver, Beverly J. 2003. *Forces of labor: Workers' movements and globalization since 1870.* Cambridge: Cambridge University Press.

Sklair, Leslie. 2001. *The transnational capitalist class.* Oxford: Blackwell.

Skocpol, Theda. 1997. The Tocqueville problem: Civic engagement in American democracy. *Social Science History* 21:455–79.

Skrbiš, Zlatko. 1999. *Long-distance nationalism: Diasporas, homelands and identities.* Brookfield, VT: Ashgate.

Smidt, Corwin E., ed. 2003. *Religion as social capital: Producing the common good.* Waco, TX: Baylor University Press.

Smith, Jonathan Z. 1982. *Imagining religion: From Babylon to Jonestown.* Chicago: University of Chicago Press.

Smith, Michael P., and Luis E. Guarnizo. 1998. *Transnationalism from below.* New Brunswick, NJ: Transaction Publishers.

Smith, Robert C. 2003. Diasporic memberships in historical perspective: Comparative insights from the Mexican, Italian and Polish cases. *International Migration Review* 37:724–59.

———. 2006. *Mexican New York: Transnational lives of new immigrants.* Berkeley: University of California Press.

Smith, Tom W., and Seokho Kim. 2005. The vanishing Protestant majority. GSS Social Change Report No. 49. *Journal for the Scientific Study of Religion* 44:211–23.

South Asia Citizens Web and Sabrang Communications & Publishing Pvt. Ltd. 2002. The funding of hate: IDRF and the American funding of Hindutva. Available at http://stopfundinghate.org/sacw/index.html.

Sowell, Thomas. 1991. In defense of middlemen: Why distribution is a valuable economic activity. *Forbes,* September 30, 56.

———. 1994. *Race and culture: A world view.* New York: Basic Books.

Spain, Daphne. 1999. *America's diversity: On the edge of two centuries.* Washington, DC: Population Reference Bureau.

Spickard, James V. 1998. Rethinking religious social action: What is "rational" about rational choice theory? *Sociology of Religion* 59:99–115.

Spohn, Willfried. 2003. Multiple modernity, nationalism and religion: A global perspective. *Current Sociology* 51:265–86.

Srivastava, Raj Krishan. 1998. *Vital connections: Self, society, God: Perspectives on Swadhyaya.* New York: Weatherhill.

Stark, Rodney. 1994. Rational choice theories of religion. *Agora* 2:1–5.

Stark, Rodney, and William Sims Bainbridge. 1987. *A theory of religion.* New York: Peter Lang.

Stark, Rodney, and Charles Y. Glock. 1968. *American piety: The nature of religious commitment.* Berkeley: University of California Press.

Stark, Rodney, Eva Hamberg, and Alan S. Miller. 2005. Exploring spirituality and unchurched religions in America, Sweden, and Japan. *Journal of Contemporary Religion* 20:3–23.

Stern, Jessica. 2003. *Terror in the name of God: Why religious militants kill.* New York: Ecco.

Swanbrow, Diane. 1997. Study of worldwide rates of religiosity, church attendance. News release, University of Michigan, December 10. Available at http://www.umich.edu/news/index.html?Releases/1997/Dec97/chr121097a.

Swyngedouw, Eric. 1992. The Mammon quest, "glocalisation," interspatial competition and the monetary order: The construction of new scales. In *Cities and regions in the new Europe: The global-local interplay and spatial development strategies,* ed. Grigoris Kafkalas and Mick Dunford, 39–67. New York: Halsted Press.

———. 1997. Neither global nor local: "Glocalization" and the politics of scale. In *Spaces of globalization: Reasserting the power of the local,* ed. Kevin R. Cox, 137–66. New York: Guilford Press.

Tarrow, Sidney G. 2001. Rooted cosmopolitans: Towards a sociology of transnational contention. Paper presented at the Workshop on Transnational Contention, Cornell University, Ithaca, NY.

———. 2005. *The new transnational activism.* New York: Cambridge University Press.

Task Force on Policy Regarding Emigrants. 2002. Ireland and the Irish abroad: Report to the minister for foreign affairs, Brian Cowen, T.D. Available at http://www.foreign affairs.gov.ie/policy/emigrant_taskforce.asp.

Taylor, Charles. 1992. *Multiculturalism and the politics of recognition: An essay by Charles Taylor, with commentary by Amy Gutmann, editor, Steven C. Rockefeller, Michael Walzer, and Susan Wolf.* Princeton, NJ: Princeton University Press.

Thakur, R. 1991. India and the Soviet Union: Conjunctions and disjunctions of interests. *Asian Survey* 31:826–46.

Toppe, Chris M., Arthur D. Kirsch, and Michel Jocabel. 2002. Giving and volunteering in the United States, 2001: Findings from a national survey. Independent Sector, Washington, DC.

Tseng, Timothy. 1999. Chinese Protestant nationalism in the United States, 1880–1927. In *New spiritual homes: Religion and Asian Americans,* ed. David K. Yoo, 19–51. Honolulu: University of Hawaii Press.

Turner, Bryan S. 1993. Contemporary problems in the theory of citizenship. In *Citizenship and social theory,* ed. Bryan S. Turner, 1–18. Thousand Oaks, CA: Sage.

———. 2001a. Cosmopolitan virtue: On religion in a global age. *European Journal of Social Theory* 4:131–52.

———. 2001b. The erosion of citizenship. *British Journal of Sociology* 52:189–209.

———. 2002. Cosmopolitan virtue, globalization and patriotism. *Theory, Culture & Society* 19:1–2.

Tweed, Thomas A. 2002. *Our lady of the exile: Diasporic religion at a Cuban Catholic shrine in Miami.* New York: Oxford University Press.

Tweed, Thomas A., and Stephen R. Prothero. 1999. *Asian religions in America: A documentary history.* New York: Oxford University Press.

Twomey, D. Vincent. 2003. *The end of Irish Catholicism?* Dublin: Veritas.

U.S. Census Bureau. 2000. Decennial census 2000, PUMS data. Summary Files 3 and 4. Available at http://factfinder.census.gov/servlet/DatasetMainPageServlet?_ds_name =DEC_2000_SF4_U&_program=DEC&_lang=en.

U.S. Census Bureau. 2004–5. American community survey data. Available at http://factfinder.census.gov/servlet/DatasetMainPageServlet?_program=ACS&_submenu Id=datasets_1&_lang=en&_ts=.

USCCB (U.S. Conference of Catholic Bishops). 2005. Demographics. Washington, DC: Secretariat for Hispanic Affairs. Available at http://www.usccb.org/hispanicaffairs/demo.shtml#2.

U.S. Department of Homeland Security. 2004. *Yearbook of immigration statistics, 2003.*

Washington, DC: U.S. Government Printing Office. Available at http://uscis.gov/graphics/shared/statistics/yearbook/2003/2003Yearbook.pdf.

U.S. Department of State. 2003a. Brazil: International religious freedom report 2003. Bureau of Democracy, Human Rights, and Labor, Washington, DC. Available at http://www.state.gov/g/drl/rls/irf/2003/24481.htm.

———. 2003b. Ireland: International religious freedom report 2003. Bureau of Democracy, Human Rights, and Labor, Washington, DC. Available at http://www.state.gov/g/drl/rls/irf/2003/24414.htm.

———. 2004. Pakistan: International religious freedom report 2004. Bureau of Democracy, Human Rights, and Labor, Washington, DC. Available at http://www.state.gov/g/drl/rls/irf/2004/35519.htm.

———. 2005. Pakistan: International religious freedom report 2005. Bureau of Democracy, Human Rights, and Labor. Available at http://www.state.gov/g/drl/rls/irf/2005/51621.htm.

Van der Veer, Peter. 2002. Transnational religion: Hindu and Muslim movements. *Global Networks* 2:95–109.

Vásquez, Manuel A., and Marie F. Marquardt. 2003. *Globalizing the sacred: Religion across the Americas*. New Brunswick, NJ: Rutgers University Press.

Ven, Johannes A. van der, Jaco S. Dreyer, and Hendrik J.C. Pieterse. 2004. *Is there a God of human rights? The complex relationship between human rights and religion: A South African case*. Leiden, Netherlands: Brill.

Verba, Sidney, Kay Lehman Schlozman, and Henry E. Brady. 1995. *Voice and equality: Civic voluntarism in American politics*. Cambridge, MA: Harvard University Press.

Vertovec, Steven. 1999. Conceiving and researching transnationalism. *Ethnic and Racial Studies* 22:447–62.

———. 2002. Transnational networks and skilled labour migration. Working Paper No. WPTC-02-02, Transnational Communities Programme, Institute of Social and Cultural Anthropology, University of Oxford. Available at www.transcomm.ox.ac.uk/working_papers.htm.

———. 2003. Migration and other modes of transnationalism: Towards conceptual cross-fertilization. *International Migration Review* 37:641–65.

Waldinger, Roger, and David Fitzgerald. 2004. Transnationalism in question. *American Journal of Sociology* 109:1177–95.

Warner, R. Stephen. 1993. Work in progress toward a new paradigm for the sociological study of religion in the United States. *American Journal of Sociology* 98:1044–93.

———. 1997. Religion, boundaries, and bridges. *Sociology of Religion* 58:217–38.

———. 2004. Enlisting Smelser's theory of ambivalence to maintain progress in the sociology of religion's new paradigm. In *Self, social structure, and beliefs: Explorations in sociology*, ed. Jeffrey C. Alexander, Gary T. Marx, and Christine L. Williams, 103–21. Berkeley: University of California Press.

———. 2006. The de-Europeanization of American Christianity. In *A nation of religions: Pluralism in the American public square*, ed. Stephen Prothero, 233–55. Chapel Hill: University of North Carolina Press.

Warren, Mark A. 2003. Faith and leadership in the inner city: How social capital contributes to democratic renewal. In Smidt 2003, 49–68.

Weber, Max. 1958. *The Protestant ethic and the spirit of capitalism*. New York: Scribner.

Wellmeier, Nancy J. 1998. Santa Eulalia's people in exile: Maya religion, culture, and identity in Los Angeles. In *Gatherings in diaspora: Religious communities and the new immigration*, ed. R. Stephen Warner and Judith G. Wittner, 97–122. Philadelphia: Temple University Press.

Werbner, Pnina. 2000. Global pathways: Working class cosmopolitans and the creation of transnational ethnic worlds. *Social Anthropology* 7:17–35.

Williams, Raymond Brady. 1992. Sacred threads of several textures. In *A sacred thread: Modern transmission of Hindu traditions in India and abroad.* Chambersburg, PA: Anima Press.

———. 1988. *Religions of immigrants from India and Pakistan: New threads in the American tapestry.* Cambridge: Cambridge University Press.

———. 2001. *An introduction to Swaminarayan Hinduism.* Cambridge: Cambridge University Press.

Wilson, Bryan R. 1982. *Religion in sociological perspective.* Oxford: Oxford University Press.

Wolfe, Alan. 1998. *One nation, after all: What middle-class Americans really think about: God, country, family, racism, welfare, immigration, homosexuality, work, the right, the left, and each other.* New York: Viking.

———. 2003. *The transformation of American religion.* Chicago: University of Chicago Press.

Wood, Richard L. 2003. Does religion matter? Projecting democratic power into the public arena. In Smidt 2003, 69–86.

Woolcock, Michael. 1998. Social capital and economic development: Toward a theoretical synthesis and policy framework. *Theory and Society* 27:151–208.

World Bank. 2006. Global economic prospects 2006: Economic implications of remittances and migration. International Bank for Reconstruction and Development, Washington, DC.

World Christian Database. 2002. Figures accessed at http://worldchristiandatabase.org/wcd/.

———. 2004. Figures accessed at http://worldchristiandatabase.org/wcd/.

Wuthnow, Robert. 1989. *The restructuring of American religion: Society and faith since World War II.* Princeton, NJ: Princeton University Press.

———. 1998. *After heaven: Spirituality in America since the 1950s.* Berkeley: University of California Press.

———. 2005. *America and the challenges of religious diversity.* Princeton, NJ: Princeton University Press.

Wuthnow, Robert, Stephen J. Stein, George Marsden, Yvonne Haddad, Hasia Diner, Frederick C. Harris, Philip Kevin Goff, Andrew M. Greeley, Bruce B. Lawrence, and Jean Bethke Elshtain. 2004. Religion and culture: Views of 10 scholars. *Chronicle of Higher Education* 51:B7.

Wyman, Mark. 1993. *Round-trip to America: The immigrants return to Europe, 1880–1930.* Ithaca, NY: Cornell University Press.

Yang, Fenggang. 2002. Chinese Christian transnationalism: Diverse networks of a Houston church. In Ebaugh and Chafetz 2002, 175–204.

Yang, Fenggang, and Helen Rose Ebaugh. 2001. Transformations in new immigrant religions and their global implications. *American Sociological Review* 66:269–88.

Yeoh, Brenda S.A., Michael W. Charney, and Chee Kiong Tong. 2003. *Approaching transnationalisms: Studies on transnational societies, multicultural contacts, and imaginings of home.* Boston: Kluwer Academic.

Yeoh, Brenda S.A., and Katie Willis. 1998. Singapore unlimited: Configuring social identity in the regionalisation process. Working Paper No. WPTC-98-08, Transnational Communities Programme, Institute of Social and Cultural Anthropology, University of Oxford. Available at www.transcomm.ox.ac.uk/working_papers.htm.

Yeoh, Brenda S.A., Shirlena Huang, and Theodora Lam. 2005. Transnationalizing the

"Asian" family: Imaginaries, intimacies and strategic intents. *Global Networks* 5:307–15.

Yeoh, Brenda S.A., Katie Willis, and S.M. Abdul Khader Fakhri. 2003. Introduction: Transnationalism and its edges. *Ethnic and Racial Studies* 26:207–17.

Yuval-Davis, Nira. 1999. The multi-layered citizen. *International Feminist Journal of Politics* 1:119–36.

Zerubavel, Eviatar. 1997. *Social mindscapes: An invitation to cognitive sociology*. Cambridge, MA: Harvard University Press.

Ziring, Lawrence. 2003. *Pakistan: At the crosscurrent of history*. Oxford, UK: Oneworld.

INDEX